D1433467

# THE EFFECTS OF CRIME AND THE WORK
# OF VICTIMS SUPPORT SCHEMES

To Ross, Jay and Ian

PREVIOUS CAMBRIDGE STUDIES IN CRIMINOLOGY

# The Effects of Crime and The Work of Victims Support Schemes

MIKE MAGUIRE
*and*
CLAIRE CORBETT
*Research Fellows,*
*Centre for Criminological Research,*
*University of Oxford*

Series Editor: A. E. Bottoms

Gower

Published by
Gower Publishing Company Limited
Gower House
Croft Road
Aldershot
Hants GU11 3HR
England

Gower Publishing Company
Old Post Road
Brookfield
Vermont 05036
USA


British Library Cataloguing in Publication Data

Maguire, Mike
  The effects of crime and the work of
  victims support schemes.——(Cambridge
  studies in criminology; 51)
  1. Victims of crimes——Services for
  ——Great Britain
  I. Title  II. Corbett, Clave  III. Series
  362.8'8'0941   HV6250.3.G7

  ISBN 0-566-05412-4

Printed and bound in Great Britain by
Biddles Limited, Guildford and King's Lynn.

# Contents

# Tables and figures

ix

## Figures

## Appendix Tables

# Acknowledgements

This report is the result of a two year study funded by the Home Office with the encouragement of the National Association of Victims Support Schemes. The authors would like to thank the many people who helped or co-operated in the project, some of whom gave us a great deal of time without complaint. We were assisted with interviewing by Anna Hallett and Jane Orwell, who did an excellent job, well beyond the call of duty. The secretaries at the Centre, especially Carol McCall and Kaye Bewley, coped uncomplainingly with copious typing and redrafting. Our colleagues at the Centre, particularly Dr. Roger Hood and Dr. Joanna Shapland, provided very helpful comments on the text.

The staff at NAVSS were always welcoming, and sent us any information we requested. In particular, Helen Reeves, Kay Coventry, Sue Tomson and John Pointing, despite the pressure of work they were under, were always ready to discuss any questions we had at short notice and at length. Similarly, the members of individual Schemes gave us every facility (including several visits to Co-ordinators' own homes to allow us to look through records), and were very keen to assist with the research. As we are not identifying the Schemes studied, we are unfortunately unable to mention names. The police in every area we studied also willingly answered our questions and helpfully facilitated our interviewing of victims.

Finally, we would like to acknowledge the generosity of the Home Office in funding the project, and to thank the members of the Research and Planning Unit, particularly Mr. Tony Marshall and Mr. J. M. Hough, who gave us advice and support throughout.

# 1 Introduction

The desire for a 'better deal' for victims of crime, which has grown world-wide over the past decade, has expressed itself very differently in different countries. In the United States, where the 'victim movement' was born in a welter of political activity, closely linked to other issues such as women's rights, the main debates and associated actions have revolved around the position and the rights of the victim in relation to both the offender and the criminal justice system (see, for example: Harding, 1982; Elias, 1983; B. L. Smith, 1985). In Canada, following very effective pressure by a small 'victims' lobby' upon and within the Ministry of the Solicitor-General, the federal government was persuaded to set up an expensive package of research and experimental programmes of services to victims, many of them special units based in police premises and staffed by fully trained 'crisis workers' (Canadian Federal-Provincial Task Force, 1983; Rock, 1986). In Great Britain, by contrast, despite the pioneering in the sixties of a state compensation scheme for victims of violent crime, the notion of 'victims' rights' has not been widely discussed, and there has been until recently little government interest in funding special services for victims. Here, the lead came - and continues to come - mainly from 'care' or 'welfare' oriented groups of volunteers, in most cases with help from sympathetic individuals within statutory service agencies. Inspired by an initial experiment in Bristol in 1974 (Gay et al., 1975; Volunteer Centre, 1976), such groups quietly courted the local police, tapped what local resources they could find, set up modest organisations - often run 'on a shoestring' from an obliging person's own house - and began calling at victims' homes to offer whatever support or assistance they could provide.

Unlike many of the victim initiatives in the United States - both government-sponsored and community-based - these early Victims Support Schemes (VSS) had no political aims or 'hidden agendas'. They took little interest in the offender, the court process, or the sentences passed. Their primary objective was very simple: to act as a 'good neighbour', or perhaps 'good Samaritan', to people who had suffered at the hands of a thief or assailant. They laid great emphasis upon personal contact, upon 'reaching out' to victims rather than leaving it to victims to ask for help, and upon establishing contact as soon as possible after the event: to these ends, they were prepared to waste many journeys on unannounced visits to the homes of victims who were out, or who did not want their assistance. The service they offered was (to some extent deliberately) neither 'professional' nor sophisticated. It could be undertaken by ordinary people who volunteered to help, most of whom received only minimal training. Indeed, the 'gesture', the 'expression of community concern', was regarded as no less important than any practical assistance given. The normal practice quickly became to visit each victim only once or twice, offering primarily a sympathetic 'listening ear' for the fears, distress and anger which many felt a need to express. The minority of cases involving more serious problems were to be 'referred on' to other agencies with which the Scheme maintained contact through its Management Committee, and which were supposedly better equipped to deal with them.

The simple primary idea, and the practices it generated, have proved to be remarkably powerful and successful. In little more than a decade, the numbers of Schemes, volunteers and referrals have grown at an impressive rate.[1] As we shall show, 'catchment' areas now cover over half the population of England and Wales; over a quarter of the adult population know of Schemes' existence; at least 50,000 victims annually are offered support in person, and many more by letter or telephone. Schemes have gained the confidence of the police in virtually every force; and they receive frequent and serious attention from politicians, the media, and the academic world.

In explaining this almost unprecedented speed of growth in a voluntary organisation, it is of course necessary to give full credit to the individuals involved, both in local Schemes and in the National Association (NAVSS). The latter, formed in 1979, has given a strong lead to the movement under an exceptionally dedicated and charismatic Director, and has encouraged both expansion and higher standards of service. It has helped to put the VSS movement 'on the map' with judicious use of publicity, as well as lobbying for more funds and for more co-operation from other agencies. Victims Support has also developed within a social and political climate increasingly sympathetic to victims of crime, a climate which it has both fed and fed upon. Rising crime rates, doubts about the effectiveness of the criminal justice system, greater knowledge about the effects of crime on individuals, publicity about the treatment of victims by the police and courts, and, indeed, the growth of an internationally campaigning 'victim movement' (which has helped to prompt both a United Nations Declaration and a Council of Europe Recommendation) have all served to push victims into the arena of public debate. Inevitably, this interest has fuelled a major rise in the 'business' of Victims Support Schemes, as more volunteers are attracted and the police are more willing to refer cases. Significantly too, it has accelerated a rise in the level of expectations, both within and outside VSS, about the scale and standards of service which should be provided for victims.

Naturally, increased attention to their work, and the concomitant increased expectations, have had a considerable impact upon the character of local Schemes. Some have developed from totally voluntary, small-scale, home-based organisations into more 'professional' modes of operation, with their own offices and one or more full-time paid officers. Many which, a few years ago, were dealing with perhaps four or five cases selected for them each week by the police, are now receiving cases under 'automatic' referral systems, running into hundreds per month. Many 'Co-ordinators', who are responsible for the day-to-day administration of Schemes, are no longer supervising the work of a small group of friends, but of perhaps 25 or 30 volunteers. And Schemes are fast branching out into demanding areas such as the longer-term support of victims of rape or relatives of murder victims. At the same time, as one Co-ordinator put it, there is a subtle 'moral pressure', from both NAVSS and from other Schemes, to 'keep doing a bit more'. Whereas a few years ago, she said, a Scheme which reported having visited 100 burglary victims in a year could expect praise at a conference, 'nowadays you can hear others thinking, "Why so few?" and "Why only burglary victims?" '

3

One of our main purposes in this research project was to take stock of the 'situation on the ground' in this fast-changing organisation. We set out both to establish a broad picture of the movement and to evaluate the work of a number of local Schemes, identifying their strengths and weaknesses, the problems they experienced, and the services they provided to victims in their area. As one would expect in what is still very much a 'grass-roots' movement, we found very wide differences between areas, not only in the level of resources at Schemes' disposal, but in their overall perceptions of their task and in their attitudes to the pressure for change and development. These ranged from Schemes which stressed above all else the 'voluntary' and 'good neighbour' aspects of VSS and were opposed to anything 'smacking of professionalism' (e.g. full training courses, paid Co-ordinators, and even NAVSS) to those with the ambition of achieving 'professional standards' and a comprehensive service to all victims in their area.

Such differences made it very difficult to select suitable criteria for evaluation: one can hardly judge a small and totally voluntary Scheme by the same standards as a large, well-funded, office-based enterprise with paid staff. Moreover, there is no general agreement, even among those with considerable resources, about their primary objective: is it to make a 'gesture that the community cares' - by offering a few words of sympathy, by letter, telephone or personal call - to (ideally) <u>every</u> victim of <u>every</u> offence, however trivial; is it to send volunteers out to act as a therapeutic 'listening ear' for the fears and worries of as many victims as possible, regardless of how major or minor these fears; or is it to identify and to concentrate the Scheme's resources upon the very seriously affected minority who most need their support?

The answers to such questions have to some extent remained obscured under the rhetoric which has inevitably grown up within the Victims Support movement. For example, one of the most common terms used in VSS circles to describe their activities has been 'crisis intervention'. This term has caused confusion owing to its association, particularly in the United States, with a set of specific counselling techniques, derived mainly from 'crisis theory', which posits a series of identifiable stages through which people 'in crisis' pass (Caplan, 1964). Such techniques have been used for many years to treat people in other crisis situations, and have been developed among professional groups to a considerable level of sophistication. The model has been adapted in various forms for use with crime victims, for example by Stein (1981), who advocates immediate on-the-spot support to help victims through the initial stage of intense emotional reaction, followed by recontact within a couple of days for a series of 'crisis counselling' sessions aimed specifically at reducing feelings of anger and fear and restoring self-esteem (see also Salasin, 1981). The Victims Support movement, although aiming at similar goals, has never developed a very clear idea of what it means by crisis intervention, and in our experience, most volunteers regarded it as a catch-all phrase to cover anything from one brief visit the day after the offence to a series of visits to sort out practical problems. Certainly, only a minority associated the phrase with specific counselling techniques requiring a considerable amount of training. Latterly, in fact, the term seems to be disappearing from NAVSS liter-ature, and becoming replaced with more neutral phrases such as 'short-term intervention'.

We have tried not to impose our own views of the 'correct' objectives, priorities and standards for Schemes, and in our broad evaluation in Chapter 8, we have assessed their work from a number of possible standpoints. However, we do think it important to look at their achievements within the con-text of estimates of the total numbers of people who are badly affected by crime, and who can be said to 'need' outside support and assistance. The fact that, as we shall indicate, Schemes are not at present capable of meeting all these needs, does not in itself imply any criticism of VSS. There is a good case for regarding it as a <u>government</u> res-ponsibility to ensure that adequate assistance is available to those suffering badly as a result of crime - whether through existing statutory agencies or by the provision of sufficient funds to voluntary agencies such as VSS.

In the remainder of this chapter, we describe briefly the basic structure of Victims Support Schemes and that of NAVSS and the Regions. We also outline our sources of data and the research methods we used, which will be described in more depth in the relevant chapters.

In Chapter 2, we present a 'statistical overview' of the Schemes existing in mid-1984 (when we sent a questionnaire to every Scheme in the country) updated to some extent by information obtained from NAVSS regarding developments in 1985. This overview includes not only basic information on the size of Schemes, numbers of volunteers, and numbers and types of referrals, but attempts to make some overall esti-mates of the extent of 'coverage' of victims, of the 'pro-ductivity' of Schemes (e.g. in numbers of victims seen per volunteer), and of their 'progressiveness' (e.g. in assis-ting victims of very serious crime, or in accompanying victims to court). We also compare urban Schemes with and without paid Co-ordinators in terms of these qualities.

5

In Chapter 3, we present findings, from our own interviews with victims and from questions we inserted in the 1984 British Crime Survey, concerning the effects of crime upon victims, and victims' 'needs'.  These include assessments, using a variety of measures, of the emotional impact of crime and of the practical problems caused for victims, both in the short term and the medium term.  The findings highlight variations between victims with different social characteristics and following a variety of types of offence.  It is also estimated how many people in an 'average' Scheme area, over a one-year period, would be expected to consider themselves badly affected by crime.  Although the concept of 'needs' is found to be problematic and confusing in this context, we provide broad estimates, based on a particular definition of the term, of the proportion of victims who can be said to need VSS services.

In Chapter 4, we look at what we call the 'filtering process' - the ways in which the total pool of victims is narrowed down to those who are (a) referred to Schemes and (b) visited by volunteers.  We explore the reasoning behind both the general referral systems ('automatic' or 'selective') adopted by Schemes, and the individual decisions made by police officers and Scheme Co-ordinators, as well as looking at examples of filtering systems in practice.  We ask to what extent the decisions made are based on sound knowledge of local crime patterns, to what extent they involve prejudice (including 'stereotyping' of victims who do and do not 'deserve' help) and, ultimately, whether the support goes on the whole to those who need it most.  Other subjects covered include the referral of 'non-crime' cases, and self-referral by victims who have not reported offences to the police.

In Chapter 5, we raise questions about the management structure of Schemes, above all about the disproportionate load which tends to fall upon the shoulders of Co-ordinators.  We also identify problems in communication between the three main sections of the typical Scheme - the Committee, the Co-ordinator, and the volunteers.  We highlight ways in which some of the Schemes studied had partly or wholly overcome these problems.  Particular issues considered include the supervision and support of volunteers, the use of report forms, and confusions about the role of the Management Committee.

Chapter 6 deals with the central issues of what Schemes actually do for victims, what victims think of the services provided and, ultimately, whether Victims Support can be said to 'work' - i.e. to ameliorate recovery from the effects of crime.  We look first at victims' reactions to contact from a Scheme, comparing responses to telephone calls, letters and personal visits, and then to the service as a whole, including both practical assistance and psychological support. We examine the nature and extent of assistance given, including the use made of other agencies, and finally report the results of a 'matching' exercise comparing the recovery of victims who received and did not receive support from a Scheme.

Chapter 7 is devoted to a category of victims upon whom the psychological effects are almost always very serious - victims of rape. We describe the effects experienced by a sample of such victims, linking these to findings from other research and to theories about the essential nature and the duration of such effects. We discuss the place of Victims Support in an area already covered to some extent by Rape Crisis Centres, and compare the differing approaches of the two organisations. We also raise questions about the kinds of training necessary to equip volunteers for undertaking what is undoubtedly a heavy responsibility, and about the extent to which they should become 'involved' with victims over long periods.

In Chapter 8, we summarise previous chapters and draw the threads together into some overall conclusions, including broad evaluations of the work of Schemes according to different criteria. Finally, in the Appendix, we deal briefly with miscellaneous issues, namely victims' accounts of how they were treated by the police, victims' views on mediation, the recruitment and selection of volunteers and the types of training offered by Schemes.


## Victims Support Schemes

Details of the structure and organisation of VSS will emerge during the report, but a brief outline may be helpful by way of introduction. Every Scheme has what might be called a 'tri-partite' structure, consisting of a Management Committee, one or more Co-ordinators, and a number of volunteer visitors, although personnel may overlap between all three. Most Schemes still pay nobody, but there is a growing trend towards paying the Co-ordinator, upon whom falls most of the responsibility for the day-to-day administration of the Scheme's business and the supervision of volunteers. According to NAVSS, in early 1986, 133 Co-ordinators and 57 deputy or assistant Co-ordinators were receiving either full-time or part-time salaries or honoraria, at a total cost of over £600,000. A small number of Schemes also pay some visitors, mainly on a temporary basis through Manpower Services Commission (MSC) funding.

Funds for salaried staff tend to come out of grants from County Councils (made to 79 Schemes in 1985/6), MSC (32 Schemes) and Urban Aid (23 Schemes). The total amount of public money received has been estimated at about £1 million (NAVSS, 1986). Nevertheless, the majority of Schemes continue to depend for their running costs upon their own local fund-raising efforts, which include pleas to businesses and charities (such as Lions or Rotary clubs), as well as fetes, bazaars, lunches, sponsored walks, and other 'self-help' methods. Various larger trusts such as Cadbury's have provided generous 'pump-priming' funds to help Schemes in their first year, and some Schemes have been 'taken under the wing' of local Probation Services, Councils for Voluntary Services or other organisations which provide them with offices and/or paid staff. Despite this generosity, the financial situation for most is volatile and precarious, and some have used short-term increases in funds to expand, only to find themselves at a later date over-stretched and in financial difficulties. As noted in the latest Annual Report:

> 'Not only the shortage of funds, but also their lack of continuity, continue serving as grievous constraints on the work of many Schemes'.

Although there are a few 'mavericks', the vast majority of Schemes belong to NAVSS, which receives a certain amount of government funding to maintain permanent staff and offices in Brixton, London. NAVSS officially 'affiliates' Schemes each year only if they meet certain basic requirements, which are gradually becoming stricter (as reflected in NAVSS' Code of Practice). It is now insisted upon, for example, that volunteers receive some training, and that Management Committees contain representatives from the police, as well as from at least one statutory service agency and one voluntary body. However, NAVSS has few direct powers over local Schemes, which remain independent members of an Association.

Schemes are also grouped into 14 separate Regions, and one representative is elected by each Region to sit on the National Council, the main national decision-making body. The National Council employs the Director and her staff at headquarters, and makes all the major policy decisions, although inevitably, as it meets only a few times a year and is composed of people from all over the country with different local interests, it is strongly influenced by the recommendations of two appointed Committees, the Executive Committee and the Policy Committee, to which it also delegates a number of tasks. The Council also sets up Working Parties on various subjects (e.g. race relations,

8

fuel meters, compensation, research), which report back at intervals. Meanwhile, the staff at headquarters deal with a wide variety of problems brought to them by individual Schemes, help set up new Schemes, circulate all Schemes with information (including a regular newsletter), deal with inquiries from the public or from other organisations, publicise the work of VSS in general, produce the Annual Report, organise the Annual Conference, and help to organise any new initiatives, particularly ventures requiring the co-operation of major organisations at national level. NAVSS has also been pressing the government for a direct grant of funds sufficient to pay a Co-ordinator in every sizeable Scheme, although to date only a small contingency fund of £136,000 has been granted. In anticipation of a better response in the future, the National Council is considering ways of changing the constitution and structure of the organisation to make it better suited to receiving, distributing and monitoring the expenditure of public funds by local Schemes.

## Research methods and sources of data

Our research methods and sources of data will be described in more detail at relevant points in the report, and here we merely outline them. As already stated, we circulated a questionnaire to all Schemes existing in July 1984, to which over 90 per cent replied. We interviewed a total of 265 victims of burglary, theft from the person, robbery, rape, and assault, 225 of whom had been visited by VSS volunteers, the remainder having had no contact with a Scheme. We also had access to computerised data from the 1984 British Crime Survey, for which we wrote a number of questions relating to the effects of crime upon victims and their attitudes to and knowledge about Victims Support.

Our main fieldwork was carried out with eight different Schemes, ranging from one in a largely rural area to one in a very deprived district of London. The smallest had only three volunteers, and the largest over 40. Three had full-time paid Co-ordinators, the remainder being either part-time or voluntary. And some had 'automatic' and some 'selective' referral policies (see Chapter 4), with large variations in workload. These Schemes should not be regar-ded as 'representative' of all Schemes, but they are typical in their diversity, and allow us to comment upon a range of practices. During our fieldwork, we spent periods, 'on and off', of between six months and a year with each. We attended numerous Management Committee and volunteer support meetings, training sessions, and other Scheme functions. We interviewed the Co-ordinators, samples of volunteers (40 in

9

all), the senior police officers responsible for referrals and the 'link officers' who passed cases on daily. We also analysed large samples of cases from the records of six of these Schemes.

We visited 13 other Schemes on a 'one-off' basis, in most cases interviewing the Co-ordinator and talking to any other Scheme members present. We visited frequently NAVSS headquarters and attended several regional meetings and conferences, a National Council meeting, the Annual Conference, regional training sessions, and other functions at which representatives of several Schemes were present. At all these we were able to 'keep our finger on the pulse' of developments on a wider scale than in simply the eight Schemes we studied in depth. We also acted as 'participant observers', in that one of us sat on the NAVSS Research Working Party, and the other underwent training courses for volunteers wishing to deal with rape cases. Apart from being excluded from meetings of the important Policy Committee at NAVSS headquarters - which surprised us - we received excellent co-operation and assistance from all concerned.

### Notes to Chapter 1

1.    The latest 'official' figures (NAVSS 1986) show a total of 293 Schemes and districts, 185,000 referrals, and 6,750 volunteers (including management). These compare with figures for 1983 of 145 Schemes and districts, 65,000 referrals and 2,900 volunteers. No reliable figures are available for previous years, but it is known that at the time of the establishment of NAVSS in 1979 there were only about 30 groups in existence.

# 2 Salient characteristics of schemes: a national survey

## Introduction

In order to obtain a broad picture of the size, resources and scope of activity of all the Schemes in the country, we distributed a questionnaire in July 1984 to each of the 193 member Schemes and districts listed in the NAVSS Annual Report as existing in May of that year.  After a certain amount of prompting, we received back 152 questionnaires containing information about 177 (92 per cent) of these bodies.  The reasons that there were fewer returned questionnaires than the number of 'Schemes and districts' described in them were (a) that in some counties, where a number of distinct local groups are linked together under the umbrella organisation of a 'County Scheme', our questionnaire was completed by the County Co-ordinator or County Chairman on behalf of more than one district, and (b) that several of the 'districts' listed as separate were not, in fact, regarded locally as separate entities, being managed and co-ordinated by one group of people and often using the same volunteers.

Such ambiguities make it difficult to decide precisely how many separate 'Schemes and districts' should be deemed to have been in existence at that time.  In this report we shall assume a total of 179, which is 14 less than that given in the 1984 Annual Report.  Like NAVSS, we have treated local districts of County Schemes as separate units,[1] but elsewhere we have preferred to follow respondents' own definitions of their local situation.  The total number of Schemes and districts responding to our questionnaire, then, will be defined as 163 (i.e. 179 less 16 non-respondents).  This figure includes two very new Schemes which, although not yet operational, were able to complete parts of the questionnaire.[2]

11

The following overview is based primarily upon data about these 163 Schemes and districts, as they were in mid-1984. However, conscious of the rapid 'dating' of information in such a fast-growing organisation, we have used more recent information from NAVSS to draw attention to the major changes which occurred in 1985 and early 1986. It should be noted, in particular, that the total number of Schemes and districts (as defined by NAVSS) increased by 62 in the twelve months after our survey was conducted, and by a further 37 by mid-1986.

## Characteristics of Schemes

(i)  Location and size

The majority of Victims Support Schemes are based in sizeable urban areas. In 1984, 71 per cent were situated in towns or cities with a population of over 50,000, and these urban-based Schemes between them covered 93 per cent of the total population covered by all Schemes in the UK.[3] Furthermore, over 1 in 5 described themselves as working in substantially or predominantly 'inner city' areas. Partly due to active encouragement from the Metropolitan Police Commissioner, Greater London in particular has seen a mushrooming of Schemes, their number trebling from 13 in 1982 to 40 in 1985. Indeed, in mid-1985, Greater London, Merseyside, Greater Manchester and the West Midlands between them accounted for nearly one third of all Schemes and districts in the country.

The most common unit of area covered by individual Schemes or districts responding to our questionnaire was one police division. Fifty-one per cent were set up in this way, while 36 per cent covered parts of one division. Just under half received referrals from only one police station, often the divisional headquarters, and another 35 per cent from only two or three. This does not mean that they were all of similar size - on the contrary, the populations of the areas covered varied between 7,000 and 500,000. Nevertheless, 60 per cent fell within the range 50,000 - 195,000. The median population was 130,000.

Many Schemes were not content to see neighbouring areas without cover, and the 'expansionist' mood of the movement is reflected in the fact that 42 (26 per cent) were considering expanding their boundaries. A large proportion of these were recently-established Schemes in big cities, where the plan was usually to take in another police sub-division,[4] but there were also twelve based in medium-sized towns which intended expanding into surrounding rural areas.

(ii)  Volunteers:  numbers, recruitment, turnover

The 163 Schemes replying possessed between them, in Summer
1984, a total of 2,468 trained volunteers - an average of 15
per Scheme - and had a further 540 in or awaiting training.
Almost half had between 10 and 19 and a quarter had 20 or
more volunteers, most of the latter being urban-based (but
not necessarily large city-based) Schemes with high populations and high referral rates.[5]  By contrast, there were 26
Schemes or districts, mainly small-town or rural-based,
which had six or fewer volunteers.

We asked respondents to state how many of the volunteers
'on their books' were in fact 'regularly active visitors'.
The overall total here came to just under 2,000, 80 per cent
of those registered.  As a general rule, the larger the
Scheme, the more difficult it is to keep in close contact
with all volunteers (see Chapter 5), so the above percentage
was lower for most Schemes with a large volunteer force.
Even so, as will be shown later, the average individual
workload - measured in visits per volunteer per annum -
remained considerably greater in the larger urban Schemes
with their high numbers of referrals.  This suggests that a
'hard core' of volunteers may be bearing an exceptionally
heavy load.

When asked to name the worst problems facing their Scheme,
one-third of our respondents, unprompted, mentioned a
shortage of volunteers or difficulties in recruitment
(Appendix, Table A).  Similarly, 38 per cent replied to a
pre-coded question that finding enough volunteers for their
present needs was a 'major' or 'considerable' problem.  On
the other hand, almost a quarter considered it 'no problem
at all'.

Schemes based in <u>inner city areas</u> were by far the most
likely to face major problems of this nature, and only four
out of 35 such Schemes claimed to have no problems at all.[6]
A further factor associated with shortage of volunteers was
that of the age of the Scheme.  Established Schemes
generally complained of more serious recruitment problems
than newer ones, and, interestingly, in every type of area
it was Schemes of 3-4 years old which were the most likely
to report at least some difficulty in finding enough volunteers (see Appendix, Table B).  We may speculate that this
is due partly to natural waning of the initial burst of
enthusiasm which tends to accompany the formation of a new
Scheme (both loss rates of volunteers and proportions of
volunteeers inactive were at their highest in Schemes two
years old),[7] but is mainly a result of rapid growth in
workload as the maturing Scheme gains in experience and

13

enjoys enhanced confidence from the police: the range and number of referrals begin to increase and finding greater numbers of active volunteers becomes a priority. Certainly, our questionnaire returns indicate that both the number of referrals and the number of volunteers per Scheme tend to increase markedly with each year of operation up to three years, and then to level off.[8]

Schemes wishing to maintain or increase their complement of volunteers had experimented with various methods of recruitment. By far the most successful, the majority asserted, had been simply to let the Scheme's needs be known by 'word of mouth' or through 'friends of friends' (see Appendix, Table C, and see also Mawby and Gill, 1986). Nevertheless, as we discuss briefly in the Appendix, this has certain drawbacks. Advertisements in the local press had been tried by two-thirds of all Schemes, but though more successful than other alternatives, only 13 per cent of those trying this method went as far as to call it 'very successful'. Requests to Voluntary Service Bureaux and talks by Scheme members to local groups had been found only moderately fruitful avenues.

On the other hand, most respondents recognised the value of a more indirect form of recruitment: publicity about Victims Support in newspapers and on radio or television. Their responses indicate that at least one in five of all volunteers had joined Schemes primarily as a result of reading articles or hearing programmes about VSS work. Co-ordinators we interviewed stated that prominent local publicity of this kind often led to many enquiries, although some stressed that they had come to expect a subsequent high 'drop-out' rate in the early stages of selection and training (cf. Mawby and Gill, forthcoming). National publicity was generally unproductive in this respect although it was regarded as important for creating general public awareness of the existence of the service.[9]

Once volunteers have commenced training, it seems, the great majority go on to complete it and become active volunteers: 77 per cent of our respondents stated that 'all or nearly all' debutants completed successfully, and only nine per cent said that around half tended to drop out. Again, the Schemes with such problems came disproportionately from inner city areas.[10] We comment briefly upon training practices, including 'drop-out' problems, in the Appendix.

Although some Co-ordinators expressed serious concern about the number of trained volunteers who stayed with their Scheme for only a short period (see below), the national picture of volunteer turnover also seemed fairly

14

satisfactory. Of 1,739 volunteers who, it was stated, had been active visitors twelve months previously, 1,378 were still active at the time the questionnaire was answered - i.e. only 20 per cent had fallen by the wayside over a one-year period.[11] As far as we can determine from contacting other agencies, this rate is well below average for voluntary organisations. For example, the Samaritans have an annual turnover nearer 40 per cent (personal communication).

However, to compound their general recruitment problems, Schemes in inner city areas had greater difficulty than others in 'holding on to' trained volunteers. Seventeen per cent of such Schemes had lost (or had to replace) over half their volunteers within the last twelve months, and less than one-third had managed to keep 80 per cent (see Appendix, Table D). The problem was particularly acute in the largest of the inner city Schemes: only one of the six with twenty or more volunteers had managed to keep over 80 per cent of the same faces for a year.

Some of the inner city Schemes we visited had experienced great difficulty in recruiting volunteers from within the most deprived areas, and many of their members lived outside the district, often several miles away. In such cases it is only a 'hard core' of exceptionally dedicated volunteers who cope successfully for long periods with both the extra travel and the stress of working in a difficult area. Moreover, the more volunteers a Scheme has, the harder it becomes for the Co-ordinator to maintain close enough relationships with them all to prevent some from feeling neglected or dissatisfied. This problem, too, almost certainly becomes magnified in a large city (see Chapter 5).

Finally, like many other aspects of the victim movement, the overall number of volunteers has been growing fast. According to NAVSS, the national total increased by 46 per cent between March 1984 and March 1985. By the latter date there were roughly 3,500 volunteers and 2,400 management committee members in Schemes in the UK. If we assume (based upon our observation of Schemes) that about one in six committee members also acted as visitors, this gives a total of trained visitors approaching 4,000.[12] As well as an increase in overall numbers, then, there was also over the year in question a rise in the average number of volunteers per Scheme or district: roughly speaking, from 15 to 16. The latest figures from NAVSS (1986) indicate that in the year to March 1986, the total number of volunteers increased, in line with the number of Schemes, by about 15 per cent.

## (iii) Coverage of victims by Schemes

We estimate that, by mid-1985, at least 33 million people (59 per cent of the population of the UK) lived in areas covered, nominally at least, by Victims Support Schemes.[13] This represents an outstanding achievement over such a short period, and, together with the widespread plans for expansion referred to earlier, suggests that the National Association's ambition of covering the whole country within the next decade (Reeves, 1985) is eminently attainable.

Of course, there is a vast difference between nominal coverage and full service provision. Living in an area with a Scheme by no means guarantees that one will be visited, or even contacted, in the event of becoming a crime victim. For example, in the 252 areas of England and Wales listed in the 1985 Annual Report as being served by a Victims Support Scheme,[14] recorded offences of residential burglary, robbery, theft from the person, theft of or from motor vehicles, and sexual or serious physical assault - which by no means exhausts all categories of crime with personal victims - together number at least 900,000 per year.[15] To deal with them all, even at the basic level of a letter or telephone call, local Schemes would have to average annually over 3,500 referrals each. And even if the service were restricted only to victims of residential burglary (the crime most often dealt with), each would have to average at least 1,200 such referrals per year.[16] In fact, both the responses to our questionnaire and NAVSS figures presented in their Annual Reports suggest that, thus far, Schemes have been averaging little more than 600 referrals per annum, about 80 per cent of which concern burglaries.[17] In short, even where the 'staple diet' offence of residential burglary is concerned, the police have been referring only about 1 in 3 of all recorded cases in areas which have Schemes.[18]

Perhaps a more positive way of describing the situation is to note that in 1985, somewhere in the region of 1 in 5 of all residential burglaries recorded by the police in the UK were referred to Schemes, and that this proportion will almost certainly grow to around 1 in 4 in 1986. For most other kinds of offence the proportions referred have been very much lower,[19] but again practices are changing fast. The official total of referrals presented by NAVSS increased from 125,000 in 1984/5 to 185,000 in 1985/6. There was a particularly rapid increase in the number of violent offences referred, these more than doubling from 8,600 to 17,500.

Unfortunately, the national picture looks a little gloomier - though still remarkable considering the short time taken to achieve it - if one takes further account of

16

the quality of service provision by looking at 'coverage' not simply in terms of referrals received, but in terms of visits made to victims' homes. We asked respondents to estimate (a) for what proportions of referred victims their first attempt at contact was by letter, telephone or unannounced visit, and (b) how many of those referred to the Scheme were eventually seen in person by a volunteer. The following analyses are based upon returns from the 159 Schemes which were able to provide at least rough estimates.

These 159 Schemes had received between them approximately 48,200 referrals over the previous six months.[20] Their estimates of the proportions of victims initially contacted by each method, combined to produce the following picture:

| First attempted contact by: | No. | (%) |
|---|---|---|
| Unannounced visit* | 27,300 | (57) |
| Letter | 11,500 | (24) |
| Telephone | 8,400 | (17) |
| No contact attempted | 1,000 | (2) |

* Includes cases where the police (but not the Scheme) informed victims about the service in advance.

It has to be recognised that some respondents, naturally eager to present a favourable picture of their Schemes' work, may have exaggerated the proportion of victims visited unannounced, so the figure of 57 per cent has to be regarded as a probable over-estimate. Certainly, from examining the records of the eight Schemes we studied in depth, we would put this proportion at around 45 per cent (see Chapter 4). In the following analysis, therefore, we shall show 'maximum' and 'minimum' contact figures, depending upon which estimate one accepts.

First of all, projecting the above percentages on to the national referral figures given by NAVSS, it would appear that volunteers were by mid-1985 making 'unannounced visits' to victims' homes at a rate equivalent to between 55,000 and 70,000 per year, and by mid-1986 to between 80,000 and 105,000 per year.

Of course, by no means all victims are found at home when the volunteer arrives, and many volunteers are too busy to make another journey later. In the Schemes we studied in depth, the overall failure rate for unannounced visits varied between 30 and 44 per cent. Some other visits were generated from replies to letters or telephone calls, but these formed only small proportions of the total number of visits achieved (see Chapter 4).[21]

Taking the above findings into account, we may calculate that between 35 per cent (according to Scheme records we examined) and 44 per cent (according to questionnaire returns) of all victims referred to Schemes are eventually spoken to, face-to-face, by a volunteer.[22] This means that in 1985 volunteers spoke face-to-face to between 44,000 and 55,000 victims of crime, 35,000 - 44,000 of them victims of burglary in a dwelling. We can therefore calculate with a fair degree of confidence that in that year somewhere between seven and nine per cent of all victims of burglary offences recorded in England and Wales spoke to a volunteer in person. Moreover, the latest NAVSS referral figures suggest that in 1986 this proportion will have risen to at least ten per cent. Such a degree of 'outreach', particularly in relation to such a common offence, is almost certainly unsurpassed by victim service agencies anywhere else in the world. Even so, it shows how far the movement has to go if it is to come anywhere near being a comprehensive visiting service.

(iv) Workload

As stated earlier, in mid-1984 Schemes and districts possessed, on average, 15 trained volunteers each. We calculate that, again on average, over the previous six-month period these volunteers had each made about ten initial unannounced visits[23] (with or without finding the victim at home) and one visit at a victim's request (i.e. in response to a Scheme letter or telephone call): in short, they had visited fewer than two new addresses per month each.

This sounds a fairly modest workload, but it should first be pointed out that victims are quite often visited more than once. Secondly, as with most statistics relating to Victims Support Schemes' activities, the national averages conceal very wide variations between individual areas. For example, the four Schemes with the 'busiest' volunteers in terms of making unannounced visits claimed to be averaging over ten new visits per volunteer every month. At the other end of the scale, over a third of all Schemes had averaged under one visit per volunteer per month.[24] It can be seen from Table 2.1 that Schemes based in large urban areas achieved considerably higher averages than those working in small-town or rural areas, despite the problems of high turnover in (and losing touch with) volunteers in inner city areas described earlier. This suggests that, in order to cope with the flood of referrals in high crime rate areas, some individual volunteers were putting a great deal of their time into VS visiting.

18

## Table 2.1
### Average number of visits made to new addresses per volunteer per month; by type of area in which Scheme is based

| | Average number of visits per volunteer | | | | |
|---|---|---|---|---|---|
| Scheme based in: | Under two per month % | 2 - 4.99 per month % | 5 per month or over % | Total % | |
| Large city (250,000+) | 53 | 31 | 16 | 100 | (N = 58) |
| Medium-sized town (50,000-250,000) | 52 | 39 | 9 | 100 | (N = 54) |
| Small town/rural | 85 | 13 | 2 | 100 | (N = 47) |
| All Schemes and districts | 62 | 28 | 9 | 100 | (N = 159) |

Finally, it is a sobering thought for those who would like to see every victim visited that, simply to go to the home of everyone referred to Schemes in 1985, the 4,000 or so trained volunteers then registered would have had to visit at a rate achieved in only nine per cent of the Schemes responding to our questionnaire. And a major increase in referral rates - for example, through the extension of 'automatic' referral systems to most Schemes - would produce an overall workload well beyond the levels so far achieved in all but a tiny handful of Schemes. By way of illustration, had it been somehow centrally agreed that a visitor would be sent to knock on the door of every victim reporting a residential burglary in the areas covered by Schemes in 1984, the then existing volunteers would have had to average at least five times the number of visits to homes they actually achieved.[25] If the same hypothetical policy had been extended to all other notifiable offences with personal victims, volunteers would have had to average 8 or more initial visits per week each - i.e. 20 to 25 times the rate actually achieved.[26] A voluntary organisation - especially one with few paid employees to organise the distribution of tasks - can hardly be expected to reach these kinds of targets. When it is remembered that crime rates are several times greater in inner city areas than in small town or rural areas - and hence the burden upon volunteers several times heavier - such tasks are seen to be bordering upon the impossible under present circumstances. This raises major questions about the tasks that Schemes should attempt to perform and the way that they should organise their resources; these will be considered further in Chapters 5 and 8.

(v)  Co-ordinators

While it is still argued in some quarters that it is wrong
to pay people to work in what is essentially a voluntary
organisation, the feeling seems to be growing throughout the
Victims Support movement that, in all but the smallest
Schemes, the task of the Co-ordinator is becoming too
onerous and time-consuming to be left to an unpaid
volunteer.  Not only is it unfair on the individual, it is
argued, but an overburdened voluntary Co-ordinator may slip
into inefficient ways, to the detriment of the Scheme as a
whole.  These problems will be discussed more fully in
Chapter 5.  Here, we simply examine the distribution of paid
and unpaid Co-ordinators, and outline some apparent differences between Schemes which do and do not pay their key
personnel.

Our national survey revealed that the 179 Schemes and
districts existing in mid-1984 possessed 255 main or
assistant Co-ordinators.[27]  Among these were 42 paid to
work full-time and 43 part-time, but the great majority of
Schemes - almost exactly two-thirds - had to depend upon Co-
ordinators who received either no remuneration at all or
only a small honorarium (see Table 2.2).

### Table 2.2
### Paid and Unpaid Co-ordinators
### Summer 1984

| Main Co-ordinator | Number of Schemes | | Number of Co-ordinators | |
|---|---|---|---|---|
| Full-time paid | 37 | (21%) | 42 | (16%) |
| Part-time paid | 22 | (12%) | 43 | (17%) |
| Honorarium | 40 | (22%) | 60 | (24%) |
| Without remuneration | 80 | (45%) | 110 | (43%) |
| | | | | |
| Total | 179 | (100%) | 255 | (100%) |

NAVSS figures for both March 1985 and March 1986 show
considerable increases in the numbers of paid Co-ordinators.
By the first date, there were 59 full-time and 80 part-time,
increases of 40 per cent and 86 per cent respectively.  The
1986 totals are not sub-divided, but they show 218 paid
staff of all kinds, including those receiving honoraria.
The Annual Report states that at least 157 Schemes and
districts  - i.e. a minimum of 53 per cent - were by that
time served by a paid Co-ordinator, although some of these
shared the same person.  Thus the proportion without paid

20

help of any kind, fairly constant between 1984 and 1985, seems to have fallen significantly over the following year.[28] On the other hand, the fact that even in 1986 only 67 Co-ordinators were receiving over £5,000 per annum suggests that the number working full-time for a proper salary is still not very large.

For those who are paid, the main sources of funds are grants from County Councils and other local authorities, the MSC Community Programme and Voluntary Project Programme, Urban Aid, and DHSS Opportunities for Volunteering. Including assistance with rents and running costs, about one-third of all Schemes received grants of over £1,000 from public funds in 1984/5, and the total amount received in 1985/6 was of the order of £1 million. However, we found during our fieldwork that many such grants are inadequate, take a great deal of time to apply for, and are uncertain of renewal (see Chapter 5). Most seriously, the termination of a grant can mean that an experienced Co-ordinator is forced to leave, with a consequent damaging loss of both continuity and expertise. It is revealing that when asked 'what would you say were the most difficult problems facing your Scheme at the moment?', 36 per cent of all respondents to our questionnaire - and 46 per cent in Schemes with paid Co-ordinators - mentioned (without any prompting) financial problems. These were mentioned, in fact, more frequently than any other type of problem (Appendix Table A).

What differences were there between Schemes with paid and unpaid Co-ordinators? First and foremost, as one would expect, the bulk of paid Co-ordinators were to be found in large urban areas: only three of the 48 small town/rural Schemes replying to our questionnaire had a full-time paid Co-ordinator, compared with 18 (31 per cent) of the 59 in large cities and 13 (23 per cent) of the 56 in medium-sized towns. Therefore, in order to avoid the distorting effects of the obvious differences between urban and rural areas, the following analysis is based only upon Schemes situated in towns with a population above 50,000.

Within urban areas, the differences revealed by the questionnaire between Schemes with and without paid Co-ordinators were by no means vast, although the overall level of activity certainly tended to be higher in those with paid staff. While there were no significant differences between them in terms of their age or of the populations of the areas they covered, Schemes with paid Co-ordinators tended to receive higher numbers of referrals than those relying purely on voluntary help. They also generally had more volunteers to deal with the workload, so more victims received visits (see Table 2.3).

## Table 2.3
Numbers of referrals, numbers of volunteers and numbers of visits in urban schemes with or without paid Co-ordinators

| Status of (main) Co-ordinator | Number of trained volunteers with Scheme | | | |
|---|---|---|---|---|
| | Under 10 | 10 - 19 | 20 or more | Total |
| | % | % | % | % |
| Full-time paid | 13 | 45 | 42 | 100 (N = 31) |
| Part-time paid | 12 | 65 | 23 | 100 (N = 17) |
| Honorarium | 19 | 52 | 29 | 100 (N = 31) |
| Unpaid | 36 | 53 | 11 | 100 (N = 36) |
| All | 23 | 55 | 23 | 100 (N = 115) |

| Status of (main) Co-ordinator | Number of referrals received in past six months | | | |
|---|---|---|---|---|
| | Under 100 | 100 - 199 | 200 or more | Total |
| | % | % | % | % |
| Full-time paid | 10 | 17 | 72 | 100 (N = 29) |
| Part-time paid | 6 | 18 | 76 | 100 (N = 17) |
| Honorarium | 19 | 13 | 68 | 100 (N = 31) |
| Unpaid | 34 | 20 | 46 | 100 (N = 35) |
| All | 20 | 17 | 63 | 100 (N = 112) |

| Status of (main) Co-ordinator | Number of victims visited in past six months | | | |
|---|---|---|---|---|
| | Under 100 | 100 - 199 | 200 or more | Total |
| | % | % | % | % |
| Full-time paid | 21 | 24 | 55 | 100 (N = 29) |
| Part-time paid | 29 | 29 | 41 | 100 (N = 17) |
| Honorarium | 26 | 39 | 35 | 100 (N = 31) |
| Unpaid | 54 | 17 | 29 | 100 (N = 35) |
| All | 34 | 27 | 39 | 100 (N = 112) |

It might be expected that paid Co-ordinators would be much more efficient than voluntary Co-ordinators in terms of handling volunteers - keeping them interested, organising their workload, monitoring their activities, and so on. However, although the statistical evidence points in this direction, the differences uncovered were not strong. For example, the proportion of volunteers regularly active was only marginally higher in Schemes with paid Co-ordinators and there were only minimal differences in the proportions of volunteers leaving the different types of Scheme.[29] Again, Schemes with paid Co-ordinators tended to hold volunteer meetings more frequently than others (see Appendix, Table E), but the difference was again small.

A superficial indication of the relative 'progressiveness' of Schemes with full-time paid Co-ordinators is provided by Appendix Table F. These Schemes were more likely than other urban Schemes to have accompanied victims to court and supported the relatives of murder victims. They were also more likely to have plans for expanding their range of services. But the most striking difference lay in the extent of assistance with CICB claims. Half the Schemes without paid staff had dealt with none at all, while 89 per cent of those with paid Co-ordinators had dealt with some.

If one can speak of the work of Schemes in terms of 'productivity' - i.e. the efficiency with which available resources such as volunteer labour are used - our question-naire produced some indications that paid Co-ordinators may be more 'productive' than others. For example, the number of victims seen per volunteer per annum was significantly higher in Schemes with full-time paid Co-ordinators than elsewhere, even when taking into account differences between Schemes in numbers of volunteers and numbers of referrals.[30] Other similar indicators, such as the number of initial unannounced visits made per volunteer (and per 'active volunteer') pointed in the same direction.

Closer inspection highlights a further important difference. While Schemes with voluntary Co-ordinators, looked at as a whole, showed lower 'productivity', there was

### Table 2.4
### Number of victims seen in home per volunteer, by payment or not to Co-ordinator (urban Schemes only)

| Status of (main) Co-ordinator | Average number of victims seen in home*per volunteer over the last six months | | | | |
|---|---|---|---|---|---|
| | Under 10 | 10 - 29 | 30 or over | Total | (No. of Schemes) |
| | % | % | % | % | |
| Full-time paid | 41 | 41 | 17 | 100 | (N = 29) |
| Part-time paid | 53 | 29 | 18 | 100 | (N = 17) |
| Honorarium | 58 | 29 | 13 | 100 | (N = 31) |
| Voluntary | 57 | 17 | 26 | 100 | (N = 35) |
| All | 53 | 29 | 19 | 100 | (N = 112) |

* Based on Co-ordinators' estimates. Our own would be somewhat lower throughout.

nevertheless among them a highly active minority which seemed to rival in every respect the most 'professional' of those with paid staff. Indeed, as can be seen in Table 2.4, there was actually a higher proportion of Schemes with unpaid Co-ordinators than with full-time paid Co-ordinators which had averaged over 30 victims seen per volunteer during the previous six months. In other words, the _range_ of levels of activity was much greater among Schemes which relied wholly upon volunteer labour. As we shall show in Chapter 5, this appears to be largely a function of the energy and dedication of individual Co-ordinators, some of whom seem to work astonishingly hard for no financial reward.

## (vi) Referral systems: policy and practice

Victims Support Schemes rely very heavily upon the police for their referrals. The extent of this dependence is illustrated in Table 2.5. Altogether, 63 per cent of functioning Schemes and districts 'never' or 'very rarely' received referrals from any other source, and only 4 per cent stated that they 'quite often' did so.[31]

Table 2.5

Do you receive referrals from sources other than the police?

|  | Number of Schemes | (%) |
| --- | --- | --- |
| Quite often | 6 | (4) |
| Occasionally | 53 | (33) |
| Very rarely | 56 | (36) |
| Never | 46 | (29) |
| Total | 161 | (100) |

Whatever the disadvantages of this near-total dependence upon the active co-operation of the police - a situation rare, if not unique, among voluntary groups anywhere - the majority of Schemes could argue that, if only in terms of the numbers of victims being referred, it has also proved increasingly productive. NAVSS figures show a sixfold increase in the annual total of referrals between 1982 and 1985/6,[32] and an increase in referrals per Scheme of more than 150 per cent over the same period. Our survey showed that in mid-1984, 29 per cent of Schemes which had been established for over six months were still experiencing a rising referral rate - and almost one-third of these a 'greatly rising' rate. However, at the same time we were surprised to find that as many as 22 per cent had been experiencing a declining number of referrals - a topic to which we shall return presently.

The type of referral system advocated by NAVSS as the ideal for established and well-organised Schemes - its increased adoption clearly being one of the main reasons for the overall increase in referral rates - is variously called 'blanket', 'automatic' or 'direct' referral. This means that, except in exceptional circumstances, the police will refer all cases of certain types of offence, whether or not the victim is known to need support and whether or not the victim's consent to the referral has been obtained.

In mid-1984, some version of this system was the agreed referral policy in 57 per cent of all functioning Schemes and districts. In many cases, the policy applied only to the offences of burglary, theft from the person and/or street robbery, although, according to our respondents, it also applied to woundings or assaults in 39 per cent of Schemes. Alternative referral policies, which we shall refer to generically as 'selective referral', included referral only with the consent of the victim, and selection by police officers (from records or from personal knowledge) of cases which seemed to be 'likely candidates' for VSS support. Such systems were complex and overlapping, but some idea of their distribution can be gleaned from the fact that nearly 20 per cent of Schemes received burglary cases only with the consent of the victim. Finally, five Schemes restricted their service purely to selected elderly victims.

Table 2.6
Number of referrals received; by whether referral system 'automatic' or 'selective'

| Referral System | Number of referrals received in past six months | | | | |
|---|---|---|---|---|---|
| | Under 100 % | 100-199 % | 200 or more % | Total % | |
| 'Automatic' | 20 | 27 | 53 | 100 | (N=88) |
| 'Selective' | 51 | 10 | 38 | 100 | (N=65) |
| All | 33 | 20 | 47 | 100 | (N=153) |

Table 2.6 shows that, as one would expect, Schemes with 'automatic' referral policies tended to receive many more referrals than those with 'selective' systems. It is also

significant that most of the Schemes in which the number of referrals had been either declining or fluctuating greatly were those relying upon police selection and/or victim consent (see Table 2.7). This is confirmed by our fieldwork experience that the flow of referrals to Schemes dependent upon initiatives by individual police officers[33] tended to slow markedly when there were changes in key personnel or pressure of work mounted (see Chapter 4).

### Table 2.7
### Trends in referral rates by type of referral policy

| | Type of referral policy | | |
| --- | --- | --- | --- |
| | 'Automatic' | 'Selective' | |
| Trends in referrals | % | % | |
| Declining greatly | 12 | 88 | (N=8) |
| Declining somewhat | 46 | 54 | (N=26) |
| Fluctuating a lot | 45 | 55 | (N=54) |
| Steady | 61 | 39 | (N=20) |
| Rising somewhat | 71 | 29 | (N=31) |
| Rising greatly | 79 | 21 | (N=14) |
| All | 57 | 43 | (N=153) |

On the whole, respondents were fairly satisfied with both the policy and the practice of their local police regarding referrals. Over 83 per cent indicated that the agreed policy was 'always' or 'usually' carried out, and 75 per cent that they were 'very' or 'fairly' happy with the current arrangements. There was, however, a significant minority of 27 Schemes (17 per cent) in which the respondent stated that members were 'very unhappy' with the arrangements. This dissatisfaction came overwhelmingly from Schemes with selective referral arrangements, particularly those in which the number of referrals was declining or fluctuating a great deal.[34]

(vii)  Types of victim referred

As mentioned earlier, around 80 per cent of all people referred to Schemes are victims of residential burglary. As recorded offences of burglary certainly constitute no more than one-third of all recorded serious crimes with a personal victim (see footnote 26), there is a significant over-representation here which demands both explanation and justification. Other offences over-represented in referrals to Schemes - although less important in terms of absolute numbers - include theft from the person (4 per cent of referrals to Schemes but no more than 2 per cent of recorded

26

offences with a personal victim) and rape (0.2 per cent and 0.1 per cent respectively). By contrast, offences of robbery, assault and wounding (6 per cent as opposed to 9 per cent) were somewhat under-represented, while those of simple theft, criminal damage and, above all, theft of or from motor vehicles were grossly under-represented.

The reasons for the concentration upon burglary appear to be partly historical, partly 'ideological', partly to do with the limitations of volunteers, and partly based upon conclusions from 'trial and error'. Out of the initial experiment in Bristol there emerged a basic working model of Victims Support which, although undergoing various trans-formations, has been adopted essentially unchanged by most Schemes. For most, their 'bread-and-butter' work still consists of unannounced 'one-off' visits to as many victims as possible, demonstrating that someone in the community 'cares', and offering simple practical assistance and a 'listening ear' to allow the expression of emotional reactions. The Bristol Scheme quickly discovered that burglary was a very suitable crime for this kind of operation. Generally speaking, victims of this offence were found to be considerably upset by the experience and were very pleased to talk to a volunteer, yet at the same time one visit (with perhaps some follow-up practical assistance with repairs or security) seemed all that was necessary. In most cases, volunteers did not have to be greatly skilled to carry out the work, but there were sufficient problems for them to 'get their teeth into' to make them feel that the visit had been worthwhile. By contrast, visits to victims of offences such as theft from vehicles were quickly discon-tinued, as a relatively small proportion of those visited seemed to need any support, and volunteers' journeys were often perceived as 'wasted' (despite their value as a 'gesture'). The sheer volume of crime meant that some priorities had to be set, and burglary victims were one of the most obvious candidates for high priority.

In fact, at many Schemes which followed the Bristol lead (although this was not the case with the Bristol Scheme itself), the offence of burglary became virtually the only object of attention. Not only did they exclude 'lesser' offences such as theft, but came to ignore equally or more serious crimes such as wounding, rape, robbery and murder. Many were - and continue to be - encouraged in this by local police officers with doubts about the value of 'non-profess-ional' intervention in more serious cases, or with 'stereo-typed' views about victims and their needs (see Chapter 4). Policemen see the initial distress of burglary victims often enough to understand the need for VSS, and also tend to regard them - in a different light to, for example, many of the predominantly young male victims of assault - as 'deserving' of assistance, having done nothing to provoke an offence committed by a complete stranger. At the same time, the 'stranger to stranger' element of burglary largely relieves the police of worries about 'naive' volunteers becoming enmeshed in disputes between victims and offenders who know each other, which is much more common in assault cases. And not least important, it is administratively convenient: there are enough burglaries to ensure a steady flow of referrals to keep Schemes happy, and not much careful 'sifting' is necessary to exclude victims who might pose a threat to volunteers and cases where a volunteer's involvement could possibly lead to legal complications. Thus 'automatic' referral can quite safely be left to a junior officer or civilian clerk.

While this situation has undoubtedly been changing rapidly over the past few years, not least because of consistent NAVSS advice to aim for automatic referral of a wide range of offences, there is no doubt that burglary remains the main focus of attention in a high proportion of Schemes. Table 2.8 shows, for all but 12 of the Schemes and districts active in mid-1984, the police referral policies applied to eleven different types of offence. It will be observed that

### Table 2.8
### Police referral policies for different offences in 161 Schemes and districts existing in Summer 1984

#### Referral policy

| Type of offence | All but a few special exceptions referred % | Certain selected cases referred % | No cases of this type referred % | Total % |
|---|---|---|---|---|
| Residential burglary | 57 | 41 | 2 | 100 |
| Attempted burglary | 53 | 46 | 1 | 100 |
| Theft from the person | 45 | 50 | 5 | 100 |
| Street robbery/ 'mugging' | 45 | 49 | 6 | 100 |
| Theft of/from car | 6 | 24 | 70 | 100 |
| Other theft | 22 | 44 | 34 | 100 |
| Criminal damage | 25 | 53 | 22 | 100 |
| Assault, wounding (not domestic) | 39 | 44 | 17 | 100 |
| Domestic assault | 6 | 29 | 65 | 100 |
| Rape | 23 | 29 | 48 | 100 |
| Indecent assault | 25 | 36 | 39 | 100 |

70 per cent of Schemes, as a matter of policy (either the Scheme's or that of the local police), received no victims of theft of or from cars, and 65 per cent none of domestic assault. Almost half received no rape victims, although a high proportion of those that did expected to have referred to them all such victims in their area. Over one in five were never given any cases of vandalism, and - a situation more difficult to justify - over one in six never dealt with cases of assault. These issues are explored further in Chapter 4.

In some areas, the concept of 'victim' has been understood to include not only victims of crime, but those of road accidents, bereavement, fires, floods, and so on. Indeed, NAVSS figures indicate that in 1985/6, one per cent of all referrals were of 'non-crime' victims. Whether Victims Support should be extended into these areas, and if so at what point to 'draw the line', are issues on which Schemes tend to be split (see Chapter 5). This is reflected in Table 2.9, which shows how many Schemes, by mid-1984, had taken on various kinds of cases outside the usual crime categories. About a third had accepted cases of sudden death or bereavement, but other 'non-crime' referrals - including racial harrassment, which many would consider to have criminal overtones if not actually leading to a recorded offence (see Chapter 3) - were much less common.

Table 2.9
Number of Schemes accepting 'non-crime' referrals over previous six months

| | Number of Schemes dealing with: | | | |
| | Several Cases | One or two cases | No cases | Total |
| --- | --- | --- | --- | --- |
| Sudden deaths, bereavements | 21 | 33 | 107 | 161 |
| Road accidents | 8 | 21 | 132 | 161 |
| Racial harassment | 5 | 24 | 132 | 161 |
| Fires, floods | 2 | 11 | 148 | 161 |

In addition to the kinds of case shown, respondents mentioned having received referrals relating to suicides and attempted suicides (15 Schemes), family or neighbourhood disputes (10), people 'found wandering' (9) and, less often, cot deaths, missing persons, accidental injury and 'hit and run' cases.

29

## (viii)   Serious crime and long-term assistance

The 'traditional' model of victim support in Britain, as
developed by the Bristol Scheme and adopted by most others
since, has been of a short-term, 'crisis intervention'
service.   Volunteers have generally been trained to expect
to see most victims only once or twice:   anyone needing
longer-term support, it has been widely agreed, should be
'referred on' to a specialist agency for professional help.
However, not only have some Schemes always disagreed with
this policy, taking on long-term cases themselves, but many
have experienced difficulty in finding agencies both
suitable and willing to accept referrals of victims.
Consequently, a considerable amount of rethinking has been
taking place, at NAVSS headquarters and at conferences and
other meetings across the country.   With specially-trained
volunteers, it has been argued, Schemes can take on the
responsibility of long-term support for victims of serious
crimes, in particular for relatives of murder victims and
for victims of rape.   We shall discuss such developments at
greater length in Chapters 7 and 8.   Here, we simply
indicate what the practices of Schemes were, nationwide, in
mid-1984, and how many were thinking of expanding their
services in new directions.

Table 2.10 shows how often Schemes had taken on long-term
support or counselling of victims.   Only two claimed to have
done so many times and it was an exceptional event for the
great majority.   However, this is a situation which has been
changing rapidly, and several Schemes are already heavily
committed to long-term work with rape victims.

### Table 2.10
Q.  Has your Scheme, or have individual volunteers, taken on
    on long-term support or counselling of victims
    (i.e. several visits over a period of months)?

|  | Number | (%) |
|---|---|---|
| Many times | 2 | (1) |
| Several times | 31 | (19) |
| Once or twice | 83 | (52) |
| Never | 45 | (28) |
|  | 161 | (100) |

We also asked whether Schemes had any volunteers who had
been specially trained to handle very difficult or sensitive
cases, such as rape, murder or bereavement.   A total of 72
(45 per cent) replied in the affirmative.   Of these, 46 had
volunteers whose training had taken place as part of their

paid profession or their work with other voluntary organisations (e.g. CRUSE or the Samaritans) and 22 had volunteers who had been to special discussion groups or courses set up by the Scheme, Region or local police. Four Schemes stated simply that such skills were taught as part of their normal training. Altogether, 83 Schemes (52 per cent) had dealt at some time with cases of rape - ten, apparently, without any special training - and 30 (19 per cent) had supported relatives of murder victims. The correctness of allowing volunteers without special training to take on rape cases is questioned in Chapter 7.

While 83 per cent of functioning Schemes had been referred at least one case of physical assault, we were surprised to find that fewer than 60 per cent had ever helped with or advised on a claim to the Criminal Injuries Compensation Board, and that only 16 per cent had helped with more than three. Moreover, only 35 Schemes (21 per cent) had actually dealt with any CICB claims on behalf of victims, as opposed to simply offering advice.

In sum, it has to be concluded that, at the time we surveyed Schemes in mid-1984, despite a growing interest in expanding VSS services to include more intensive work with victims of serious violent crime, this had not yet been translated into practice in the majority of Schemes and districts, which remained primarily geared to 'one-off' visits to burglary victims. However, we re-iterate that we know from many visits to Schemes in 1985 and from conversations with Co-ordinators and others at conferences and workshops in 1986 that this situation has been changing very rapidly.


### Notes to Chapter 2

1.    Where a County Co-ordinator has responded on behalf of more than one Scheme, we have, as far as possible, 'unpacked' the replies to represent each district separately.

2.    Altogether, six of the 179 Schemes were not yet operational, four of which were among the 16 Schemes failing to reply to our questionnaire.

3.    By comparison, only 65 per cent of the population of England and Wales lives in urban areas of 50,000 and above (Social Trends, 1985). It is true that almost half of the urban-based Schemes also cover some surrounding rural areas, but, even so, large urban areas are certainly over-represented in Scheme coverage as a whole.

4.    Of the 26 Schemes under three years old which were based in cities of over 250,000, 17 were considering expanding their boundaries.

5.   The highest numbers of volunteers were by no means always found in Schemes in large cities.  For example, six of the 14 Schemes with over 30 volunteers were based in medium-sized towns, all but one covering an area with a population of under 100,000.

6.   29 per cent of inner city Schemes said they had 'major problems' in finding enough volunteers, compared with only 8 per cent elsewhere.

7.   Fifty-five per cent of Schemes two years old had experienced a turnover in volunteers of at least 30 per cent during the past year (compared with 30 per cent of other Schemes);  and 40 per cent (compared with only 18 per cent of others) had at least a third of their registered volunteers inactive.

8.   The percentages of Schemes receiving over 500 referrals in the previous six months, and of Schemes with 20 or more volunteers, are shown below, in relation to the age of the Scheme:

|  | % receiving over 500 referrals in six months | % with 20 or more volunteers |
|---|---|---|
| 1st year of operation | 0 | 10 |
| 1 year old | 8 | 12 |
| 2 years old | 12 | 30 |
| 3 years old | 24 | 41 |
| 4 years old | 22 | 28 |
| 5 years old | 21 | 29 |
| 6 years or older | 28 | 22 |
| All | 17 | 24 |

9.   One unsolicited source of volunteers was from among victims themselves.   In the course of research we met several who had been so impressed by the gesture of an offer of help that they had offered their own services to their local Scheme.  To our respondents' knowledge, 170 (7 per cent) of the total of 2,460 volunteers had been recruited in this fashion - despite reservations in some Schemes about the possible unsuitability of people who were still suffering effects themselves.

10.   18 per cent of inner city Schemes had 'drop-out' rates from training near 50 per cent, compared with 6 per cent of all others.

11.  The above figures are based on replies from the 132 Schemes and districts which had been in existence for over 12 months.

12.  The total number of volunteer visitors is calculated as follows:

Number in 186 Schemes responding  to NAVSS inquiry (March 1985)  2,633
plus:  number (estimated) in non-responding Schemes               905
plus:  number (estimated) of visitors on management committees     400
                                                                   -----
Total                                                              3,938

Calculations based upon returns to our questionnaire and the NAVSS rate of increase give a very similar total:

| | |
|---|---|
| Number in 163 responding Schemes | 2,460 |
| plus: estimated number in 16 non-responding Schemes | 240 |
| plus: increase of 46 per cent 1984-85 | 1,243 |
| Total | 3,943 |

13.   The total population covered by the 92 per cent of Schemes and districts which responded to our questionnaire in 1984 was 24,990,000. We estimate the population covered by those not responding as approximately 1,800,000, while the 60 or so new Schemes subsequently created by mid-1985 added coverage to approximately 7 million more.   Indeed, by the time of publication, it is likely that 3-4 million more than this will be covered.

14.   For the following calculations we have used as a base the Schemes and districts listed in the 1985 Annual Report as existing in June 1985. As discussed earlier, it is likely that, on local definitions, the total would be 15-20 fewer:   the projected burdens per Scheme would thus in reality be somewhat heavier still.

15.   Calculated from the total number of offences recorded by the police in these categories in England and Wales, and the proportion of the population of England and Wales estimated to live in areas covered by Schemes (64 per cent).   900,000 is probably a considerable underestimate, as existing Schemes already cover most urban, high-crime areas and those not yet covered are mainly low or medium crime-rate areas.

16.   Moreover, the gulf in crime rates between inner city and rural areas means that certain Schemes would have to bear a burden several times higher than the above average figures indicate.

17.   The 159 Schemes and districts (according to our definition) for which we have a fairly reliable estimate of the number of referrals received over a six-month period in 1984, together produced a total of 48,246 - an average of approximately 600 each projected over the whole year.   NAVSS figures yield rather lower averages per Scheme/district, as more small areas are defined by them as separate districts, and their average reached 600 only in 1985/6.

18.   According to NAVSS estimates, about 100,000 burglary victims were referred to Schemes between April 1984 and March 1985.   Over the same period, we calculate, at least 300,000 offences of burglary in a dwelling were recorded in areas covered by Schemes.   However, the ratio improved somewhat in 1985/6, as referrals grew by 45 per cent while the number of Schemes grew by only 15 per cent.

19.   Nevertheless, the calculation in the NAVSS Annual Report 1984/5 that 16 per cent of all recorded cases of rape in England and Wales in

1984 were referred to Schemes, is worthy of note, if perhaps a slight over-estimate. (The more 'progressive' Schemes were more likely to reply to the NAVSS questionnaire.)

20. Where Schemes had been operational for less than six months, we projected their current referral rates forward.

21. A few more visits were generated from replies to letters or cards put through the letter-boxes of victims who were out when called upon.

22. We also asked respondents to estimate how many referred victims were 'actually seen in their homes'. These totalled 23,800 for the six-month period in question, i.e. 48 per cent of the total referrals. The fact that respondents' estimates of 'successful contact' were higher than our own was not unexpected. Several Co-ordinators we spoke to were unaware of the high proportion of victims whom volunteers found to be out when they visited. Others completing the questionnaire clearly assumed (as could be seen when their answer to this question was compared with that to the question about the percentage of unannounced visits) that all victims whose names were given to volunteers were actually seen. Moreover, it is natural for committed workers, when asked to make such an estimate, to 'blow their own Scheme's trumpet' a little by giving the highest figure which seems possible. (Few Schemes keep records from which the true figures can be easily extracted.)

23. Between 9 and 11, according to which estimate one uses (see previous section).

24. The differences can also be expressed in terms of personal contact: volunteers in three Schemes had spoken in person to over 50 victims each over the previous six months - i.e. two per week each - while in 49 Schemeseach volunteer had averaged personal contact withunder five.

25. The average required would have been about 1.8 initial visits per volunteer per week, to burglary victims alone. This assumes 250,000 offences of burglary in a dwelling recorded in the Scheme areas existing in England and Wales in mid-1984 - an estimate (and almost certainly on under-estimate, considering the urban bias in the location of Schemes) made by multiplying the number of offences known to the police in 1984 (476,700) by the proportion of the population of England and Wales then living in Scheme areas (52 per cent).

26. It is impossible to tell how many of the offences in the largest categories in Criminal Statistics - theft and criminal damage - had personal as opposed to institutional victims, but a conservative estimate would be 1,500,000 (or 800,000 in the 1984 Scheme areas). With burglaries and sexual and violent offences, the total number of offences in Scheme areas, to be handled by 2,700 volunteers, would have reached 1,200,000. Certainly, the number of volunteers increased markedly in 1985, but so did the number of areas to be covered, so the basic task per volunteer would not be not greatly changed.

27.   Information about the 16 Schemes which did not reply to our questionnaire was added from NAVSS records.

28.   The Annual Report give figures of 53 per cent for 1983/4 and 55 per cent for 1985.   These, it will be noted, are considerably higher than our figure (Table 2.2) of 45 per cent.   The difference is explained by the fact that NAVSS officers have counted every small district as a separate Scheme, whereas we have taken the local interpretation of which districts are or are not separate.

29.   47 per cent of urban Schemes with voluntary Co-ordinators, and 55 per cent of those with full-time paid Co-ordinators, reported 90 per cent or more of their volunteers to be 'regularly active'.   50 per cent of urban Schemes with voluntary Co-ordinators, and 58 per cent of those with full-time paid Co-ordinators, had kept at least 80 per cent of their volunteer force for over a year.

30.   Among urban Schemes with 10-19 volunteers which were receiving referrals at a rate above 400 per year, 8 of the 9 with full-time paid Co-ordinators achieved a 'victims seen per volunteer' rate of over 20 per annum, compared with 16 of the 25 without full-time staff.   (These figures are based on Co-ordinators' estimates of numbers of visits achieved, so may be somewhat inflated.)

31.   Asked to name the most common source, if any, other than the police, 21 per cent mentioned Social Services departments, 20 per cent self-referrals, 7 per cent Citizens' Advice Bureaux and 7 per cent voluntary welfare agencies such as Age Concern or church groups.

32.   The figures were originally given for the year January to December, but in 1984 NAVSS changed its official year to run from April to March.

33.   Co-ordinators received referrals from a wide variety of personnel within police stations, the most common principal contacts being Collators (27 per cent), Inspectors or Chief Inspectors (20 per cent), Community Liaison Officers (13 per cent), Desk Sergeants (12 per cent) and 'CID Admin' (9 per cent).   Eight of the Schemes with selective referral policies had no fixed liaison point, relying upon investigating officers or 'any PC' to let them know when there was a case thought to deserve their attention.

34.   Dissatisfaction also varied with the job or rank of the officer(s) who usually passed referrals to the Scheme:   while 84 per cent of Schemes receiving them from Inspectors, Collators or 'CID Admin' staff were very or fairly happy, the equivalent figure for those relying upon the investigating officer or 'any PC' was only 50 per cent.

# 3 The effects of crime and victims' 'needs'

## Introduction

### (i) Conflicting results

Members of the Management Committee of any Victims Support Scheme aiming to provide an appropriate level of service would certainly like answers to two related (but separate) questions: how many victims of crime in their area are likely, in any one year, to be badly affected by the experience, and how many are likely to need their support or assistance? However, a perusal of research findings relevant to such questions would probably leave them more confused than when they started. For example, how would they reconcile, on the one hand, statements such as:

> 'A large proportion of victims reported neither practical nor emotional problems.' (Hough and Mayhew, 1985:32)

or:

> '... the extent of need should be kept in firmer perspective. Past victimisations often do not seem memorable enough to be recalled for survey interviewers, and even those which are remembered are frequently trivial and of little import; they are part of life's vicissitudes, not ineffectively coped with by victims with help from family, friends and insurance premiums.' (Mayhew, 1984:30)

with those of, for example, Friedman et al. (1982), that:

'... the most common problems, affecting three-quarters of the sample ... were psychological problems including fear, anxiety, nervousness, self-blame, anger, shame and difficulty sleeping ... We were stunned at the general impact of a crime on the victim's psychological state, and at the alterations to daily life which were so often a part of the victimization experience.'

One simple reason for the existence of such differences - and for the unnecessary confusion which they can easily produce - concerns a basic point which is often ignored where statistics are quoted second-hand or presented in a brief form for public consumption. Obviously, a sample of victims of petty theft will show less distress than a sample of rape victims. Yet findings based upon samples of very different victim populations (e.g. of crimes reported to victim surveys, of miscellaneous offences recorded by the police, or of specific serious offences) have quite often been erroneously equated, or used to draw unjustified conclusions about 'victims' as a whole. Mayhew (op. cit.) notes that most misinterpretations of this kind have been in the direction of overstatement of the impact of crime:

'At least part of the victims lobby may, with more emotion than judgement, have exaggerated victims' needs ... Insofar as many in the victim movement have based their case on firm evidence at all, they have relied mainly on studies of serious victims, implicitly suggesting the need to consider the whole victim 'pool' as in need of extended provision.'

On the other hand, what she calls the 'victims lobby' might argue back that it is equally misleading to use survey data, composed substantially of property-related incidents too trivial to be reported to the police, as the basis for statements about the impact of crime upon 'typical victims'.[1] Although justifiable theoretically, this might be said to stretch the scope of the term 'victim' beyond how it is understood in everyday language.

Secondly, as Maguire (1985) has pointed out, researchers have sometimes contributed to the confusion by using words like 'needs', 'problems' and 'effects' loosely and inter-changeably, and without recognition of their ambiguity and subjectivity. Empirical results in these slippery areas are greatly affected by the interpretations put upon such terms. Measurement of levels of 'need', for example, can be based upon interviewed victims' perceptions of their own needs, upon inferences drawn from measures of the impact of crime, upon volunteers' assessments of cases they have dealt with, or upon actual take-up rates of services (cf. Mawby, 1984).[2]

37

To complicate matters further (see again Maguire, 1985, for examples), the levels of 'effects' and 'needs' reported seem to vary widely according to how the questions are asked. Telephone interviews, broad survey interviews in person, and 'in-depth' interviews about particular types of incident, all give very different estimates, while prompting about possible effects substantially raises the proportion of victims who report having suffered them. It seems, in fact, that many victims are reluctant to admit to problems or needs (particularly of an emotional kind) until a certain amount of personal rapport has been established with the interviewer: partly, perhaps, because they fail to realise, until thinking carefully about it, how much damage the event has caused to their lives or what kinds of support might have speeded their recovery.[3] The latter point has been made well by Shapland et al. (1985):

> 'Expressed needs are to some extent culturally based. They are related to the expectations of victims as to the potential effects of the offence and to their knowledge of what remedies exist.'

This also accords with the common experience of many volunteers, that victims who have at first denied any need for the Scheme's services quite often reveal serious effects in the course of later conversation or when the volunteer is on the point of leaving - a phenomenon called the 'door-handle effect' by one Scheme.

In the present study we have made efforts to untangle some of these knots and, by understanding better the distorting effects of different methods of inquiry, to arrive at a balanced overall view of the size of the problem facing Victims Support Schemes or any other agency concerned with assisting victims. We have used both survey data and material from in-depth interviews, including in both cases prompted and unprompted questions. We have measured the impact of crime in a number of alternative ways, including self-ratings by victims, check-lists of effects, and scores on a version of the General Health Questionnaire (Goldberg, 1978). The assessment of 'needs', too, has been approached from a number of different angles. Though unavoidably complex, the argument is conducted as far as possible with an eye to its practical relevance for Victims Support.

(ii) Sources of data and structure of samples

The survey data used stem from questions we were permitted to include in the 1984 British Crime Survey. Although limited by tight constraints upon interviewers' time and subject to the reservations about 'rapport' mentioned above, these data are important in that they provide, for the first time, a nationwide and statistically reliable set of responses concerning the impact of crime and the needs of those who have experienced it. This includes, of course, information about both reported and unreported incidents and about victims of a wide range of offences. Our 'in-depth' interviews, which were aimed at answering questions about Victims Support as well as the effects of crime, were focused, by contrast, mainly upon victims of more serious crimes who had been referred to Schemes. The two sets of data can therefore be compared directly only on selected sub-samples of each.

Before presenting the results, a few words of explanation are necessary about the structures of the samples of victims that we shall be analysing, both from the British Crime Survey and our own interviews.

For the British Crime Survey, interviews were conducted in early 1984 in 11,030 households drawn from electoral registers in 300 Parliamentary constituencies in England and Wales. Respondents were asked to recall incidents potentially classifiable as criminal offences which had been perpetrated against them or their household since the beginning of 1983. For each such incident (up to a maximum of four per respondent) a 'victim form' was completed, containing over 80 questions about the offence and its consequences.[4] The result, after questionable cases had been excluded, was a set of information about nearly 5,000 offences, under 40 per cent of which had come to the notice of the police. It should be noted, however, that these data can be considered fully representative only after correction, by means of weighting, for the deliberate over-sampling of inner city areas and for differences in the sampling of 'personal' and 'household' crimes.[5] Unless otherwise stated, any percentages we give from this source will be based upon weighted data. And as VSS work is concerned almost entirely, for the present at least, with crimes recorded by the police, we shall concentrate chiefly upon those BCS offences which, according to the respondent, became known to the police.

Our 'in-depth' interviews were designed to cover a variety of issues concerning a number of quite separate groups of victims - for example, the needs of victims of specific serious offences, the views of 'supported' victims about the service provided, the reactions of those contacted by tele-phone, and so on. (Several of these issues are discussed in later chapters.) We therefore took random samples of several distinct victim populations, rather than (as would have been more appropriate for this particular chapter) just one representative sample from police records. We also limited the offence categories to be included in these samples primarily to those with which Schemes have generally been most concerned - burglary, robbery, assault and theft from the person.

We interviewed 242 victims of the above offences, as well as 23 victims of rape, who are discussed separately in Chapter 7.[6] Excluding rape cases, all but 35 were drawn from the records of five Victims Support Schemes.[7] Three of these received referrals of (in theory, 'all') burglaries from the police on an 'automatic' basis, and a different sub-set of three, in practice, received most recorded cases of robbery, theft from the person and serious assault. As Table 3.1 shows, the largest group we interviewed consisted of victims who had been visited by volunteers. Over two-thirds of these had been visited without prior arrangement, but the remainder had 'selected themselves' for VSS visits by responding to postal or telephone invitations. We also interviewed 51 victims who had declined to take up such invitations. The other 35 were selected at random from police records in areas not currently served by an active Scheme, and had had no VSS contact at all. Most interviews were conducted between three and six weeks after the offence, but in order to acquire information about longer-term effects, a number were carried out either three to four months or more than one year after the event.[8]

Table 3.1
Interviewed population, by type of offence and type of contact with VSS

Type of Contact with VSS

| Type of offence | Visited unannounced | Visited after letter/ phone call | Telephoned letter only | No contact with VSS | Total |
|---|---|---|---|---|---|
| Burglary | 72 | 26 | 12 | 26 | 136 |
| Robbery, assault, theft from the person | 37 | 21 | 39 | 9 | 106 |
| Rape | - | 18 | - | 5 | 23 |
| All | 109 | 65 | 51 | 40 | 265 |

While these data are valuable for exploring issues related to specific victim groups, and for comparing findings between them, the interviews cannot be simply aggregated to approximate to a representative sample of victims of recorded offences of the above types. Not only would certain groups (such as victims of robbery and assault) be over-represented, but the sample would be 'skewed' towards victims with serious effects by the facts that some had been individually selected by police officers for referral and others had 'selected themselves' for visits. Thus when, as in this chapter, we wish to use information from a substantial set of our interviews to make more general statements about victims of recorded offences, we can justifiably include in the analysis only the 35 cases sampled from police records, together with 140 cases which were referred to Schemes on an 'automatic' (or near-automatic) basis and which did not involve 'self-selection' by victims. To complicate matters further, it will be necessary to weight responses within the latter group to compensate for our deliberate over-sampling of victims of violence (as opposed to burglary) and victims visited by volunteers (as opposed to telephoned or sent letters).[9] The sample thus created, albeit in a somewhat artificial manner, is a fairly good approximation to a representative sample of victims of recorded offences of burglary (with loss), robbery, serious assault and theft from the person - i.e. of the basic 'pool' of offences from which most Schemes draw their referrals.[10] For the sake of convenience, this sample will be referred to throughout the report as our 'composite sample' of victims.

## The effects of crime

### (i) The initial impact of crime

We set out first to assess the extent, nature and intensity of the initial effects produced by different types of offence upon different kinds of victim. We attempted to measure these rather elusive phenomena in a number of different ways, but our main starting-point was victims' own assessments of how badly affected they had been. The very simple measure we used for this - but one which, despite its apparent crudeness, correlated highly with alternative measures of initial impact (see footnote 28) - was a four-point self-rating scale. British Crime Survey respondents reporting one or more crimes were asked, for each incident:

'Thinking back to the first few days after it happened, how much would you say the incident affected you or your household at that time? Very much, quite a lot, a little or not at all?'

Our interviewees were asked a similar question, except that they were asked to rate how much the incident had affected them _personally_ (effects on others being rated in a separate answer). In comparing the two sets of data, we shall adjust our interviewees' responses to take account of this difference.[11]

(a) Survey and 'in-depth' interviews:  contrasting results

Table 3.2 illustrates the range of results derived from responses to the above question.  It provides first of all a graphic warning of how important it is in making statements about 'the effects of crime upon victims' to specify precisely _which_ crimes and _which_ victims. Here, between 11 per cent and 79 per cent of 'victims' emerge as badly upset, depending upon the population one chooses to analyse.  The first line of the Table could be used to support Mayhew's

Table 3.2
Victims' ratings of level of impact upon themselves or household:
by selected groups of respondents from BCS and 'in-depth' interviews.

| | Ratings of level of impact | | |
|---|---|---|---|
| | % 'very much' affected | % 'a little'/'not at all'affected | (N)[*] |
| BCS Respondents Victims of: | | | |
| All incidents | 12 | 71 | (N = 4,882) |
| Incidents known to police only: | | | |
| (a) All offence categories | 21 | 55 | (N = 1,927) |
| (b) Burglary, robbery, wounding, snatch theft | 36 | 36 | (N = 345) |
| 'In-depth' interview respondents Victims of: | | | |
| Burglary, robbery, wounding, snatch theft: sample from police records | 60 | 23 | (N = 35) |
| Burglary, robbery, wounding, snatch theft: all those visited by Scheme volunteers | 79 | 8 | (N = 151) |

[*] Unweighted N. Percentages are based on weighted data.

(1984) assertion that the bulk of offences committed do not have serious consequences for their victims. Of all incidents reported to the survey interviewers, under 12 per cent were said by the respondent to have affected him, her or the household 'very much', while the answers 'a little' and 'not at all' were given by 32 and 40 per cent of respondents respectively. On the other hand, if we look only at offences reported to the police, the percentage of victims 'very much' affected almost doubles. If we go further and (following a more everyday use of the term) limit the definition of 'victims' to, for example, those who have been physically attacked, robbed or burgled, the proportion badly affected rises to well over a third.

Even this remains low compared with the results from our 'in-depth' interviews. Other researchers who have interviewed samples of victims from police records (e.g. Friedman et al., 1982; Shapland et al., 1985) have also found strong emotional effects to be fairly common, so the figure of 60 per cent 'very much' affected among our sample from this source (Table 3.2) comes as no surprise.[12] However, it is not clear from this Table how much of the divergence from survey results is due to the different context of the interviews (i.e. unhurried discussion with the focus upon the victims' reactions, as opposed to rapid collection of data in a rigid format), and how much to differences in the structures of the samples. Obviously, before any two groups of respondents can be meaningfully compared, it must be certain that each group has experienced similar types of incident and contains a similar balance of gender, age and social class.

In order to achieve a valid comparison, we selected from both BCS and our interview data only those offences of burglary in a dwelling in which entry was forced or damage caused inside the house, property valued at 25 or over was stolen, and the respondent was aged below 60. We also excluded from the 'in-depth' interview group all cases from areas in which victims might have been individually selected for VSS referral (e.g. because a policeman knew them to be upset) and all cases where victims themselves had requested a visit. The structures of the two populations thus created turned out to be very similar in terms of gender and occupational class.[13]

When the responses of the two groups were compared (Table 3.3), it was found that 47 per cent of the BCS group, and 66 per cent of the 'in-depth' interviewees, reported themselves or their household 'very much' affected. This gap was not as wide as that indicated by Table 3.2,[14] but still suggests that survey-based attempts to measure the proportion of

## Table 3.3
## A controlled comparison of 'self-rating' responses produced by survey and 'in-depth' interview methods

Percentage of victims (aged under 60) of forced entry burglary, with loss of £25 or over, rating self or household:

|  | 'very much' affected % | 'quite a lot' affected % | 'a little'/ 'not at all' affected % | Total % |
|---|---|---|---|---|
| British Crime Survey | 47 | 27 | 26 | 100 (N=111) |
| 'In-depth' interviews | 66 | 23 | 11 | 100 (N=53) |

victims badly affected will produce estimates almost a third lower than those that would have been obtained had the same questions been put to the same victims in longer, 'in-depth' interviews.

## (b) Variations by offence type

The above point should be borne in mind during the next part of our discussion, where we consider what proportions of victims (or their families) are likely to be badly affected by each category of offence. Table 3.4 shows BCS findings on this question for both reported and unreported offences. It also shows the proportions in each category claiming to be totally unaffected by the incident.

This Table should be of interest to Victims Support Schemes for the indications it gives about the relative impact of categories of reported crime which do and do not normally come to their notice. (Unreported crime, with which few Schemes deal regularly, but which also deserves attention, will be discussed later.) In fact, the Table gives considerable support to the general consensus of opinion - and consequent practice - which has grown up among experienced members over the years. The highest proportions of victims rating themselves badly affected - between 36 and 40 per cent in the case of offences known to the police - are to be found among the kinds of offence most often referred to Schemes, namely burglary (with loss), 'snatch' theft, robbery and serious assault.[15] Conversely, most of the offences which normally receive low priority in both referral and visiting (e.g. theft from motor vehicles and 'ordinary' personal theft) duly reveal only small proportions of victims reporting serious effects.

Table 3.4
Proportions of respondents reporting self or household 'very much' and
'not at all' affected; by offence type and whether known to police

| Type of Offence | Offences known to police | | Offences not known to police | |
| | 'very much' affected % | 'not at all' affected % | 'very much' affected % | 'not at all' affected % |
| --- | --- | --- | --- | --- |
| Robbery/snatch theft | 40 | 21 | 8 | 25 |
| Wounding | 36 | 20 | 11 | 28 |
| Burglary (theft) | 36 | 10 | 23 | 29 |
| Threats | 36 | 15 | 15 | 42 |
| Major vandalism | 29 | 21 | 9 | 40 |
| Theft person (sneak) | 22 | 19 | 6 | 32 |
| Minor vandalism | 21 | 24 | 4 | 51 |
| Theft of m/v | 21 | 16 | ** | ** |
| Burglary (attempt) | 17 | 18 | 7 | 37 |
| Bicycle theft | 13 | 32 | 7 | 47 |
| Other h/h theft | 13 | 32 | 3 | 54 |
| Common assault | 12 | 42 | 12 | 46 |
| Theft from m/v | 10 | 33 | 2 | 57 |
| Other pers. theft | 10 | 31 | 5 | 50 |
| All | 21 | 25 | 7 | 47 |

** Numbers too small for analysis.
Source: BCS 1984. Weighted data.

On the other hand, there are some surprising results which
deserve closer attention. Two categories which stand out
are 'major vandalism' (criminal damage to the value of over
£20) and 'threats'. The proportions of victims seriously
affected by these offences were similar to those of
burglary, robbery and serious assault. The obvious
conclusion is that both should receive higher priority than
at present.

Certainly, there seems to be no reason why the police
should not pass on routinely to Schemes cases of criminal
damage where there is an individual victim. This already
happens in some areas, but it seems to be a neglected
offence in most (see Chapter 2). Threats are more
problematic, because unless there is clear evidence of a
threat to kill or to commit criminal damage, the police are
in most cases unable to take any action and only rarely
record such reports as notifiable offences.[16] There may,

however, be a case for the police to refer particularly worried or frightened complainants to Victims Support Schemes even if no offence is officially recorded. The same applies, of course, to criminal damage.

A particular aspect of the above two offences makes attention to them even more important. This is that they are more likely than most other offences to be associated with <u>racial harassment</u>.[17] The Islington Crime Survey (Maclean <u>et al.</u>, 1986) has recently found evidence that not only is 'harassment' of a general kind experienced by high proportions of Afro-Caribbean and Asian groups, but that this is also true of a much more tangible indicator of harassment - that of repeated vandalism. The survey found that 32 per cent of Afro-Caribbean households, compared with 19 per cent of white households, in Islington had suffered at least one incident of criminal damage in 1985, and, moreover, that 'vandalism as well as burglary is ... directed at the same target again and again'.

As well as differences in levels of effects between offence categories, significant variations were found <u>within</u> the official categories. For example, victims were much more likely to report bad effects from burglaries in which property was stolen (36 per cent of victims 'very much' affected) than from those where nothing was taken or an attempt not completed (25 and 15 per cent respectively). And, as we have already seen, the addition of damage to loss pushes the figure up towards 50 per cent. Similarly, the offence of theft from the person is much more likely to be badly upsetting when it involves a 'snatch' than when it involves theft by stealth.

Finally, in discussing features of offences which influence the level of impact, it is important not to miss a general point which seems to apply to almost all kinds of offence. Crimes in which <u>the offender was known to the victim prior to the event</u> tend to have stronger adverse effects upon victims than those where the offender is a complete stranger. Over all BCS offences reported to the police in which respondents 'were able to say anything at all about the people who did it', 39 per cent of those previously acquainted with the offender, compared with 22 per cent who knew the offender to be a stranger, reported themselves 'very much' affected. Two types of incident where prior acquaintance was found to be quite common, and where the difference this made to levels of effects was especially striking, were reported cases of wounding, and threats. In both instances, well over half of the victims who had previously known the offender reported themselves 'very much' affected compared with under a quarter of those

46

who were sure they had not (see Appendix, Table G). This finding deserves attention from Victims Support Schemes, who tend on the whole to limit their work to victims of 'stranger to stranger' offences. There is supporting evidence (Resick, 1985) that victims of domestic violence, in particular, experience effects on a level comparable to that of burglary.

(c)   Numbers badly affected

We have so far discussed effects chiefly in percentage terms. However, it has to be remembered that there are large differences between offence categories in the numbers of incidents occurring. In order to provide a fuller picture of the situation - and one which is directly relevant to Schemes - Table 3.5 translates BCS results into the context of a putative 'average-sized' Victims Support Scheme area (130,000 population) with an average crime rate. Estimates, based on BCS responses and Criminal Statistics, are shown of how many personal and household offences would have been officially recorded by the police in such an area in 1983, how many others would have failed to reach the official returns, and how many in each category would have affected victims or others in their household 'very much'.[18] (Similar estimates for the numbers so affected in the whole of England and Wales are given in the Appendix, Table H). It is suggested that these should be treated as minimum estimates of the numbers of victims perceiving themselves to have been badly affected: as we have shown above (section (a)), if 'in-depth' interview results were used as a base, these latter totals might emerge as nearly half as high again.

In separating recorded offences from non-recorded and non-reported offences, this Table also sheds light on the question of whether, by relying so heavily upon the police for referrals (rather than actively encouraging self-referrals), Schemes are unwittingly excluding large numbers of people who might urgently need their assistance. We have seen (Table 3.4) that offences not reported to the police - which, of course, tend to be less serious than reported offences in terms of loss or injury[19] - are on average three times less likely than reported offences to be associated with a strong emotional impact upon the victim. On the other hand, they greatly outnumber offences which end up in official crime reports - i.e. the pool of recorded offences from which Schemes draw most of their victims.

As Table 3.5 shows, it can be calculated from the survey data that in 1983, the average-sized Victims Support Scheme area would have contained about 4,000 victims considering

## Table 3.5
BCS-based estimates of numbers of victims or households 'very much' affected by crime in an 'average-sized Scheme area', 1983[a]; by type of incident and whether known to and/or recorded by police

| Type of incident | Estimated number of offences occurring in area | | Estimated numbers of victims/ households 'very much' affected | | |
| | Number of offences recorded by police | Number of incidents not recorded[b] | Offence recorded by police (range) | Incident reported to but not recorded by police (range) | Incident not known to police |
|---|---|---|---|---|---|
| Burglary | 1,250 | 1,300 | 420-460 | 30-70 | 100 |
| Vandalism | 600 | 7,200 | 180-360 | 60-240 | 310 |
| Theft of mv | 700 | ** | 150 | ** | ** |
| Theft fr mv | 1,050 | 2,500 | 110-140 | 10-40 | 50 |
| Other personal theft | 950[c] | 3,700 | 100-110 | 30-40 | 160 |
| Robbery/theft from person | 150 | 1,900 | 40-90 | 70-120 | 70 |
| Wounding | 200[c] | 900[c] | 80-120 | 110-150 | 50 |
| Other hh theft | 550[c] | 3,800[c] | 70-90 | 10-30 | 110 |
| Bike theft | 400 | 400 | 50-60 | 10-20 | 20 |
| Sex offences | 50 | 200[d] | 10-20 | 0-10[d] | 60[d] |
| Threats | ** | 2,900 | ** | 310 | 300 |
| Common assault | ** | 3,400 | ** | 120 | 290 |
| All | 5,850[c] | 28,200[c] | 1,210-1,600 | 760-1,150 | 1,520 |

** Numbers too small for analysis.

Notes

a. Assuming an average crime rate and a population of 130,000.
b. Includes incidents reported to police which were not recorded.
c. Approximations only, as some BCS offences do not overlap fully with police recording categories.
d. Sexual offences tend to be underestimated by survey data (Hough and Mayhew, 1984; 9).

Numbers of offences are rounded to nearest 50.
Numbers of affected victims are rounded to nearest 100.

Sources: BCS 1984; Hough and Mayhew (1985: Appendix, Table A); Criminal Statistics 1983.

themselves very much affected by incidents potentially classifiable as crimes. About 2,500 of these would have reported the matter to the police, although in perhaps 1,000 of the reported cases no crime would have been officially recorded.

Given how difficult it is to persuade more than a small percentage of victims to come forward and ask for assistance (cf. Chesney and Schneider, 1982; Van Dijk, 1983; Reeves, 1984; Kilpatrick, 1985), this finding suggests that ventures advocated in some quarters to help victims who have not been to the police (such as 'hot lines' and even 'walk-in centres') cannot expect - if designed to cover areas only the size of those presently covered by single Schemes - to attract large numbers of people badly in need of support. Nevertheless, it may be felt, particularly in large cities where several Schemes might co-operate, that the numbers are sufficiently disturbing to demand some experiments to encourage self-referral. In this context, we would draw attention particularly to three categories of incident which have relatively low reporting rates but which clearly cause a lot of distress. The first is sexual offences, which show the highest proportion of severe effects among all non-reporting victims.[20] While Rape Crisis Centres already meet some of the need in this area, and while it would be unproductive to directly 'compete for victims', there may be a case for suitably equipped Schemes to provide an alternative service based on self-referral, if only for women not attracted by the Rape Crisis Centres' 'image' (see Chapter 7).

The other two categories are 'threats' and vandalism, which again stand out prominently. In particular, a relatively high proportion (15 per cent) of respondents who had received a threat but failed to report it to the police stated that they had been very much affected, and as it was also a relatively common event, the total numbers badly affected were higher than in most other categories of crime. Moreover, the very low recording rate mentioned earlier, combined with the high self-rating of effects, suggests that many victims who go to the police may fail to find the comfort or protection they seek. Although some of the threats involved might not be legally classifiable as crimes, the level of impact on those receiving them seems to us to demand attention. It is also worthy of note that threats, particularly threats to assault or kill (which made up two-thirds of those reported), were quite likely to be repeated: 40 per cent of the latter were not isolated events, but one of a series of similar incidents.[21] They can in many cases, then, be regarded as a serious form of 'harrassment', a problem in which, particularly where there is a racial element involved, the Victims Support movement is beginning to take an interest. Much the same applies to vandalism, which (as mentioned earlier) the Islington Crime Survey identifies as a crime directed particularly against ethnic minority groups. A BCS-based estimate of the proportion of cases of vandalism reported to the police which do not end up officially recorded as crimes is 63 per cent (Hough and Mayhew, 1985:61), and Maclean et al. (1986: Fig. 3.4) would put it as high as 76 per cent. We repeat that attention could fruitfully be paid by VSS to ways of being put in contact with victims of possible racial harrassment who do not find their way into the official crime statistics.

(d)  Variations by victim characteristics

We next examine the extent to which ratings of the level of impact varied according to the social characteristics of the respondent. The larger numbers of cases make BCS data better suited to this type of analysis than our interview data, but we shall use the latter for comparison later.

Table 3.6 shows (for offences known to the police only) the proportions of BCS victims rating themselves or their household very much affected, in relation to respondents' age, sex, social class and marital status, and the size of the household. One of the clearest differences - which is even more striking when it is remembered that the question put referred to effects upon the whole household - is that between male and female respondents.[22] In almost every individual category of offence (the main exceptions being vehicle theft and miscellaneous personal theft), a significantly higher proportion of female than male respondents reported themselves or their household 'very much' affected. Of course, whether this represents a 'real' difference, or is caused by a greater reluctance among men to admit to being emotionally upset - what someone suggested we should call the 'macho effect' - is difficult to state with any certainty.

The other two factors which emerged as clearly significant were those of socio-economic group (defined here according to the Registrar-General's classification of the occupation or previous occupation of the head of household) and marital status. Victims in households headed by a manual worker were much more likely than people in non-manual households to say that they had been very much affected. And respondents who were separated, widowed or divorced generally reported worse effects than those who were married or single. These findings largely echo the results of earlier work on burglary victims (Maguire, 1982).

Table 3.6
**Proportions of offences (known to police only) in which victims rated themselves or their household 'very much' affected over the first few days; by category of offence and social characteristics of respondent**

Percentage of incidents where victim or household
'very much' affected

| | Sex | | Age | | Occupational Class (SEG) | |
|---|---|---|---|---|---|---|
| | Male | Female | Under 60 | 60 and over | Non-manual (I, II, 3M) | Manual (3N, IV, V) |
| Type of offence | % | % | % | % | % | % |
| Burglary/theft dwelling | 27 | 40 | 34 | 31 | 32 | 35 |
| Assault/Wounding | 17 | 39 | 21 | 32 | ** | 27 |
| Robbery/Snatch | 31 | 51 | 37 | 75 | ** | 36 |
| Threats | 9 | 57 | 37 | 18 | ** | 39 |
| Vandalism | 16 | 32 | 20 | 41 | 20 | 31 |
| All other theft | 13 | 12 | 13 | 11 | 8 | 14 |
| All BCS offences known to police | 16 | 27 | 20 | 27 | 12 | 24 |

| | Marital status | | Household | |
|---|---|---|---|---|
| | Married/ Single | Divorced/separated/ widowed | Living with others | Living alone |
| Type of offence | % | % | % | % |
| Burglary/theft dwelling | 34 | 33 | 38 | 23 |
| Assault/wounding | 20 | 59 | 18 | 55 |
| Robbery/'snatch' | 24 | 54 | 43 | ** |
| Threats | 37 | 31 | 38 | 16 |
| Vandalism | 21 | 45 | 23 | 35 |
| All other theft | 12 | 18 | 13 | 12 |
| All BCS offences known to police | 20 | 33 | 21 | 25 |

** Numbers too small for analysis.
Source: BCS 1984 (weighted data).

51

While the above factors were strong predictors of levels of impact throughout the whole victim population, the factors of <u>age</u> and <u>whether or not living alone</u> were unimportant except in combination with certain other factors.[23] First of all, while men over 60 were no worse affected than men under 60, female pensioners were clearly worse affected than younger women (Table 3.7(A)). Yet when the group of females over 60 was sub-divided further, it emerged that it was only those among them who were living alone and/or were widowed, who were significantly more affected than comparable groups of younger women (Table 3.7(B)).[24]

### Table 3.7
Proportions of incidents (known to police) in which victim or household 'very much' affected; by age and sex of respondent and whether living alone or with others

| | (A) Sex of respondent | | | (B) Type of household | | |
|---|---|---|---|---|---|---|
| Age of respondent | Male % | Female % | (All) % | Female living with others % | Female living alone % | (All) % |
| Under 60 | 16 | 24 | (20) | 24 | 25 | (24) |
| 60 and over | 14 | 23 | (25) | 25 | 49 | (33) |

Source: BCS 1984. All BCS offences known to police (weighted data).

It is difficult to unravel the relative importance of these factors, as they are often closely inter-related in the case of older people: for example, living alone is likely to be the result of the death of a partner, rather than (as among younger people) a matter of choice. Nevertheless, whatever the contributions of the various factors of 'age', 'femaleness', 'aloneness' and 'widowhood', we can say that in combination they identify a group significantly more likely than all others we can find to be badly affected by crime. This emerges not only on self-rating scales, but on measures of specific effects (see next section). In other words, the widely-held belief that VSS services are most needed for the elderly (what is sometimes rather disparagingly known as the 'stereotype' of the 'little old lady') has a certain foundation in reality, although it is only a particular sub-set of the old - women widowed or living alone - who can be shown to be significantly worse affected than equivalent younger groups. It is not unlikely that among elderly <u>men</u>, too, living alone or widowhood increase the impact of crime, but even in the BCS there were too few victims in the relevant categories to test this.

Our 'in-depth' interviews produced results broadly confirming BCS indications of the worst affected groups. Among our 'composite' sample of victims, those in manual occupations and those divorced, separated or widowed (young and old alike) were significantly more likely than other groups to report being 'very much' affected. Women over 60 also emerged as the group most likely to rate themselves badly affected - particularly those living alone.[25] Surprisingly, however, among younger victims of burglary there was no significant difference in self-rated levels of effects between males and females. This puzzled us for some time, for, although it is quite possible that men are in reality as likely as women to be emotionally disturbed by crime, all previous findings indicate that they do not express this to interviewers. However, the mystery was largely cleared up when we introduced a more finely differentiated measure, as will be explained shortly.

Finally, it is worth mentioning our respondents' ratings of the levels of effects upon others close to them. Among our 'composite' sample, 47 per cent stated that others had been 'very much' affected; and among victims with children, 70 per cent stated that the children had been badly frightened or upset. This underlines the point that most crimes have more than one 'victim', and that Victims Support Scheme volunteers need to be aware of others in the house who may need their support.

(e)  Specific emotional effects

We move on now to consider the substance of the effects of crime, first in terms of emotional impact and later in terms of the practical problems created. Here our interview data will be more helpful, being more detailed than the BCS data, but in order to gain some idea of differences over a wider range of offences, we shall again begin with some findings from the latter. Unless otherwise stated, BCS findings quoted are based upon offences which became known to the police.

BCS respondents were asked to describe 'any kinds of emotional or personal problems which this incident has caused you or your household'. Only 29 per cent of all respondents named any such problems, but this proportion rose to 41 per cent among victims of offences reported to the police. Moreover, female respondents were much more likely than males to mention specific emotional problems (see Appendix, Table I).[26]

The kinds of effect most often mentioned were anger, fear and worry, although this varied considerably by offence type. The offences which produced the most mentions of anger were thefts of personal items (among men), and vandalism (among women). Those producing the most fear and worry were threats, violence and, to a lesser extent, burglary. General health problems, too (stress, depression, sleeplessness), were mainly associated with these latter offences (Appendix, Table J).

We can now complement the above findings, for some offences at least, with more detailed information from our interviews with victims. A free response question asking them to describe their first reaction to the event found shock, panic and confusion together mentioned by almost 40 per cent of victims, and anger and general 'upset' each mentioned by nearly a third (Appendix, Table K). Differences by sex in the type of reaction expressed were again very apparent, with twice as many men as women mentioning anger, but women much more likely to mention fear or (after burglary) shock.

In order to document early reactions more precisely - and at the same time to produce an alternative measure of effects to the self-rating scale - we next gave each interviewee a list of 22 (primarily emotional) effects they might have experienced over the first few days, and asked them to say whether they had experienced each intensely, to some extent, a little, or not at all.

Altogether, 65 per cent of our composite sample of victims said that they had experienced four or more of these effects at an intense level. Victims of violence mentioned considerably more effects than did those of burglary, and female victims more than males. The pattern according to the sex of the victim, among burglary victims aged under 60, largely solves the 'mystery' described in the previous section. It will be remembered that on the four-point self-rating scale this group showed no difference by sex in levels of effects. However, a more differentiated scale, based on how many of the 22 prompted effects were mentioned, shows that although there are no major differences by sex among those at the 'less affected' end of the spectrum, there are important differences at the 'worst affected' end. The numbers of male and female burglary victims who stated that they had experienced listed effects 'intensely' were as follows:

|                 | Male under 60 | Female under 60 |
|-----------------|:-------------:|:---------------:|
| 0-3 effects     | 15            | 12              |
| 4-6 effects     | 10            | 3               |
| 7 or more effects | 2           | 15              |
|                 | 27            | 30              |

Although there was only a small difference between males and females in those naming four or more effects, the difference at the 'seven or more effects' level was marked: no fewer than 15 of the 17 individuals naming the highest number of effects were female.[27] In other words, as most of those with four or more effects had put themselves into the highest ('very much affected') category on the four-point scale, this difference at the extreme had earlier remained concealed.[28]

Table 3.8

**Specific effects experienced by victims in the first few days after the event: by type of offence**

Percentage of victims in composite sample[*] experiencing each effect 'intensely'

| | Burglary | Robbery/assault | Theft person |
|---|---|---|---|
| | % | % | % |
| Feeling angry | 75 | 53 | 37 |
| Difficulty sleeping | 46 | 47 | 15 |
| Unsettled or uneasy | 45 | 46 | 19 |
| Feeling dazed, confused, unreal | 38 | 45 | 22 |
| Feeling depressed | 38 | 33 | 4 |
| Feeling frightened | 34 | 53 | 22 |
| Shaking, shivering | 33 | 40 | 15 |
| Feeling contaminated, dirty | 32 | 4 | 5 |
| Afraid to go out | 29 | 29 | 11 |
| Helpless, vulnerable | 28 | 36 | 19 |
| Afraid to enter house/room | 28 | 7 | 4 |
| Unable to do ordinary tasks | 25 | 47 | 4 |
| Crying or on verge of tears | 25 | 31 | 7 |
| Loss of appetite | 24 | 36 | 11 |
| Feeling weak, loss of strength | 21 | 41 | 15 |
| Not wanting to be alone | 21 | 21 | 7 |
| Loss of interest in work/hobbies | 20 | 43 | 11 |
| Feeling or being sick | 19 | 24 | 4 |
| Afraid to stay in house | 12 | 5 | 7 |
| Feeling guilty, 'your fault' | 9 | 7 | 11 |
| Headaches, feeling ill generally | 5 | 35 | 4 |
| Loss of memory of what happened | 4 | 7 | 0 |
| (Unweighted N) | (N = 90) | (N = 57) | (N = 28) |

[*] Best approximation to a representative sample of victims of recorded offences of burglary (with loss), serious assault, robbery and theft from the person.

Table 3.8 shows the 22 reactions which were listed in the interview schedule and the proportions of various categories of victims stating that they had experienced them intensely. (The reactions of rape victims are discussed separately in Chapter 7.) The reaction most commonly picked out was that of anger, which was also one of the few effects reported more frequently by men than by women. It was felt most strongly by burglary victims, of whom three-quarters recalled intense anger, but it also headed the list of reactions to violent offences.[29]

Difficulty in sleeping and feeling 'unsettled' or 'uneasy' were the next most frequently chosen reactions, each experienced very strongly by about 45 per cent of victims. The type of offence made less difference here, although where difficulty in sleeping was concerned, female victims of burglary were particularly badly affected (60 per cent).

Fear and shock, as already indicated by our 'free response' findings above, were also prominent. Fifty-three per cent of all victims of robbery or assault, and 52 per cent of female victims of burglary, reported intense fear. 'Shaking or shivering' and feeling dazed, confused or unreal, symptoms associated with shock as well as fear, were also at high levels among female victims of burglary, and among both sexes in the case of assault. This latter finding, together with the fact that there was no significant difference in these reactions by age in the case of male victims, helps to underline one of the key points to emerge from this exercise: the effects of violent crime are severe for a high proportion of men, including young men, as well as for women. The findings strongly suggest that the low priority given by some Schemes to young male victims of violence (see Chapter 4) may be a mistaken policy.

Among effects experienced less often than might have been expected (according to some of the previous literature) were feelings of guilt and loss of memory of what happened. Apart from a few assault cases in which the victim was knocked unconscious, respondents seemed to remember all too vividly what had occurred. Feelings that the offence had been precipitated by one's own mistake were also quite rare. It might be thought that those who feel guilt tend to be worse affected emotionally than those who do not, but this was the case neither among our interviewees nor the BCS victims.[30]

(f)  Practical problems

Following many types of offence, the victim is typically faced with a number of practical tasks (such as repairing windows, replacing stolen cheque cards, travelling to hospital appointments, or making insurance claims) which have to be carried out in order to deal effectively with the immediate consequences and 'put things back to normal'. Previous research has come up with widely varying findings concerning the magnitude of these problems, and to what extent people are in need of assistance with them. In fact, this is one of the areas where we believe it is most important to separate the concepts of 'effects' (or 'problems') and 'needs'. For example, Friedman et al. (1982) found that 39 per cent of a sample of victims of burglary, robbery and assault needed to change or repair locks, but this does not mean that they all needed help from a victim support agency: many were perfectly able and willing to arrange it for themselves. We would describe the 39 per cent as experiencing the 'effect' or 'problem' of having to get locks repaired, while we would reserve the term 'needs' for the unknown percentage among them who were unable (for whatever reason) to get the necessary job done within a reasonably short time. The latter are clearly those who would most benefit from VSS assistance - although, of course, this does not preclude VSS from giving assistance also to people who could have solved the problem themselves. We shall discuss immediate effects or problems here. 'Needs' will be discussed in the last part of the chapter.

Measurement of the extent of the practical problems caused by crime is in some ways easier than that of the emotional effects, as one is talking about physical events and actions rather than mental states. Even so, victims may have differing ideas about what constitutes a practical problem. And as Brown and Yantzi (1980) have shown, the extent to which prompting is used makes a big difference to the results.

We begin by looking at responses to the general BCS question, 'Looking back over the time since it happened, could you describe to me any kinds of practical problems or particular inconvenience which this incident has caused you or your household?'. According to the results obtained, a high proportion of victims, even among those reporting fairly serious crimes to the police, had no practical problems. In approximately 60 per cent of all BCS incidents, the respondent - unprompted - could recall none at all; and even where offences were reported to the police, only just over half the respondents mentioned a practical problem. However, this varied considerably according to the type of offence. In contrast to emotional problems, practical problems were mentioned more often by victims of 'ordinary' property offences than by victims of either burglary or violence. Furthermore, whereas we showed earlier a close correlation between the types of offence with a strong emotional impact and those paid most attention by VSS, a different picture emerges where practical problems are concerned. Table 3.9 shows the rank order of BCS offences known to the police, according to the percentage of victims mentioning 'practical problems or particular inconvenience'. Only two of the first seven (burglary and theft from the person) are offences regularly dealt with by most Schemes.

Table 3.9
Proportions of victims mentioning practical problems; by type of offence (BCS offences known to police only)

Percentage mentioning (unprompted) a practical problem

| Type of offence | % |
|---|---|
| 'Sneak' theft from person | 79 |
| Other personal theft | 71 |
| Theft of vehicle | 67 |
| Vandalism | 61 |
| Burglary (with theft) | 58 |
| Other theft | 58 |
| Threats | 45 |
| Burglary (attempted/nil stolen) | 40 |
| Wounding | 40 |
| Robbery/'snatch' theft | 30 |
| Common assault | 11 |
| All BCS offences known to police | 52 |

Source: BCS 1984 (weighted data).

The substance of the problems in question was not recorded in great detail in the BCS, but it is clear that most of them could be subsumed under the general heading of 'inconvenience'. The largest group mentioned having to replace or repair stolen or damaged articles, and a substantial number mentioned the inconvenience of temporarily being without such articles. 'Top of the list' of offences for mentions of inconvenience was theft of a vehicle (59 per cent),[31] with vandalism and other personal theft quite close behind (around 50 per cent). The financial cost resulting from the offence was mentioned as a problem particularly by victims of 'sneak' theft from the person, which usually involves the theft of cash from a handbag or wallet (37 per cent). Victims of other personal theft (20 per cent) and major vandalism (18 per cent) were also quite likely to mention the cost. Finally, problems in 'dealing with authorities' were mentioned by a small proportion of victims, most often

by those of 'sneak' theft from the person (mainly, one
assumes, because of having to replace personal documents)
and burglary (mainly concerned, presumably, with dealing
with Councils over repairs or with fuel Boards when meters
were 'broken' - see below).

When we put a similar unprompted question to our interviewees, the proportions naming at least one practical
problem were somewhat higher than those of victims in equivalent crime categories in the BCS. For example, 72 per
cent of burglary victims in our composite sample mentioned
such problems compared with the BCS proportion of 58 per
cent.[32] As Table 3.10 shows, effecting repairs - mainly to
windows and doors broken or forced during entry - was the
specific practical problem most often mentioned by burglary
victims. Victims of violent crime, who (as in the BCS)
mentioned considerably fewer practical problems overall,
spoke mainly of problems caused by injuries (such as
inability to move around freely) and financial problems
(e.g. loss of cash in robberies or 'snatches', and loss of
earnings through inability to work).

Table 3.10

**Practical problems to be dealt with over the first few days: unprompted
and prompted responses, by type of offence**

| | Burglary (N=90) | | Robbery, assault 'snatch' theft (N=76) | |
|---|---|---|---|---|
| | Unprompted % | Prompted % | Unprompted % | Prompted % |
| Repairs | 45 | 71 | 1 | 1 |
| Clearing up | 10 | 34 | 3 | 3 |
| Changing locks/improving security | 7 | 31 | 13 | 21 |
| Replacing stolen goods | 6 | 10 | 7 | 10 |
| Insurance claims | - | 40 | - | 9 |
| Notifying/dealing with authorities | 12 | 35 | 1 | 25 |
| Financial problems | 7 | 13 | 14 | 22 |
| Getting medical attention/ lack of mobility | - | 4 | 28 | 46 |
| General inconvenience | 23 | N/A | 14 | N/A |
| None | 28 | 6 | 47 | 12 |

(Columns do not sum to 100% as more than one reply was allowed.)

N = 166 victims of burglary (with loss), robbery, serious assault and
     'snatch' theft ('composite sample', weighted to approximate to a
     representative sample of above offences from police records)

59

When we prompted victims, asking them whether they, or anybody else, had had to deal with any of a list of specific problems over the first few days, the numbers in each category grew considerably (Table 3.10) - indicating, as mentioned earlier, that victims are put to considerable inconvenience which they do not necessarily recall as 'practical problems' in answer to general questions. For example, 40 per cent of burglary victims had to deal with insurance claims and 35 per cent had to spend time replacing stolen documents (e.g. cheque cards, pension books), negotiating with the DHSS, or making arrangements with fuel boards or rental companies concerning stolen or damaged property which belonged to the latter. Victims of 'snatch' theft also often engaged in the time-consuming replacement of documents, and several either changed their keys or made security improvements to their homes. Altogether, after careful prompting by us, only 6 per cent of burglary victims and 12 per cent of victims of violence maintained that they had had no practical problems at all to deal with.

We had no direct measure of the seriousness of the practical problems caused - although in a relatively small number of cases dealt with by volunteers (see Chapter 6) these were sufficiently serious to demand several visits and a great deal of 'telephoning around' by volunteers or Co-ordinators on the victim's behalf. What we do know, however, is that in crimes of the kind most often dealt with by VSS, the emotional impact is generally regarded by victims as much more serious and significant than the practical problems caused. Among our victims of burglary, assault, robbery and theft from the person, only a small minority mentioned practical problems or inconvenience as the 'worst thing' about the whole affair (Appendix, Table L), a result echoed in the BCS (Hough and Mayhew, 1985: Table 6). In other property offences included in the BCS, certainly, practical problems were named more frequently than emotional responses as the 'worst problem'. But in most of these cases the average rating for the offence on the BCS 'seriousness scale'[33] was anyway much lower, and many victims named no problems of any kind.[34] The major exception was theft of a car - an offence rated by victims almost as seriously as burglary. Here, 49 per cent of all victims - and over 90 per cent of those naming any problems at all - mentioned practical problems or inconvenience as the worst aspect. (For interview-based data on car theft victims, see May, 1986.) Other offences where such problems loomed quite large were bicycle theft and vandalism.

To sum up, the evidence we have clearly indicates that crime causes widespread inconvenience among victims of many different offences. This consists largely of the chores of

60

repairing property, replacing articles, and (often mentioned as the most time-consuming and frustrating) dealing with organisations such as Housing Departments, DHSS, rental firms, and insurance companies. As one victim of a 'snatch' theft put it, 'You don't realise how many different people you have to write to and forms you have to fill in to replace what you carry in one handbag!' On the other hand, this inconvenience is not immediately thought of as a 'problem' by a large proportion of those who experience it: prompting was needed to get many people to mention it as such and, moreover, practical problems were considered the worst aspect of the offence by under 10 per cent of the victims we interviewed. When we come later in this chapter to discuss victims' needs, we shall also find that most victims cope successfully with practical problems, time-consuming and annoying as this can be, and that the number who think that VSS volunteers could help with practical matters is comparatively low. This general picture, however, should not distract attention from the minority for whom practical problems are very serious, whose situation will also be discussed later (Chapter 6).

(ii)   Longer-term effects

(a)   Patterns over the first few weeks

We now consider how the effects of crime changed over the first few weeks after the event. As VSS intervention may change the pattern, we show here the responses only of the 72 victims interviewed after 3-6 weeks who had not been visited or otherwise assisted[35] by Scheme volunteers (those who had will be discussed in Chapter 6).

Table 3.11 shows such victims' ratings of how badly affected by the experience they remained. Although the majority had by that time largely recovered, 15 per cent rated themselves still 'very much' affected, and only 20 per cent claimed to have shaken off the effects entirely. These results are comparable with those of Maguire and Bennett (1982), which showed 65 per cent of burglary victims still affected to some degree 4-10 weeks after the event.

When asked to describe how they felt now, over two-thirds named, unprompted, a specific lingering effect. The effects most frequently mentioned were persisting fear or insecurity (by 44 per cent). Several victims of violent crime spoke of continuing fear of places which reminded them of the attack, while burglary victims tended to feel a more generalised sense of insecurity or unease. Four of the 39 victims of violence crime spoke of severe restrictions on their work or social life, and four of the whole 72 wanted to move house.

## Table 3.11
### Effects of crime after 3-6 weeks: victims not visited or assisted by volunteers

#### Ratings of level of impact

| | Over first few hours: | | 3-6 weeks later: | |
|---|---|---|---|---|
| | Self | Others in household (where appropriate) | Self | Others in household (where appropriate) |
| Affected | % | % | % | % |
| Very much | 52 | 39 | 15 | 7 |
| Quite a lot | 26 | 31 | 22 | 11 |
| A little | 22 | 20 | 43 | 41 |
| Not at all | 0 | 10 | 20 | 41 |
| | 100 (N=72)[*] | 100 (N=56)[*] | 100 (N=72)[*] | 100 (N=56)[*] |

[*] Victims of burglary, robbery, assault, theft/person not visited or assisted by VSS. Weighted to allow for oversampling of violent offences.

When they were prompted by being asked to say which of a list of 22 effects (similar to that used for measuring initial effects) they were still experiencing, 32 per cent pointed to at least one which they felt very strongly, and 10 per cent to at least four. As Table M (Appendix) shows, anger, fear, feeling 'unsettled', constant thoughts about the crime, and sadness about the loss, all figured prominently. Fewer than half said they were not at all afraid or nervous, or not at all angry. Moreover, a quarter stated that others in their household were still affected to a considerable extent - mainly feeling afraid or worried - and a third of those with children in the house said that the latter were still frightened or upset.

We asked the same victims to describe, in broad terms, how their feelings about the crime had changed over the weeks since it had happened and, in particular, when they had felt at their lowest point. Table 3.12 shows the patterns which emerged. It seemed that, while for an unfortunate few the effects continued unabated for weeks (or longer - see next section), the majority were affected worst within the first 24 hours and the effects wore off gradually after that. The most common 'low point' identified was a few hours after the event, when the police had left, the victim was perhaps alone, and the impact of what had happened 'sank in'. One elderly widow, for example, said, 'I felt terribly isolated after the police had left, and very cold'.

## Table 3.12
### Patterns of emotional effects over first few weeks

Q. When did you feel at your lowest point?

|  | Burglary % | Robbery, assault, theft % |
|---|---|---|
| Immediately afterwards | 15 | 20 |
| A few hours later | 33 | 26 |
| 24 hours later | 24 | 23 |
| 2-3 days later | 6 | 10 |
| 4-6 days later | 3 | 8 |
| About a week later | 6 | 5 |
| Over a week to a month later | 9 | 5 |
| No lowest point | 3 | 3 |
|  | 100 | 100 |
|  | (N = 33) | (N = 39) |

Q. How have your feelings about the crime changed over time? For instance, did any bad feelings about it wear off over the first few days, did they get worse and worse, did you feel better and then worse, or what?

|  | % |
|---|---|
| Not affected/wore off quickly | 20 |
| Gradually better throughout | 39 |
| Bad for a few days, then better | 7 |
| All right, then bad period, then better | 6 |
| On and off/fluctuating | 6 |
| Bad, continuing bad | 20 |
| All right at first, then bad period, continuing bad | 2 |
|  | 100 |
|  | (N = 72)[*] |

[*] Victims of burglary, robbery, assault and theft from the person not visited/assisted by VSS. Weighted to compensate for oversampling of violent offences.

However - a finding which should be of particular interest to Schemes in deciding when to visit - over a quarter said that their lowest point came rather later. Several of these referred to a sort of 'relapse', 'delayed shock', or 'sudden depression' after being relatively unaffected initially. A victim of burglary and one of assault stated, respectively:

'I was not upset for the first week, but it hit me two weeks later. My mother asked why I was upset, but I didn't want to tell her it was the crime - it sounded wimpy for a thing that had happened two weeks earlier.'

'About a week later I started shaking with anger - it was my own stupidity partly - I could have avoided it.'

In fact, 'delayed reactions' of some kind were mentioned by about a third of the composite sample. It is worth noting that victims of <u>assault</u> (45 per cent) were particularly likely to mention delayed effects. Indeed, the (predominantly young) male victims of assault were as likely as female victims of burglary (each 37 per cent) to mention a delayed emotional/psychological effect of some kind - a finding which contradicts views about relative need held by some policemen responsible for VSS referrals (see Chapter 4). Other reasons given for a later 'low point' were instances of what has been called 'secondary victimisation' - e.g. unsympathetic treatment by organisations such as the DHSS, Electricity Board,[36] police or hospitals; the general inconvenience of repairs or renewals; and (following assaults) pain or immobility.

One BCS question gives roughly comparable kinds of information for all offence types. BCS victims who said that they would have accepted an offer of assistance from a Scheme, had it been offered, were asked at what point a call would have been most welcome. The great majority replied 'the day of the incident' or 'the next day', only 18 per cent naming a later point (see also Chapter 6). The offences most likely to produce a preference for a later call were robbery, assault, 'snatch' theft and (above all) threats.

To what extent did victims feel the event had changed their lifestyle or personality? Long-term changes will be discussed later, but among those we interviewed after 3-6 weeks who had not been visited or assisted by Schemes, 52 per cent felt that the event would have some lasting effect:

Q. Do you think this crime will have a lasting effect
       on your life in the future?

|  |  |
|---|---|
| Yes - very strong | 6% |
| Yes - quite strong | 17% |
| Yes - but not strong | 29% |
| No | 48% |
|  | 100% (N = 72) |

It is interesting that the figure of six per cent of victims who thought it would have a very strong lasting effect, is the same as that given by Maguire and Bennett (1982) as the proportion of burglary victims suffering 'very serious' lasting effects. It is also is similar to several other estimates of the incidence of 'trauma' (see Waller, 1982; Mayhew, 1984).

More specifically, the same victims were asked whether they thought the crime had 'changed [them] at all as a person', and prompted with five possibilities (as shown in Appendix, Table N). While only a few felt that there had been major changes, almost a half felt 'a little more afraid of unpleasant things happening to them' and over a quarter felt 'a little less cheerful' or 'a little less in control of their own lives'. In addition to effects on the prompted list, 20 per cent of victims mentioned other 'personality changes', mainly that they felt less 'sociable', less 'trusting', less 'confident' or less 'tolerant'. Three of the latter admitted to new 'anti-black' feelings after being assaulted by a black offender.

As many as 41 per cent of victims of violent offences not assisted by Schemes said that they felt 'more punitive' towards offenders than they had before the event. About a fifth of burglary victims also reacted in this way. Yet, despite this, 27 per cent of the whole group agreed that 'something positive' had come out of the whole affair. Most of these explained that they had become more conscious of the importance of security, but a sizeable minority (7 of the whole 72) said that they felt more self-confident, more self-aware, or had less fear of the unknown as a result. Two examples of this are:

> 'This was probably one of the worst things that could have happened, but beforehand it was an unknown quantity. Now it has, I know it was less worse than the violence I've suffered from my husband throughout my married life.'

> 'I feel less afraid, because now it's happened, one doesn't need to be so apprehensive any more.'

When asked what difference the offence had made to their actual behaviour, over two-thirds of the burglary victims (prompted with a list of possibilities) answered that they were now more careful in locking up. However, of more concern may be the findings that a quarter said that they went out less and over 20 per cent that they invited fewer people into their homes. Indeed, 15 per cent were still disturbed enough to sleep in a different room or with the light on. Victims of violence tended to mention a different set of behaviour changes: 38 per cent stated that they 'went out less at night' and 26 per cent that they 'avoided certain places or people'. (See Appendix, Table O.)

Finally, in order to obtain a measure of the degree of recent psychological change in victims which can be compared broadly with that of groups of non-victims, we used a version of the General Health Questionnaire, originally developed by David Goldberg at the General Practice Research Unit (Goldberg, 1978).[37] This is a well-tested instrument which has often been used to detect possible psychiatric disturbance in particular populations, such as those consulting their GPs. In a random sample of the adult population of Manchester, Goldberg et al. (1974) found that the probable prevalence of psychiatric disturbance of the kind that psychiatrists consider deserving of treatment was 11 per cent for males and 23 per cent for females. These proportions rose to 34 and 38 per cent respectively among a sample of patients in GPs' waiting-rooms.

Among our sample of victims of burglary, robbery and assault who had not been visited or assisted by VSS volunteers (interviewed 3-6 weeks after the offence) the GHQ scores which emerged were much higher than those of the general population and, in the case of female victims, were considerably higher even than those of patients in waiting-rooms. The relevant scores were as shown in Table 3.13 (see Appendix, Table P, for more details).

Table 3.13
Indications from responses to GHQ.60 questionnaire of
probable prevalence in population of psychiatric disturbance

|  | Probable percentage in population with disturbance | |
|---|---|---|
|  | Males % | Females % |
| Victims of burglary (after 3 - 6 weeks) | 16 | 45 |
| Victims of robbery/assault (after 3 - 6 weeks) | 18 | 48 |
| Random community sample (Goldberg) | 11 | 23 |
| Primary care attenders (Goldberg) | 34 | 38 |

It can be seen that our female victims were twice as likely as the female 'non-victims' in the Goldberg study to have symptoms of psychological disturbance. This is one of the clearest pieces of evidence we have that the types of offence under discussion have serious consequences, for several weeks at least, for more than just a few of their victims.

(b)  Effects after three months or longer

With the exception of rape, the aftermath of which has been studied in some depth (see Chapter 7), knowledge about the long-lasting effects of crime is limited and to some extent contradictory. As Kilpatrick (1985) points out, research on effects over the long term - which he defines as commencing at three months after the offence - poses enormous methodological problems. And although it is clear that some victims of burglary, robbery and assault are badly affected for very long periods, it cannot be said with certainty how many or how seriously. In England, the longitudinal study by Shapland et al. (1985) has provided evidence that serious offences of violence cause long-lasting fear, depression or anxiety in a significant minority of cases. About one in five victims in a sample of serious assault cases taken from police records were found to be still psychologically affected to some degree two years after the event. Elsewhere, Brown and Yantzi (1980) found few 'emotional needs' among a sample of victims of mixed offences interviewed a year after the event; Friedman et al. (1982), who re-interviewed a sample of victims of robbery, burglary and assault (i.e. similar to our own 'composite' sample) four months later, found that most problems originally rated as serious were by then no longer regarded as such; but by contrast Stuebing (1984) found effects such as distrust of others (54 per cent) and fear of walking alone at night (33 per cent) persisting in substantial proportions of a not dissimilar sample of victims for several months.

The British Crime Survey data is a useful addition to the evidence on long-term effects, in that it provides comparable measures of effects for offences occurring in each month up to a year prior to interview. Table 3.14 shows selected categories of BCS offences (reported to the police), according to the three-month period in which each occurred. For each category, we show the proportion of respondents rating themselves or their household still (at the time of interview in early 1984) 'very much' or 'quite a lot' affected by the event. It can be seen that 8 per cent of all respondents were still affected by incidents which had occurred about a year previously. The BCS evidence also

67

suggests that the only major fall in the level of effects among the whole victim population occurs during the first few weeks, and that most of those who are still badly affected by the event at around the three-month point continue to be badly affected for up to a year afterwards. This gives some support to the pattern predicted by crisis theory: the normal duration of the 'crisis stage' following serious offences has been put at around six weeks (Friedman et al., 1982), after which all but a small proportion of victims will be expected to make a satisfactory recovery in the 'reorganisation stage' (see Chapter 7).

### Table 3.14
Proportions of victims of selected BCS offences (known to the police) occurring in different periods, who were still 'very much' or 'quite a lot' affected at time of interview (early 1984)

| | Period in which offence occurred | | | | |
| Type of offence | Jan/Mar 83 % still affected | Apr/Jun 83 % still affected | Jul/Sep 83 % still affected | Oct/Dec 83 % still affected | Early 84[*] % still affected |
| --- | --- | --- | --- | --- | --- |
| Burglary | 15 | 27 | 22 | 26 | 34 |
| Wounding/robbery/snatch | 25 | 27 | 20 | 12 | 61 |
| Vandalism | 8 | 3 | 18 | 19 | 62 |
| Theft | 4 | 1 | 7 | 8 | 12 |
| All offences | 8 | 10 | 11 | 12 | 28 |

[*] The majority of interviews were carried out in February-March 1984
Source: BCS 1984. Weighted data.

Even so, it can be seen from the Table that some offences leave a much larger minority of victims than others suffering long-lasting effects. Those standing out in this respect were serious assaults and robberies, where a quarter of victims considered themselves still 'very much' or 'quite a lot' affected a year after the event. Some 15 per cent of burglary victims said the same.

Nearly all the 64 victims we interviewed three to four months after the offence had been visited by VSS volunteers, and several of these had originally been selected individually by the police for referral as cases deserving attention. We cannot therefore generalise from these findings. Nevertheless, it is worthy of note that - despite having received VSS visits at an early stage - seven of the

68

28 victims of robbery, 'snatch' theft and serious assault still rated themselves in the 'very much affected' category. None of the burglary victims rated the effects this high, although a third were still 'quite a lot' affected. This difference, in fact, accords with the small amount of evidence so far available (e.g. Smith et al., 1985) that while burglary is equally disturbing in the short term, victims of violence are more likely to be badly affected for longer.

The types of continuing psychological effect reported most frequently by the victims of robbery, assault and 'snatch' theft were persistent thoughts about the crime (still 'very strongly' experienced by 25 per cent), anger (32 per cent) and fear of going out (18 per cent). The patterns of reaction they described indicated that over a quarter felt that they had not been 'getting better' at all over the past three months, and 7 per cent felt they had been 'getting worse'. Over a half said they felt 'less cheerful' and similar proportions that they felt 'less warm towards other people' and had 'less energy' as a result of the offence; over 40 per cent went out less than before the offence or avoided certain places; and - perhaps of most concern - over one in five thought that the offence would have a 'very strong' effect on their life in the future. The burglary victims scored much lower on all these measures,[38] although under 20 per cent said that they had recovered entirely from the incident: the most widespread continuing effects - experienced to some extent by over 50 per cent - seemed to be anger, fear of the event being repeated, and a loss of trust in other people.[39]

Finally, the small group of 15 victims we interviewed a year after the event - all of whom had been visited early on by VSS volunteers after being referred under a selective referral system - acted as a further illustration that the effects of crime can seriously disrupt peoples' lives for a very long time. Four of these (one burglary victim, one robbery victim and two assault victims, all of whom had completely recovered from any physical injuries) were obviously still very badly affected by the offence. One could not bring herself to travel on public transport since being attacked on a bus a year previously. Two of the others hardly ever went out, and the fourth - the burglary victim - still felt that she was 'being watched' and had devised elaborate changes to her daily routine. Their eagerness to tell us every detail of what had happened was one indication of how vividly the incidents had remained in their minds.

Taken together, the evidence we have suggests that, although some unpleasant memories, unease and nervousness may remain for quite a long period, the majority of victims of most types of crime recover from the worst psychological effects within a few weeks - the 'crisis' period, according to crisis theory. However, a substantial minority - perhaps as high as 20 per cent - of victims of serious violent crime, and a small percentage of victims of other offences, do not recover in the same way. The event causes lasting changes in their personality and behaviour. Early results from an important American study of long-term effects on robbery victims (Resick, 1985) suggests that this applies to both male and female victims, although the former are more likely to show changes in levels of self-esteem and 'interpersonal problems' and the latter in levels of fear or anxiety. Whether intervention by organisations such as Victims Support Schemes at an early stage can either facilitate the recovery of those who would anyway have recovered from the worst effects within a few weeks, or can significantly reduce the problems of those vulnerable to long-term effects, are major questions we leave until Chapter 6.

## Victims' 'needs' for support and assistance

Although we have shown that substantial proportions of victims are quite badly affected emotionally and/or face practical problems as a result of the offence, this does not mean that all these victims 'need' VSS intervention. Many are fully capable of dealing with the practical problems themselves (and may indeed prefer to do so), while others receive adequate emotional support from family or friends.

Taking the above points into account, we attempt in this last section to arrive at a broad estimate of the number of victims who can be said to 'need' VSS intervention to solve particular problems. We have limited our definition of this group to a combination of (a) those who define themselves as badly affected by the crime but receive little emotional support from family, friends or neighbours, and (b) those whose practical problems are not resolved within a reasonable period after the offence. To these can be added the smaller (but, we believe, most important) group, consisting mainly of victims of serious sexual and physical assault, who may receive good support from families, but who are so disturbed by the event that they may need regular visits from an experienced outsider to help them overcome persisting psychological effects. It should be noted, finally, that we have ignored here a 'need' whose satisfaction, we would argue, is squarely the responsibility of the police - the desire for information about the progress of the case.[40]

Of course, this is only one of many possible ways of defining the slippery concept of 'need' in relation to victims (see Mawby, 1984; Maguire, 1985). It does not imply that others would not benefit from support, nor that they should not be contacted in order to 'show that someone cares'. Rather, it defines the <u>minimum</u> number of badly affected victims with 'needs' which they themselves would readily recognise - and hence, perhaps, the minimum population which, in an ideal world, Schemes would wish to contact with an offer of support or assistance.

(i)  Need for emotional support

In an effort to discover to what extent emotional support was already available, we first asked victims how many people (excluding the police and VSS volunteers) they had spoken to about the offence. Only two among the whole 265 we interviewed had mentioned it to nobody at all, but 17 per cent of the 'composite' sample had spoken about it only to 'one or two' people. Moreover, 8 per cent had told no-one outside their own household. (A similar number, conversely, deliberately had not told others in their household, usually for fear of upsetting them.) The great majority, nevertheless, had told 'several' or 'a lot' of people, most often family members living elsewhere (Table 3.15).

Table 3.15
Responses from friends and family

| Q. Whom did you tell about it? | % |
| --- | --- |
| All in household | 94 |
| Family elsewhere | 76 |
| Friends | 68 |
| Neighbours | 55 |
| Workmates | 30 |
| No-one outside household | 8 |

| Q. Did any of these provide moral support or a 'listening ear'? | % |
| --- | --- |
| Yes | 68 |
| A little | 28 |
| No | 4 |
| | 100 |

| Q. Were those told about it generally ...? | % |
| --- | --- |
| Very sympathetic | 68 |
| Fairly sympathetic | 16 |
| Some sympathetic, some not | 12 |
| Unsympathetic | 4 |
| | 100 |

| Q. Who was most supportive? | % |
| --- | --- |
| Members of household | 7 |
| Family elsewhere | 34 |
| Neighbours | 17 |
| Workmates | 4 |
| Police/professional agency | 3 |
| Nobody | 3 |
| | 100 |

Weighted data. Unweighted N = 175 victims of burglary, assault, theft from the person, and robbery ('composite' sample,see Table 3.8).

Telling others, of course, will not always produce a supportive or even an interested response.  Table 3.15 shows that about 70 per cent of victims said that they had received an attentive and very sympathetic 'listening ear' from their friends or family.  The bulk of the remainder had received at least some support, but 12 per cent had found some people unsympathetic and 4 per cent had found no 'listening ear' at all.  (Most of the latter lived alone.)  One in ten, too, had noticed some people avoiding them as a result of the incident.  One victim of robbery told of a range of reactions:

> 'I didn't tell my parents for fear of worrying them.  My friends gave me a bit of support.  I avoided telling people who would not be sympathetic, but some made me more frightened by telling me about what had happened to them.  My daughter didn't really want to know either.'

A victim of burglary similarly remembered:

> 'I started to tell my neighbour, but she had no time - said her husband was coming home for his dinner.  My son and husband have rarely mentioned it even though they were there when it happened.  I suppose they think I'll be reminded of it all over again.'

When asked to identify the person or persons who had been most sympathetic, many more named friends and relatives living elsewhere than mentioned members of their own household (Table 3.15).

It was clear that victims found talking to others helpful in ameliorating the emotional impact of the offence.  About half said that it had made them feel very much better and a quarter a little better.  Moreover, the more people spoken to, and the more sympathetic they had been, the more likely victims were to report having felt very much better.[41]

To what extent did victims express a wish for more support than they had received?  Of those who had not been visited or telephoned by Scheme volunteers, 26 per cent said that they definitely would have liked to talk more about their feelings, and a further 5 per cent were undecided.  Most of those who did not want to talk any more about them gave the reasons that they had already had sufficient opportunity to do so, that they were not upset, or simply that they wanted to forget the matter.  On the other hand, those who would have liked to talk more but had failed to do so, explained that they felt reluctant to impose upon other people, that others 'did not want to know', and that they found it difficult to express feelings (see Appendix, Table Q).

The above findings may be compared with responses to our questions in the BCS designed to measure self-expressed need. Most pertinently, victims were asked whether they had needed (but did not get) among other things, 'someone to talk to about the crime and your feelings'. Twenty-eight per cent of the BCS victims of burglary, robbery or wounding (reported to the police) admitted to such a need - a figure very similar to the 26 per cent of our (non-VSS visited) interviewees who had wanted to 'talk more'.[42] At a more general level, 33 per cent of the same group of victims said that they would have liked to have been contacted by a Victims Support Scheme, and 51 per cent said that they would have accepted assistance if offered. (The equivalent figures were 26 per cent and 45 per cent respectively for all BCS offences reported to the police.)

A general picture can now be constructed, taking account of the main findings in this chapter, of the level of 'need' for emotional support by volunteers. At the lowest level, it will be recalled that in the BCS only about 10 per cent of victims of 'ordinary' theft which had been reported to the police rated themselves as badly affected. If we assume, drawing upon our interview findings, that in about two-thirds of these cases the victim's family or friends provided a sympathetic 'ear' when required, the 'need' for VSS intervention to provide emotional support is limited to only 3 per cent of all personal victims of thefts known to the police. Even allowing for the tendency of survey data to under-estimate effects, the figure remains below 5 per cent.

On the other hand, using our findings from interviews, we may take 60 per cent as the proportion of victims of serious assault or burglary badly enough affected to be said to 'need' emotional support. If we again assume that two-thirds of these will receive strong support from friends or relatives, we are left with 20 per cent of the total 'needing' VSS intervention on the grounds of insufficient support from elsewhere, plus perhaps 5 per cent who are so badly affected that they need outside support in addition to full support from friends and family (cf. Maguire, 1982; Waller, 1982).

Thus in broad terms (and excluding those who have suffered rape, which has yet to be discussed), victims of recorded crime can be said on our definition to 'need' emotional support from VSS in between 1 in 20 (theft) and 1 in 4 (burglary, wounding) cases. An overall estimate, based on all BCS offences which were reported to the police, would show roughly 1 in 10 victims of all personal or household offences needing VSS intervention on the criteria described.

(ii)   Practical needs

The concept of 'needs' is almost as problematic in
relation to the practical consequences of crime as it is to
the emotional consequences, and estimates of the proportions
of victims 'needing' practical assistance also vary
considerably (Sebba, 1984;  Villmow, 1984;  Maguire, 1985).
There is little doubt that prompting is necessary in
questioning victims on this subject if one is to gain a set
of meaningful responses.  This was discovered by Brown and
Yantzi (1980), who initially perceived all tasks for which
help was not immediately available as 'practical needs'.
However, they found that victims did not tend to think of
them in this way.  When asked, unprompted, to name any
'practical needs' they had had, under 5 per cent of their
sample recalled a 'need' for repairs - although a high
proportion had had to make some.

In order to gain a broad idea of what practical tasks
remained undone, or were not satisfactorily resolved, after
help had been received from family or friends (i.e. what
practical assistance might be needed from VSS volunteers),
BCS respondents were asked whether there were 'Any kinds of
information, help or advice ... which you needed but did not
get', and were prompted with a list of possibilities.
Fifteen per cent of all victims (of offences which became
known to the police) mentioned at least one 'practical
need',[43] but this figure rose to over 30 per cent where
victims of burglary and serious assault were concerned.  The
most frequently mentioned overall were advice about
compensation, crime prevention, legal matters and insurance.

Our interview data can also be used to give a broad idea
of practical needs, in the sense of unresolved practical
problems, for specific offences.  As described earlier, we
first asked our interviewees which of a list of practical
tasks or problems had had to be dealt with by anybody as a
result of the offence.  We then followed this up by asking
how many of these had been successfully dealt with and how
many remained unresolved.

Table 3.16 shows, for victims of burglary in the
'composite' sample only, the main tasks which had to be
carried out, the extent of outside help received (excluding
VSS) and whether or not the outcome was considered
satisfactory.  Even though (after weighting) about half of
this sample had been visited by volunteers, the great
majority of practical tasks had been dealt fairly quickly
with by the respondent or by others in the household.  The
small amount of outside assistance reported - usually in the
form of security improvements or repairs - was generally

## Table 3.16
### Practical problems: proportion not satisfactorily resolved

| Type of problem | (A)<br>% of victims experiencing problems | % of cases in (A) where victim received some outside help (excluding VSS) | % of cases in (A) not satisfactorily resolved | % of all cases where an unresolved problem remained |
|---|---|---|---|---|
| Repairs | 71 | 12 | 27 | 19 |
| Changing locks/<br>making secure | 31 | 29 | 8 | 3 |
| Insurance claims | 40 | 4 | 16 | 6 |
| Financial<br>difficulty | 13 | 14 | 23 | 3 |
| Dealing with<br>authorities | 35 | 0 | 53 | 19 |

\* Based on response to question: Did any of the following problems have to be dealt with by you or anyone else?

N = 90 victims of burglary: 'composite' sample weighted to approximate to a representative sample of cases of burglary (with loss) from police records.

limited to older people helped by members of their family living elsewhere. And even among the respondents who had been visited by volunteers, only 13 per cent mentioned having received any practical help from the Scheme (these answers are excluded from the Table).[44] Moreover, most of the tasks had been completed or problems solved to the victim's satisfaction. For example, only 8 per cent of those who had felt it necessary to change their locks or otherwise make their home secure again, failed to achieve this satisfactorily; and even though 27 per cent of those who had needed to make repairs were dissatisfied with the result, nearly all these were concerned about incomplete repair-work, rather than a total failure to repair damage. The exception lay in victims' dealings with various authorities - particularly disputes with Gas or Electricity Boards over how much had to be repaid after 'meter breaks' - where over half the problems had not been resolved to the victim's satisfaction. This was an area in which no victims reported having received assistance from people (excluding VSS) outside their household.

The final column of Table 3.16 shows what proportions of all burglary victims were left nursing dissatisfaction about different kinds of practical matters: one in five were unhappy with incomplete repairs, and a similar proportion (overlapping to a considerable extent with the first group) were dissatisfied with the results of negotiations or disputes with authorities. In one sense, all the victims appearing in this column, who together made up about 30 per cent of the total, could be said to have been 'in need of practical assistance'. To them, too, might be added another 15 per cent who had failed to replace satisfactorily expensive stolen articles. However, in many cases, victims recognised that there was nothing a body like VSS could do to assist them: they had called the outcome 'unsatisfactory', for example, because they had not been insured, or because the rules of fuel boards, though fairly applied, seemed to them unfair in principle. Thus, it may be more realistic to limit the definition of 'practical needs' further, by excluding cases of financially-motivated dissatisfaction in which (unless the victim was so short of money that emergency funding was justified) there was patently nothing an outside body could do to help. On this basis (and also, at this point, using only those cases in the composite sample where the victim had not received a VSS visit), our best estimate of the proportion of burglary victims with at least one 'practical need' (unresolved practical problem after 3-6 weeks) is 25 per cent. For victims of violent offences, it is somewhat lower, at 15 per cent.

(iii) The need for support or assistance: a broad conclusion

As we have stressed several times, the concept of victims' 'needs' is a highly elastic one. At one extreme, virtually all victims could be said to have a need - to be given the symbolic reassurance that 'the community' is sorry about what happened to them. At the other extreme, a definition of people in 'real' need - as would be drawn up if services to victims were ever put on a statutory footing - might exclude all except the small proportion who experience severe trauma (under 10 per cent even in the case of burglary or serious assault). Ultimately, although recognising its practical and indeed political value (Maguire, 1985), we are sceptical of the analytical value of the concept of 'need' in the context of crime victims. For this reason, we have spent most of this chapter discussing the effects of crime rather than the 'needs' it produces. Others can draw their own conclusions as to where the latter line should be drawn. We have, however, offered one working definition of victims' needs, based upon victims' own assessments of the level of impact of the offence, and the amount of support or assistance available to them from family and friends. This is the closest we can come to what, in our experience, Scheme members tend to understand by the term. According to this definition, about 1 in 4

76

victims of the crimes (excluding rape) found to have the greatest emotional impact - i.e. burglary, robbery, 'snatch' thefts and serious assault - and 1 in 10 of all recorded offences against individuals, can be shown to 'need' a visit from a volunteer to provide some form of psychological support or reassurance. Among these victims, too, it should be remembered, there will be differing levels of need according to their social characteristics, with, for example, elderly widows and people of low socio-economic status more likely than other groups to need support.

Finally, we have calculated that 15-25 per cent of victims of recorded offences of violence and burglary have 'practical needs', in the sense of problems still unresolved after some weeks. If we then combine both practical and emotional needs - many of which are anyway intertwined in the same victims - we may conclude that the proportion of victims of these more serious offences 'needing' a VSS visit (according to our definition) lies in the region of 30-40 per cent. Figures around this level emerge from various different sources in addition to those described above. For example, about 30 per cent of BCS victims of such offences reported unsatisfied needs for either 'someone to talk to' or for practical advice or assistance. About 33 per cent, too, said they would have liked a visit from a volunteer.[45] And, as we shall see in Chapter 6, this accords fairly well with the experience of volunteers when visiting victims unannounced: they tended to identify a need for support or assistance on about 40 per cent of such occasions.

## Notes to Chapter 3

1. Only one in three of the 'offences' reported to the 1984 British Crime Survey were reported to the police. Over 50 per cent of 'victims' who failed to report the matter to the police gave the reason that it was insufficiently serious. And it is calculated that about one third of the survey offences which were reported to the police were not subsequently recorded by the police (Hough and Mayhew, 1985; cf. Sparks, Genn and Dodd, 1977).

2. For discussions of the general problems of measuring 'need', see Bradshaw (1972), Townsend (1972), Culyer et al. (1972) and Armstrong (1982). For examples of attempts to measure victims' needs using each of the methods outlined above, see Maguire (1985).

3. There is a possibility, of course, that when interviewed in depth, some victims who have been only mildly affected will try to please the interviewer and describe 'problems' which do not have any real significance for them. We can only say that we were well aware of this possibility, and took care not to encourage reporting of spurious effects.

4. For 'series' offences, however - several very similar crimes, committed usually by the same person - only one victim form was completed.

5. Burglary, thefts of and from vehicles, vandalism and theft from the home were defined as crimes against the household, while violent and sexual offences, together with personal theft, were treated as crimes against an individual. Respondents completed victim forms for all household offences, whether or not they were the prime victim, but not for personal crimes committed against other members of the household. For full details of weighting procedures and other technical adjustments, see Hough and Mayhew (1985:77-84) and NOP (1985).

6. We also interviewed small numbers of victims of miscellaneous offences including minor theft, criminal damage and 'autocrime', but these cases have been excluded from statistical analyses.

7. Three of these Schemes were located in large cities, the other two in medium-sized towns. The overall response rate was 67 per cent. In two areas, a researcher was permitted to call unannounced at victims' homes but in the others, at VSS or police insistence, a letter was sent first, requesting an interview. If no reply was received, efforts were made to contact them by telephone or a further letter. Eight per cent of those approached refused to be interviewed, and the rest we failed to contact.

8. Excluding the 23 interviews with rape victims (all of which were conducted more than two months after the event), 64 took place between three and four months after the offence, and 15 more than a year afterwards. Most of these had been visited by volunteers shortly after the offence. Despite the length of time that had elapsed, none of these victims had trouble in recalling the event or its immediate consequences and there were no significant differences between those interviewed 3-6 weeks and 3-4 months after the offence in terms of the levels of impact recalled.

9. Those visited by volunteers contained disproportionate numbers of elderly female victims, as this is the group to which Co-ordinators tend to give priority when there are insufficient volunteers to visit all victims referred (see Chapter 4). Based upon comparisons of the sex and age structure of the sample of visited victims, with samples from police records, a weight of 0.22 was applied to the responses of female victims of burglary aged over 60. Victims of violence, who were over-represented in a ratio of approximately 3:1 were given a weight of 0.33.

10. For example, in terms of measures of impact (see next section), there was very little difference between the 'real' police records sample of 35 cases and this 'artificial' sample (see also footnote 12).

11. Relatively few respondents (13 per cent of our whole sample) rated 'others close to them' as worse affected than themselves. Nevertheless, where we make direct comparisons between our interview data and BCS results, we have adjusted our data, using these cases, to ensure that

ratings apply to any member of the household, rather than only to the one we interviewed.

12. If we use the 'composite sample' - i.e. also include in the analysis appropriate cases of victims referred to Schemes under automatic referral systems (see footnote 9) - the proportion 'very much' affected emerges, almost unchanged, at 66 per cent.

13. The proportions of male respondents were 52 per cent (BCS) and 51 per cent ('in-depth' interviews), and of non-manual heads of household 54 per cent and 57 per cent respectively. The reason for the exclusion of respondents over 60 was that, as Co-ordinators tended to give priority to older people when sending out volunteers, our interview data contained an over-representation of over-60s (see footnote 9 above).

14. It seems, therefore, that about a third of the gap in Table 3.2 is explained by differences in the seriousness of the offences sampled. This reflects the fact that the BCS picks up many offences reported to the police which the latter do not record: these are likely to be less serious than those recorded.

15. Too few serious sexual offences were reported to BCS interviewers for a comparative measure to be made, but there is ample evidence (see Chapter 7) that the effects on victims of such offences, particularly rape, are the most severe of all.

16. In 1983 in the whole of England and Wales the total number recorded as notifiable offences was only 1,248 (688 threats to kill and 560 to commit criminal damage). A threat to assault can normally be charged only as a summary offence of threatening behaviour, if at all.

17. The number of BCS interviewees from ethnic minorities was too small to provide reliable data on racial harrassment, although it is worthy of mention that 19 (8 per cent) of the 245 threats reported to the Survey were to non-white victims, mainly of Asian origin.

18. The total numbers of reported and unreported offences likely to be committed in such an area were calculated as follows: for 'household' offences (burglaries, thefts of and from vehicles, thefts from the home and vandalism) BCS rates were applied to a nominal total of households (48,500) and for 'personal' offences (assaults, robberies, thefts from the person, other personal thefts, sexual offences and threats) BCS rates were applied to a nominal population over the age of 16 (102,500). For similarly-produced estimates of the total numbers of offences in various categories committed in England and Wales, see Hough and Mayhew (1985:61-2).

19. For example, only 14 per cent of non-reporting victims of robbery or assault had attention from a doctor, compared with 60 per cent of those who reported such offences to the police.

20.   It is likely, moreover, that such offences were substantially under-reported to the BCS interviewers (Hough and Mayhew, 1985:9).

21. And any 'series' of more than five offences is counted as only five in the BCS, so the incidence of threats may be considerably greater than the results of the survey suggest (cf. Maclean et al, 1985).

22.   Obviously, respondents who were themselves unaffected might answer 'very much' because of effects upon a spouse or others in the house of the opposite sex.   In fact, in cases where the respondent lived alone, the difference between the sexes was even greater;   over all BCS offences, only 10 per cent of men living alone, compared with 26 per cent of women, reported themselves 'very much' affected.

23.   Step-wise regression analysis largely confirmed the basic picture we have outlined.   This indicated that for offences which became known to the police, being male was the best predictor (low level of impact) and that being widowed, separated or divorced and having or being a man head of household were second and third best (high levels of impact). These factors were all statistically highly significant.   Neither age nor living alone were significant indicators of impact in this analysis.

24.   This, of course, is complicated by the fact that the BCS question referred to effects on other members of the household as well as the respondent.   However, this appears, from the evidence of our interviews to make only a marginal difference to the results (footnote 11 above).

25.   Eighty-seven per cent of this group who had suffered a forced entry burglary rated themselves 'very much' affected.

26.   While the percentage of women mentioning emotional effects varied widely by type of crime - from 88 per cent in the case of robbery and 'snatch' theft to 23 per cent in thefts from vehicles - there was much less variation among men.   However, if anger if not counted as an 'emotional problem', this difference largely disappears (Appendix, Table I).

27.   Eleven of these named more than half the effects on the list.

28.   Despite this difference, there was a fairly close correlation between victims' self-ratings (as discussed in the previous section) and the number of listed effects they mentioned.   For example, 160 of the 174 victims in the interviewed population mentioning four or more effects also rated themselves as 'very much' affected, and vice versa, 160 of the 188 'very much affected' mentioned four or more effects.

29.   However, as will be seen in Chapter 7, immediate anger was strikingly infrequently reported by victims of rape:   only 6 of 23 victims recalled intense anger, while 13 (57 per cent) recalled none at all.

30.   For instance, 12 per cent of all BCS victims who said that neither they nor their family were in any way responsible reported themselves

'very much' affected, compared with 8 per cent of those who thought that they personally were to blame. (The proportion blaming themselves in any way was rather higher among BCS victims than in our samples: 15 per cent of victims of all offences (reported and unreported) and 12 per cent of victims of offences known to the police.)

31. Unless otherwise stated, BCS figures in this section refer only to offences which became known to the police.

32. The difference seems, once again, to be accounted for partly by the slightly higher proportion of less serious cases in the BCS, and partly by the previously mentioned general tendency of survey methods to uncover fewer effects than 'in-depth' interviews. On the first point, 60 per cent of BCS burglaries with loss (known to the police) involved some form of damage, compared with 68 per cent in our sample. Similarly, there was a loss of over 100 in 55 per cent of BCS burglaries known to the police, compared with 66 per cent of our sample (attempts excluded).

33. For information on the BCS seriousness scale, which was generated from victims' ratings of the seriousness of their 'own' crime on a 20-point scale, see Hough and Mayhew (1985:20).

34. A good example is theft from a vehicle, which, across all incidents reported to the BCS, had an average seriousness rating of 4.1 compared to 7.5 for burglary. While emotional responses (4 per cent) were outweighed by practical problems (23 per cent) as the 'worst problem', 69 per cent named no 'worst problem' at all. By contrast, 37 per cent of burglary victims named emotional responses, and 19 per cent practical problems, as worst, only 35 per cent naming no problem at all. (These figures include cases known and not known to the police.)

35. For this analysis, we excluded from the group who had been telephoned (but not visited) a small number of cases in which the victim said the call had made a lasting difference to how they felt or had resulted in practical assistance from elsewhere. Those remaining contained a disproportionately high number of victims of violent offences, which were weighted in any overall analysis by 0.33 as before. The group was not grossly unrepresentative where the age or sex of victims was concerned (24 per cent over the age of 60, 39 per cent male).

36. Several victims we interviewed had to make good the value stolen from meters under the threat of being cut off. Another was extremely upset at having her slot meter removed and replaced with an ordinary meter, simply because she had been burgled twice within one year. The letter she showed us from the Board was couched in an unsympathetic tone, and virtually implied that she could not be trusted. In this case, there was no doubt at all that the burglary had been 'genuine'.

37. The version we used (GHQ.60) consisted of 60 questions, designed to measure somatic symptoms, anxiety, insomnia, social dysfunction and severe depression (see Goldberg, 1978).

38. For example, the continuing emotional reactions reported most frequently by burglary victims - 'anger' and 'lack of trust in others' - were being experienced strongly by only 12 per cent; only one of the 34 thought the offence would have a very strong lasting effect on her life; and 30 per cent (compared with 54 per cent of victims of violence) felt generally 'less cheerful' than before it happened.

39. These findings, again, are similar to those by Maguire and Bennett (1982), where 65 per cent of burglary victims reported emotional effects of some kind, though not necessarily severe, after 4-10 weeks.

40. It has been shown elsewhere (e.g. Shapland et al., 1984; Burns-Howell et al., 1982; Maguire, 1984, 1985) that failure to keep victims informed is one of their main causes of dissatisfaction with the police. This was confirmed in our interviews (see Appendix). Moreover, when prompted, about half of all those interviewed agreed that they had 'felt the need' for such information but had not received it.

41. Only two of the 175 said that discussing the event had made them feel worse. One, a robbery victim, stated: 'No, I felt worse after. People kept saying I was lucky, and the medical profession did not show much care either. Friends have said I should be grateful for not being killed or raped and I find this attitude hard to take. I don't feel grateful and it's terrible that we should have to be grateful.'

42. Responses in this area also seem to be very dependent upon whether or not victims are prompted. For example, only 10 per cent of Brown and Yantzi's (1980) sample of victims of a wide range of (recorded) offences volunteered a short-term, and 5 per cent a long-term, need for 'someone to talk to'. After prompting, however, the first figure rose to 31 per cent - again similar to our findings above. A rather higher level of this kind of need comes from Stuebing (1984), who presented interviewees with a list of possible crisis needs: it was found that 47 per cent wanted 'someone to talk to after the police had left'.

43. This excludes the 'need for someone to talk to about your feelings', which we have discussed earlier as an emotional need. It also excluded a desire for information about the progress of the case, which, it can be argued, should be a police responsibility.

44. It will, however, be shown in Chapter 6 that a slightly higher proportion than this of all burglary victims visited received some form of practical assistance. Of course, the 'composite' sample used here is weighted to compensate for selectivity by police and Co-ordinators in deciding who should be referred or visited, and it is clear that, within any offence category, those eventually visited have more serious problems (emotional and practical) than those not visited.

45. Shapland et al. (1985) also found that just over a third of victims of violence they interviewed would have liked help or support from VSS. These included a fair proportion of young male victims.

# 4 The filtering process: referral and allocation of cases

In Chapter 2 we showed that - inevitably, given present resources - only a small proportion of crime victims in any area will receive a visit from a VSS volunteer. In this chapter we discuss the 'filtering processes', deliberate or accidental, which reduce the total numbers of potential recipients of Scheme services down to the manageable numbers eventually given support. These processes include both agreed referral policies and individual decisions made by police officers, Scheme Co-ordinators and volunteers. We examine both Scheme and police views about priorities, and look in some detail at how referral and allocation systems work in practice. Attention will be focused upon the eight Schemes we studied in depth, although these will be discussed within the context of a wider picture gained from one-day visits to 13 others, and from our questionnaire to all Schemes.

## Referral policy and practice

As all but a tiny fraction of referrals to Schemes come through the police, the filtering process could be said to begin with the victim's decision to report or not to report a crime. As the British Crime Survey has revealed, this effectively removes at least three-quarters of all victims from the possibility of VSS assistance - although, happily, only a small proportion of these are badly upset or express a desire for support. In this Chapter, however, we are concerned with the subsequent filtering of offences which have already been reported to, and recorded by, the police. The first of these filters, obviously, is the system of referral from the police to Scheme Co-ordinators.

(i) The importance of planning and review

We noted in Chapter 2 the distinction between 'selective' and 'automatic' referral systems. However, it will be shown later that this distinction is not always as clear-cut as might be imagined. Not only are there various hybrid systems, but 'automatic' referral systems almost inevitably retain considerable leeway for referring officers to exercise discretion. Moreover, such systems rarely work perfectly in practice and can change considerably when police personnel change or pressure of work mounts.

Schemes appear to be particularly vulnerable to such vagaries because of a widespread failure to make clearly defined, formally recorded arrangements with local police about precisely what kinds of case, under what circumstances, will and will not be referred. Indeed, we found that, with some exceptions, members of Schemes gave surprisingly little serious thought to the overall shape of their referral system, and did not monitor or review it regularly. As long as they received sufficient numbers of cases to keep their volunteers active, most Co-ordinators and Management Committees seemed content to 'take what they were given'. Hardly any of the Scheme members we interviewed had a clear idea of the total number of offences recorded by the police in their area, nor of the balance between different types of offence. It was apparent, too, from the answers to our national questionnaire, that several respondents believed that they were receiving virtually all offences of a particular kind recorded in their area, when in fact they could only have been receiving a small fraction. Similarly, as we observed several times even in areas with 'automatic' referral, Management Committees became worried by major fluctuations in the numbers of cases referred, but had insufficient information to do more than speculate about imaginary changes in the crime rate. In two meetings we witnessed, fluctuations were put down to 'the weather', when the problem was almost certainly accounted for by a decline in either the willingness or the spare time of referring officers to pass on lengthy lists of cases. Sometimes, it has also to be said, senior police officers sitting on Management Committees were not anxious to disabuse other members of such notions.

We would argue that joint planning with the police of referral systems, in full knowledge of local crime rates, is important to any Scheme. At the extreme, failure to plan can be damaging to the whole enterprise. This is most clearly the case when unconsidered decisions are made on whether referrals should be selective or automatic. A change from the first to the second system has two major

84

consequences. It has the (in our view desirable) consequence that, in essence, it will be the Scheme Co-ordinator,
rather than the police, who decides which victims should be
visited and which not. On the other hand, it opens the
floodgates to a much larger proportion of the daunting
volume of crime which passes through police 'books' every
day: without proper preparation, volunteers can be asked to
do too much, and Co-ordinators can be overwhelmed by the
increase in paperwork alone.

The best illustration of this is provided by the aftermath
of the Metropolitan Police Force Order of February 1984,
which stated that (with certain named exceptions) all
offences of burglary in a dwelling, minor assault, small
personalised frauds, theft from the person and kindred
offences could be brought automatically to the attention of
the local Victims Support Scheme. With the co-operation of
local senior officers thus largely assured, many London
Schemes took the widely recommended step of changing within
a few months from a selective to an automatic referral
policy. In a high crime-rate area like London, even where
such a change was carefully planned, it was liable to
produce pressures upon individuals and finances.
Unfortunately, owing to the unexpectedness of the Force
Order, several Schemes introduced the policy hastily and
without adequate preparation, the result being that Co-
ordinators in particular found their workload suddenly and
dramatically heavier. For example, one Scheme studied,
which had been receiving referrals from six police stations
on a selective basis, decided, without a great deal of
thought about the consequences, to try an automatic referral
system at two stations for a three-month period. The
outcome was an immediate <u>eight-fold</u> increase in referrals.
Not wishing to, as she put it, 'over-pressure' the volunteer
visitors, the unpaid Co-ordinator responsible for the two
areas coped with the increase almost entirely by herself -
mainly by writing letters to, or telephoning, the majority
of victims. Like several other London Co-ordinators at this
time, she experienced a period of intense overwork and
stress, which may have played a part in her later decision
to leave the Scheme.

This kind of experience, we emphasise, is not an argument
for choosing selective rather than automatic referral, but
is a strong argument for <u>forward planning</u>. None of the
relevant Schemes we visited had produced well-informed
estimates of how many referrals might be expected under the
new system, so that they could ensure the availability of
sufficient manpower and resources to deal with the increase.
Essential steps - such as recruiting more volunteers,
providing clerical assistance to Co-ordinators, and

budgeting for increased travelling, telephone and postage expenses - were either taken 'in the dark' or not at all.

(ii)    Scheme viewpoints on referral

(a)    'Automatic' versus 'selective' referral

Generally speaking, the Co-ordinators and volunteers we interviewed formally, or spoke to informally at conferences, were in favour of automatic referral.  Those in Schemes with selective referral tended to claim that it was only problems of manpower and resources - or, sometimes, police resistance to the idea - which prevented them from adopting such a system.  As many pointed out, under automatic referral, victims needing support were much less likely to 'slip through the net', referrals were not affected by the whims, prejudices, or degree of diligence of individual police officers, and their number was more likely to remain steady over time.  Even so, a few actively preferred selective referral, and their views deserve a hearing.

Three main reasons emerged.  The first was what might be called a 'small is beautiful' argument.  Members of some Schemes, particularly those which had been run for several years by the same closely-knit committee with a small group of loyal volunteers, seemed to feel that any major increase in referrals might spoil an organisation which had worked smoothly, if at a modest level, for a long period.  One Chairman suggested, for example, that new recruitment to cope with such a change might upset the 'harmony of the group'.  Mawby (forthcoming) found these kinds of attitudes quite common among the small-town and rural Schemes he was studying in the west of the country.

The second reason, often related to the first, was that automatic referral was another step in the direction of an unwanted 'professionalisation' of VSS.  Two Chairmen we spoke to were quite vehement on this subject, insisting that Schemes should be entirely voluntary enterprises and refusing to entertain the notion that a paid Co-ordinator should be sought to enable them to expand.

The third, and most commonly used, argument was that volunteers responding to selected cases would be more likely to be 'needed' and 'able to do something' than those 'arriving blind' at the homes of victims referred automatically.  For example, the only cases taken by one Scheme were those where police officers thought a visit necessary and the victim's consent had been obtained, thus guaranteeing that anyone visited would welcome the visit. The Co-ordinator commented:

'Only the most seriously emotionally affected cases are referred. Nearly all come with the victim's consent. We're very happy with this arrangement, although it does depend on the police always being aware of what our Scheme can offer.'

Despite her happiness with this system, it is the Co-ordinator's cautionary final remark which found most echoes among the comments of people we interviewed who had experience of referral based upon victim request or consent. Such systems rely heavily upon the active co-operation of large numbers of individual police officers, who have to remember to mention Victims Support, explain its purposes, obtain consent and mark the case for referral; but it was commonly reported that, even after regular briefings, the majority either forgot to mention the subject to many victims or failed to convince them that the service could be of value to them.[1]

An example of this came to light in one of our study areas, where a small number of complaints by victims led a newly appointed senior officer to abandon briefly the existing automatic referral system and to instruct his officers to refer victims with consent only. Not only was there a predictably dramatic fall in referrals, but several cases (documented by the Co-ordinator) later came to light where victims who would have liked support had had their crime report forms marked 'Not for VS', when the investigating officer had in reality forgotten to mention the Scheme to them. The Management Committee, alerted by the Co-ordinator (who took an unusually keen interest in referral patterns), made strong representations to the senior officer, who agreed to return to a form of automatic referral.

The other type of 'selective' referral system - which does not necessarily include victim consent - involves the selection of 'suitable' cases from crime reports, often by a fairly junior officer. Examples of this kind of system, which has been criticised for its vulnerability to police 'stereotyping' of victims who do and do not 'deserve' assistance, will be described in some detail later in the chapter. Generally speaking, Co-ordinators we interviewed who received their referrals in this way were less critical of it than those who relied solely upon victim consent, although there were still some complaints of fluctuating numbers, of difficulties in contacting 'link officers' (who did not have to make the regular contact demanded by an automatic referral system) and of 'being treated as unimportant'.

(b) 'Automatic' systems: which categories to include?

'Automatic' referral systems, it is important to remember, already contain an in-built element of selection, in that they apply only to particular pre-selected categories of victim.[2] The factor which distinguishes them from 'selective' systems is that, barring exceptional circumstances, every member of those categories should be referred. While this is clearly advantageous in that 'needy' victims in the chosen groups are far less likely to slip through the net, there is a danger that the system will becomes totally rigid and exclude other badly affected victims simply because their offence category does not qualify them for referral. This problem was highlighted by the fact that, in several Schemes we visited, despite a strong belief in automatic referral, there appeared to be little internal discussion about, or even interest in, the question of which categories of victims should be referred. The systems in use seemed to be primarily a matter of tradition, stemming from fairly arbitrary decisions made some years previously by past Committee members or, more often, police officers.

One Scheme we studied, for example, dealt almost exclusively with victims of residential burglary. These were referred in large numbers, automatically and efficiently, by the local police Collator. However, it being his understanding that (with the exception of street robberies or handbag snatches from the elderly - both relatively infrequent in this area) the Scheme wanted no other type of referral, he ignored almost all other victims, however likely it might be that they needed help. Members of the Scheme, who were kept very busy by the flood of burglaries, rarely questioned the system or discussed possible alternative sets of priorities, either among themselves or with the police. A similar situation was found at another Scheme we visited for a day, where the Co-ordinator, questioned about the Scheme's support for victims of 'only one type of offence', replied indignantly:

> 'We get loads of different offences referred: break-ins, unforced entries, meter breaks, 'cons' and attempted burglaries!'

In other areas, however, the categories selected for automatic referral had been chosen after more careful consideration and closer consultation with the police, and were discussed occasionally at committee meetings. The normal criterion used was the official offence classification, although we did visit one area where only victims above the age of 60 (irrespective of offence type) were automatically referred - this being a conscious decision to channel very limited resources to the section of society where need was perceived to be greatest. Conscious choice of offence types for automatic referral was usually based upon the dual considerations of which were thought to cause most distress, and how well equipped the Scheme and its volunteers were to handle both the numbers of cases and the kinds of problems associated with each type. As mentioned in Chapter 2, the most common conclusion arrived at - by discussion or by default - was that residential burglary was the major priority. Nevertheless, we found many individual voices wondering whether violent crime had received enough attention. One Scheme we visited, in fact, had adopted a very different set of priorities and received (with police concurrence) only a few burglary cases, but virtually all offences of robbery and wounding. This policy was based largely on the view that help with CICB claims was one of the most important functions a Scheme could perform.

In addition to the abovementioned considerations, Schemes' referral policies were sometimes affected by their views on the 'appropriateness' of certain types of crime for referral to their kind of organisation. Offences of domestic violence and sexual abuse of minors were cases in point. It was quite widely felt that victims of domestic violence were unsuitable for referral since the situation might call for attempts at conflict resolution, a skill in which few VSS volunteers are trained or experienced.[3] Moreover, it was said by several that this kind of work was 'not what Victims Support is all about' - a reflection of the ideology of 'lack of interest in the offender' which has so far characterised the victims support movement in this country. (Similar reservations were expressed about VSS involvement in mediation - see Chapter 9.) The Co-ordinator of a North London Scheme which was finding its workload of such cases increasing, probably spoke for most when saying:

> 'We will take on domestic violence cases, but not if we're going to be piggy in the middle. If it's to help one party, then yes, perhaps when the wife is going to court to get an injunction.'

It was also felt that such cases could place the volunteer in a potentially dangerous situation. Certainly, of five volunteers (among the 40 we interviewed) who could recall ever finding themselves in a frightening situation while visiting, two recounted unnerving experiences during their intervention in domestic assault cases. Despite all these reservations, however, 35 per cent of all Schemes responding to our survey reported that they did at least occasionally receive domestic assault referrals.

Where sexual offences involving a minor were concerned, the general feeling seemed to be that professional agencies, including Social Services, are better equipped for intervention. But, as one London Scheme reported, provided that the parents are already fully conversant with the details of the incident, and that the Scheme possesses volunteers with relevant experience, useful work can be carried out with them and perhaps later with the child after consultation with Social Services or a child counsellor.

(c)  Non-crime referrals

It may be recalled (see Chapter 2) that our 1984 survey showed that in the previous six months, 55 per cent of Schemes had received at least one 'non-crime' referral and 25 per cent had received several (most often involving sudden death or serious injury resulting from fires or road accidents). These figures give only a hint of the widely different attitudes and practices to be found. As the National Association points out in a discussion paper (NAVSS, 1984), some Schemes are actively seeking to increase their non-crime caseload, others are wholly opposed to the idea, some accept a few where the police especially request this, and yet others are beginning to encourage non-crime referrals from other than police sources. While emphasising that 'we should not seek uniformity for the sake of tidiness', the paper suggests that NAVSS would like to see a greater consistency of approach among its member Schemes than exists at present.

It has been suggested that Schemes tend to accept non-crime referrals when their resources are under-used - chiefly in small-town or rural areas. However, our 1984 survey found no association between the volume of referrals received, or the location of Schemes, and their acceptance or not of non-crime referrals. We also found no proponents of the argument that there is no intrinsic difference between becoming a victim through accident and becoming a victim of crime - and therefore that support of accident victims should form a normal part of VSS work - although we know that a small number of Schemes hold this view. Rather, the main reasons given for accepting non-crime referrals were simply a dislike of seeing people in need of support neglected, and a wish to be helpful to the police. For example, the London Scheme mentioned above was accepting an increasingly higher number of troublesome domestic disputes (often where no crime was recorded) 'because the police just don't know what to do with them'. Such acceptance was not always uncomplaining. Thus one Chairman, temporarily coord-inating a hard-pressed, over-stretched Scheme, expressed his dismay at a Regional decision to accept victims of fire:

'My heart sank when they decided as a Region they'd take on fire referrals. It's all right for them with their nice salaries, offices and deputy Co-ordinators'.

Members we interviewed from Schemes which refused to take non-crime cases largely echoed the reasons mentioned in the NAVSS discussion paper (op cit.), i.e. that a different set of specialist skills are often required in such cases, and that this may be the 'thin end of the wedge' leading to VSS becoming a 'general service for the police'. Some felt that branching out into other areas is like running before one can walk: there is not yet a comprehensive, specialist service for the crime victim population, and there may be dangers in adding new purposes before the original ones are achieved. Others were either indignant at being 'used to do somebody else's job' or concerned that their intervention might serve only to direct attention away from the short-comings of statutory agencies. Thus two Coordinators commented:

'We're under pressure to take victims of car accidents, attempted suicides, etc. This is mainly a backlash from a police lack of confidence in Social Services. Even Social Services are trying to push things our way when they should themselves be statutorily involved. We're trying to keep out, because it's easy to get sucked in.'

'Social Services rang and asked me to tell some parents that their children had been sexually molested. That's not our function, and they shouldn't try to pass that on to us. It's a police job anyway.'

Their message, then, was that not only are some police forces attempting to involve VSS in cases which should be the responsibility of statutory agencies, but, vice versa, the statutory agencies are by-passing the police in favour of VSS.[4]

(d)    Self-referral

Another issue on which Schemes seemed to be both confused and of divided opinions concerns 'self-referrals' - i.e. people who contact Schemes directly for assistance, often without having first reported the offence to the police. At present this is a relatively rare event: in our 1984 survey, 20 per cent of Schemes stated that they accepted occasional self-referrals, and four of the eight we studied in depth received one or two during our period of fieldwork. Nevertheless, self-referral could potentially become a more sensitive issue in the future if ideas being floated in some

91

areas of developing 'hot lines', or even 'walk-in offices in the high street', come to fruition.

Some Co-ordinators seemed very confused on the issue. For instance, one who 'ideally' wanted a hot-line telephone service for victims also said:

'I feel uncertain whether I would wish to help anybody not reporting to the police. I feel that all offences should be reported'.

and a committee member of the same Scheme said uncompromisingly: 'If they've not reported, we can't help.' One Co-ordinator objected on the more practical grounds of potential dangers to volunteers:

'It has to be reported, or else we will check with the police first before taking any action. We must protect our volunteers. One indirect referral was a burglary victim. When we checked with the police, we found out he was a past sex offender'.

This case raises another major issue which the Scheme in question seemed to us to take too lightly. Should they pass on to the police the name of someone who asks them for assistance in order to check if he or she is 'all right to visit'? Such victims may expect confidentiality, and may have good reasons for not reporting the offence in question to the police. Similar questions occasionally arose when victims referred in the normal way told volunteers in confidence about further offences, or revealed the identity of the offender, when these facts were unknown to the police. (One woman, for example, officially a victim of robbery, told a volunteer that she had in fact been raped.) If, as seems likely, Schemes are going to become involved increasingly in incidents other than the generally 'straightforward' stranger-to-stranger offences like burglaries and street robberies, and are going to take more self-referrals, the issue of confidentiality will inevitably loom larger. Indeed, as one serious breach of trust taken up by the media could have major repercussions for the credibility of Victims Support, this is an area in which the development of a firm and nationally-agreed policy seems to us a matter of some urgency.

On the general question of whether or not to accept self-referrals, the Schemes we studied tended to follow the local police 'line'. Two senior officers who were strongly opposed to the practice easily won agreement to their point of view at meetings we observed where the question was brought up. On the other hand, in areas where the police felt that such cases were none of their concern, self-referrals seemed to cause few problems or conflicts. Co-ordinators we interviewed who regularly accepted self-referrals did not seem concerned about the potential practical dangers of visiting, nor did they have any qualms about the police not being informed. The generally relaxed view taken is reflected in the following comments:

'We accept self-referrals even if they are not reported. We'll encourage them to report, but there's no over-insistence.'

'Exactly one per cent are self-referrals. Even though one case was unreported, we suggested the two male robbery victims filled in a CICB claim form.[5] One rape was an unreported self-referral. The police said to encourage her to report, but they're very respectful here. The police acknowledge the potential conflict in issues of confidentiality quite often at our meetings, but I have never felt any pressure.'

(iii)    Police views and practice

We have been discussing Schemes' policies towards referral, but it has to be remembered that (except as regards self-referrals) these can ultimately be put into practice only with the agreement and active co-operation of the local police.  It is therefore important to examine police views about victims and police attitudes towards Victims Support, as well as the mechanics of how referral systems actually work in practice.

(a)    The views of senior officers

As we shall see in a moment, the attitudes and actions of the (normally fairly junior) officers who pass on cases to Co-ordinators are important both to the nature of cases referred and to the continuity of flow.  However, the overall shape of referral systems and the degree of effort put into 'getting them right' depend primarily upon the attitude towards Victims Support of senior officers.  Where Chief Constables have taken a special interest in the subject, their influence has had a marked effect at ground level, but in most areas the key figures have been the Superintendents or Chief Inspectors in charge of stations.

Until very recently, as several such officers admitted in interviews, serious interest in, or commitment to, Victims Support was the exception rather than the rule.  While, in many areas, senior officers were friendly towards Schemes and co-operated to a reasonable extent, they tended to know

93

little about them.  Contact was left almost entirely in the hands of an officer of junior rank, who was neither closely supervised nor made to feel that this job was of any great importance.  Within a surprisingly short time, however, awareness of and knowledge about the work of Schemes has increased enormously at senior management levels, and with this has come a perceptible change in attitudes. (See also Shapland and Cohen, 1986 for evidence on this from a survey of 35 police forces.)

Nowhere has this change been more noticeable than in the Metropolitan Police District, particularly since the abovementioned landmark of the Force Order of February 1984.  To some extent, we have no doubt, the sudden enthusiasm for Victims Support to be found among senior officers in the MPD is less than deeply felt.  Some more junior officers were cynical enough to note that VSS is 'one of the Commissioner's hobby-horses' and one said plainly that 'the top boys only do it to go places'.  However, in several cases, in London and elsewhere, we observed an undoubtedly genuine police interest, reflected in time spent voluntarily at unimportant Scheme functions, in help with fund-raising,[6] and in care taken to sort out 'hiccups' in referrals due to inefficiency or disinterest at a lower level.  The main reason seems to be that (influenced both by NAVSS national policy and by the MPD Force Order) it is becoming almost standard practice in areas with Victims Support Schemes for the head of the local division or sub-division to join the local Scheme's Management Committee - and, in our experience at least, to attend a high proportion of meetings.  Close personal relations have consequently been established in many areas, and the police members have come to understand the value of VSS work both in its own right and as a potential source of good public relations for the police.  Some have also noted - and said so openly to us - that the existence of Schemes helps remove pressure upon the police to do more for victims themselves.  Though most senior officers wanted to see their juniors handle victims more sensitively, few felt that this was of sufficiently high priority to justify more time being spent with victims. (For a brief summary of victims' comments on their treatment by the police, see Appendix.)

Despite the increasingly favourable attitude of senior officers towards Victims Support, by no means all are ready to accept the NAVSS policy of 'automatic' referral of victims.  The Superintendents and Chief Inspectors we inter- viewed in our fieldwork areas expressed sharply differing views on this subject, usually matching the referral policy operated at their respective Schemes (although in one case an officer new to the job was planning to stop automatic referral). The main disadvantage associated with an automatic policy was said to be the risk of complaints to the police arising from a perceived breach of confidentiality - i.e. the victim's name and address or telephone number being passed to the Scheme without permission. It was also commented more than once that it was a police responsibility to protect the Scheme's volunteers from 'dangerous situations' - although most officers referring cases 'automatically' were confident that they could fairly easily, as one put it, 'weed out the dodgy ones' (see below).

Another argument put forward against automatic referral was much more spurious. This was that volunteers want to feel needed and able to 'do something' when they go on a visit. One Superintendent asserted (in this case wrongly, according to the Co-ordinator) that 'VSS aren't interested in young, confident males who don't need anything', and an officer in another area, trying to justify the reversion from automatic to selective referral which his colleague had imposed upon the Scheme, argued to a committee meeting that the volunteers were better off now that they had some 'good' cases to 'get their teeth into' and had 'got rid of the wishy-washy ones'.

Nevertheless, where the senior officers interviewed did not have to accept ultimate responsibility themselves for any breach of confidentiality - for example, those who could quote the MPD Order advocating automatic referral of many offence types as the 'goal' for VSS - the objections to automatic referral tended to fade. Thus the problem of complaints was regarded quite differently by the Chief Superintendent of a Division in the MPD:

> 'Bearing in mind the small number of complaints that are received,[7] there's no need to ask consent. If the investigating officer forgets to ask, then the time resources of the CID are wasted in going back. And if the victim is in immediate shock, they won't take it in.'

He also pointed out that asking for consent raises expectations of a visit, in which 'the Scheme may sometimes let them down'.

Another MPD Superintendent observed that the three-month pilot project of automatic referral in his area had had a good feedback:

> 'It seems the police are seen in a better light, even from blacks who have said they didn't realise the police cared.'

He asserted that more contacts by VSS meant less worries for his Home Beat Officers, since there was 'someone else to go round and chat', and that the method of referral by consent, used previously, had been very much a 'hit and miss' affair.

We also asked senior officers about the 'appropriateness' of various types of case for VSS. Racial harassment was generally considered inappropriate, either because of doubts about its prevalence (an extreme view put by one Superintendent being that 'There are no, or nearly no, racial incidents nowadays. We are an integrated society.') or because it was felt that specialist training was required to tackle the problem and that Community Liaison Officers were anyway available to deal with it. It was also argued that if black people were the victims of a criminal offence, they would be referred in the normal way, and that involvement in areas beyond recorded crime was not the business of VSS. We found no instances of referral of 'racial incidents' (without an officially-recorded offence) of the kind dealt with by CLOs, although one CLO we spoke to thought that volunteers could be of help in following up some of his cases.

Finally, as among Scheme members, questions about the possible referral of cases of domestic violence provoked varying responses from senior officers. For example, one felt that his local Scheme should not become involved since counselling was required, while another said that some domestic incidents were suitable for referral providing conflict resolution between the parties was not the aim, this being the province of other agencies.

In sum, local senior police views about victims - which could change suddenly with a change in personnel - had a considerable influence upon the numbers and types of cases referred to many Schemes. Committees rarely seemed to question such views or to enter into a debate about the needs of other types of victim than those being referred (although they were quicker to complain about any major fall-off in numbers). This reflects our general observation that the thinking within Schemes about the overall pattern of need in their area, or about how to make the best use of their available resources in relation to this need, was often not fully developed, and to a large extent they had become used to 'taking what they were given'.

(b)    Referral systems in practice

Although senior officers 'set the tone' for the police-VSS relationship, they quite often give only broad guidance to the 'link officers' whose job it is to pass cases on to

96

Schemes, leaving them with wide discretion. Indeed, responses to our 1984 survey indicate that the most frequent reason for any deviation from agreed referral policy was changes in personnel at the referring stations. Some Co-ordinators reported that they had spent many months building up and improving relationships with their link officers, all the time increasing the officers' knowledge of what VSS could and did do for victims, only to find that a smoothly running and negotiated system of referral could evaporate overnight through the transfer of a key officer. Temporary falls in referral rates, whether involving a selective or automatic system, were also common where link officers were sick or on leave, being replaced by someone less sympathetic to or knowledgeable about VSS.

The vulnerability of referral systems to individual whim, prejudice or predilection can be illustrated in many ways. All such systems we examined depended upon regular telephone communication between the link officer and the Co-ordinator,[8] but since both tended to be busy people, problems quite often arose in maintaining contact with each other. In the absence of strict instructions from senior officers, perceptions about the quality of the Co-ordinator or the Scheme could substantially affect the amount of effort made by link officers to maintain regular contact, and hence affect the numbers of referrals. At the crudest level, this could depend on personality alone, as with the link officer who admitted to avoiding a particular Co-ordinator because he 'could never get her off the phone'. Another voluntary Co-ordinator suffered neglect for the more general reason of disinterest in the concept of Victims Support. She finally got in touch with her referral officer after eight 'blank' days and numerous efforts to contact him (despite it being the agreed policy that he should contact her), only to be greeted in patronising fashion:

'I said, "Has crime ceased?" His reply was, "No, we've got garage, school and shop burglaries - all not suitable for VS. But now you're on, here are a couple of assaults and a burglary by artifice."'

According to a senior officer, this attitude was partly a reaction to her voluntary status and the 'amateur' nature of the Scheme. Some policemen, he said, would not take an organisation like the VSS seriously unless the Co-ordinator was paid, and hence a 'fellow-professional'. However, the very fact that the junior officer could behave in this way without thought of recrimination from 'above', suggests that little attempt had been made to persuade him that VSS referral was an important part of his work.

The views, perceptions and interest of the link officer can be important even in Schemes with automatic referral. But in selective referral systems where the link officer is allowed, with little supervision, to decide himself which cases merit a visit, this one individual's views can be crucial, not only to the numbers referred, but to the whole shape of the Scheme's work. The views of three such officers - all of whom, although of low rank, were largely left to develop their own criteria for referral - are worth closer examination.

The first, a young PC, explained his method of selecting cases for referral as follows. 'Ordinary' burglaries were referred on the basis of age only - 'old, over 40, but more normally over 60'. If the house had been ransacked or the occupants injured, victims of any age were passed on. No 'do-it-yourself meter breaks' or 'criminal types' were referred:

> 'Why should Victims Support give their time and sympathy when next week the victim or their family won't give the police the time of day?'

Also excluded were assaults arrising from pub brawls, or involving football supporters, neighbour conflicts, 'love disputes', marital disputes and 'motorist punch-ups'. In respect of assaults not excluded by these criteria, but involving young, single males, this officer said, 'I think how I would feel and whether I'd want a visit'. As the answer was generally in the negative, few young, single males were passed on to the Scheme. Sexual offences were not referred without first asking the investigating officer about the victim's reactions. Rape victims, apparently, quite often requested referral, but complainants in indecent exposure cases were 'usually not bothered, so I don't refer', while indecent assault cases 'are often a personal thing, so they might not want outside interest'. His overriding concerns, he said, were that VSS time should not be wasted, that a visit would be useful to the victim, and that the volunteers should be protected from any potential danger.

The second officer's system was less complex. Where burglary was concerned, he normally excluded married couples under the age of 60, people suspected of committing the offence themselves ('own goals'), and 'well-off' owner-occupiers. Again, no young male assault victims were referred since 'many are offenders as well'. On the other hand, 'all elderly females' were referred and any other cases 'where there is a need for support', although how this was inferred remained unclear.

The third - and most experienced - liaison officer said
that his first criterion was whether or not a Home Beat
Officer had made a follow-up visit to the victim:

> 'I won't bother to refer that case to the VSS, because
> the Home Beat is his own Victims Support Scheme.  He
> does locks, windows, insurance and DHSS stuff himself,
> and I also have a friend at the DHSS for special
> problems of victims.'[9]

Otherwise, in the case of burglary, he tended to refer
single people and pensioners, but to exclude families with
children:  'If they've brought up kids, they can handle most
things, including burglary'.  Small shopowners were omitted
for similar reasons:  'If they've managed to get and run a
shop, they can handle a burglary'.  On the other hand, he
referred burglary victims from ethnic minorities over the
age of 35:

> 'I handle those with care because they may not speak
> English, may not know what to do, may have no friends,
> and tend to be of low intelligence.'

> He was 'one hundred per cent suspicious of meter
> breaks', but said he would refer if 'given the all clear
> from the SOCO' (Scenes of Crimes Officer).  He
> acknowledged that theft of or from motor vehicles was
> upsetting, but felt that there were too many cases to
> make referral practicable.  All offences of theft from
> the person were referred 'because of the shock', and all
> assaults with female victims.  Male assault victims were
> 'not a priority' and anyway demanded caution:  'He may
> have suffered GBH, but may have murdered the other
> person'.  Where rape was concerned, he tended to check
> with the investigating officer first to see if referral
> was 'necessary'.

> 'There are so many professional ladies around, and only
> half the rapes reported are genuine.  When they find
> their clients won't pay, they shout 'rape', but after a
> chat, they may admit that it wasn't really rape, but
> just that the man didn't pay.'

Finally, when asked to sum up his decision-making process,
he described it as based primarily on his 'gut reaction' to
a Crime Report.

Comparison of the foregoing sets of criteria for referring
or not referring victims reveals that, while they differ
considerably in detail, they embody a broadly consistent set
of attitudes towards victims.  They are based in part upon

broad assumptions about 'need', but also to no small degree upon the notion of 'desert'. The above accounts, read together, give a fairly clear idea of what is meant by the 'stereotyping' of victims.

Individual discretion is, of course, considerably reduced by the introduction of an 'automatic' system, but it is not eliminated. We interviewed the link officer (an experienced Collator) operating the system which came closest to being truly automatic, and asked him to indicate his reasons for every exclusion he had made (burglary victims only) during a one month period. Table 4.1 documents the outcome.

### Table 4.1
**A Collator's reasons for excluding cases from referral to a Scheme operating an 'automatic' referral policy (burglary in a dwelling only)**

Burglary victims not referred because:

|  | No. | (%) |
|---|---|---|
| 'I know them' | 12 | (5) |
| 'Do-it-yourself job' | 13 | (5) |
| Attempted burglary only | 14 | (6) |
| Nothing stolen | 1 | (-) |
| Offender caught | 3 | (1) |
| Other/reason forgotten | 3 | (1) |
| Total excluded | 46 | (18) |
| Total passed to Scheme | 202 | (82) |
| Total for month | 248 | (100) |

Twelve of the 248 possible cases for referral were not passed on because, as an experienced Collator, he 'knew' the families involved: 'Would you send an elderly volunteer into a den of thieves?'. Thirteen were, he guessed, perpetrated by the occupants themselves, these having occurred mainly in 'rough' areas or roads. Fourteen attempted burglaries were not referred because although he had no objection to passing them on, he did not wish to 'overload the Scheme'. Three cases failed to reach the Scheme on the grounds that the offenders had been arrested immediately, and therefore the victims 'would get help from the investigating officer'. One address he knew was an empty house, and in two instances, the reasons for exclusion had been forgotten.

So, even with an automatic referral system where 'all but a few special exceptions are excluded', and with a link officer favourable to the Scheme and with enough time to speak to the Co-ordinator at length every day, 18 per cent of cases were still filtered out, about half of them being assessed as 'undeserving'. Moreover, as Table 4.2 shows, the proportion referred by the police in another area under 'automatic' referral was considerably lower.

### Table 4.2
**Proportions of recorded cases of burglary in a dwelling referred to VSS, comparing Schemes with automatic and selective referral systems**

|  | Automatic | | Selective | | | | |
|---|---|---|---|---|---|---|---|
|  | $A^a$ | D | $A^b$ | B | C | F | G |
| Total burglaries recorded$^c$ | 154 | 363 | 1351 | 308 | 314 | 992 | 48 |
| Total referred to Scheme | 108 | 308 | 84 | 163 | 186 | 282 | 28 |
| (% referred to Scheme) | (70) | (85) | (6) | (53) | (59) | (28) | (48) |

Notes
   a. Figures in this column relate to the part of Scheme A (2 of 6 stations) which operated an automatic policy for a short period.
   b. Figures in this column relate to the whole of Scheme A (6 stations covered) before automatic referral was tried.
   c. Total number of burglary dwellings and attempts recorded by police in relevant division or subdivision covered by Scheme during a period varying between one and six months.

Finally, it is also instructive to note, in Table 4.2, the wide variation in the proportions of burglaries referred to Schemes under selective systems: these ranged from only six per cent passed on to Scheme A (in the three month period before it implemented an automatic policy) to 59 per cent passed to Scheme C. Both these Schemes were located in inner city areas, had similar numbers of volunteers, and accepted victims of several other types of offence in addition to burglary. Part of the reason for this striking degree of variation may lie in Scheme A's practice of waiting for the police to telephone the Scheme, compared with Scheme C's arrangement whereby the Co-ordinator contacted her link officer at a set time every day. It was also noticeable that, over the period monitored, the senior police officers from the division covered by Scheme C were regular attenders at Management Committee meetings and seemed genuinely interested in Victims Support, while those from the Scheme A area were often more conspicuous by their absence.

To sum up, the preceding pages have indicated that the 'filter' at the referral stage cuts out considerable proportions of victims - even of burglary victims in nominally 'automatic' referral systems. Moreover, selective systems are not only vulnerable to waning police interest or changes of personnel, but are wide open to the prejudices or arbitrary decisions of referring officers, who may exclude whole categories of victims because of ideas about what they 'deserve'. While senior officers are increasingly knowledgeable about, and sympathetic towards, the Victims Support movement - and while this can have a strong influence on referral practice even under selective systems - their instructions to, and supervision of, referral officers need to be tighter than they were in most police stations we visited if the effects of personal prejudices and of varying degrees of commitment are to be significantly reduced.

## Allocation of referrals within Schemes

The next major stage of the filtering process occurs when the Co-ordinator, having received his or her (normally daily) list of referrals, either allocates them to volunteers or deals with them personally by letter, telephone or visit. Co-ordinators may also advise volunteers on what method of contact to use (although in some Schemes only one method is ever used) or may leave this to the individual volunteer. As we shall see, these decisions are very important to the eventual nature and extent of the services delivered to the Scheme's total caseload.

### (i)  Initial methods of contact

### (a)  Aims, preferences and practical constraints

'Outreach' to victims is one of the attractive features of Victims Support in the UK which distinguishes it from most agencies serving victims elsewhere (Maguire, 1985). The VSS practice of contacting victims rather than waiting to be contacted <u>by</u> victims, is carried out, in different areas, with one or more of three separate aims in mind. One aim - in which the act of making contact is largely an end in itself - is simply to send a message to as many victims as possible that 'someone in the community cares about what happened to you'. This may have the supplementary message that actual assistance is available if required. A second possible aim is to get the available volunteers into as many victims' homes as possible - ideally, unless there are special circumstances, for 'one-off' visits lasting perhaps an hour. This rests on the belief that most victims of crime are psychologically damaged by the experience to some extent (whether they realise it immediately or not) and the provision of a 'listening ear' and/or simple practical advice helps to repair the damage and to diffuse destructive anger. A third possible aim is to identify those individuals in greatest need and to use the Scheme's resources as efficiently as possible to assist them. In this case (unlike aim 1) the initial contact is a means, not an end.

The method of contact which, given unlimited resources, would best serve all three aims, is the unannounced visit. As we shall see later in this chapter and in Chapter 6, victims are generally pleased that a volunteer has taken the trouble to come and see them (aim 1, above); those called upon will normally invite the volunteer in and talk about the incident (aim 2); and the most serious cases are relatively easy to identify during the course of a face-to-face conversation (aim 3). Unfortunately, this is not only the most time-consuming and expensive means of contact, but travel time and costs are often wasted when nobody is found at home. While a number of Schemes had few enough referrals to be able to visit virtually all of them (20 per cent of those responding to our questionnaire claimed to do so), this was impossible in any area with a high referral rate. The most common 'compromise solution' was to send volunteers out to those victims who appeared from the available information to be the most likely to need support, and to telephone or send letters to the remainder. Another variation was to ring up everybody who had a telephone and offer to visit them, either writing to or calling at the houses of those without telephones. Which system an individual Scheme adopted depended partly upon its resources, partly upon its beliefs about how victims react to each form of contact, and partly upon its underlying (if not always articulated) assumptions about which one of the above three aims was the most important.

Views about the value of letters and telephone calls certainly varied widely among all the Co-ordinators we spoke to. The main area of agreement was that letters were the least productive method of contact in terms of generating subsequent visits or identifying serious need (aims 2 and 3 above): few replies were received and it was likely that some of the worst affected would be reluctant to ask for help. Even so, some believed that the reply rate could be increased considerably by thinking carefully about the wording. Co-ordinators were more divided in their opinions of the value of letters as a meaningful way of expressing community concern (aim 1). At one extreme was a dedicated voluntary Co-ordinator who was continually pressing the police for genuinely 'blanket' referral and who took the trouble to write sympathetic messages in longhand to large numbers of victims. At the other was a Co-ordinator at a Scheme we visited briefly, who was convinced that letters were not a useful strategy on any grounds at all:

> 'Letters are not important enough to justify the expense. We operate a selective referral system where investigating officers contact us direct, so all victims with needs are seen.[10] Other victims may say "how nice", but a letter will only make a momentary difference.'

Telephone calls were also considered to be difficult to 'convert' into visits, as most victims tended to refuse offers on the grounds that they were not seriously affected. They were, however, generally thought to be much more effective than letters as a means of identifying people particularly badly affected. Schemes again differed in their views of the value of telephone calls as a method of passing the message of community concern, for their quickness and cheapness had to be weighed against the risk of frightening some recipients (see below). Finally, while most Schemes viewed telephone calls primarily as a preliminary method of contact for arranging visits or for 'sifting the wheat from the chaff', a small group of volunteers at one Scheme were unusual in their belief that a great deal of genuine support work could be carried out over the telephone. They tended to make lengthy initial calls, and quite often to follow them up with further calls, providing advice and a 'listening ear' if needed. Unless the victim appeared particularly badly affected, no effort was made to persuade him or her to accept a visit. They argued that successful telephone counselling was perfectly possible, if one paid attention to basic rules of 'telephone manner'.

(b)  Contacting victims in practice

As noted in Chapter 2, responses to our 1984 questionnaire suggested that, nationally, 57 per cent of all first attempts at contact were by unannounced visit, 24 per cent by letter and 17 per cent by telephone, while in 2 per cent of all referrals no contact was attempted. However, these overall figures - which, we believe, exaggerate somewhat the proportion visited (see later) - conceal extremely wide variations. For example, the proportion initially sent letters varied between nil and 90 per cent, and while over one in three Schemes said they never contacted victims initially by telephone, 5 per cent said they used the telephone in more than 75 per cent of cases. We now briefly describe the practices of some of the Schemes we studied in depth and the reasons given by members to explain or justify these practices. Table 4.3 shows the methods of contact utilised at five of these Schemes, and the percentages of victims (sampled from Scheme records) which the Co-ordinators or volunteers initially attempted to contact by each method. As expected, the differences between Schemes turned out to be quite striking.

### Table 4.3
#### Initial method of contact (attempted) at five Schemes

|  | Scheme | | | | |
|---|---|---|---|---|---|
|  | A | B | C | D | E |
| Method of contact | % | % | % | % | % |
| Unannounced visit | 16 | 56 | 24 | 33 | 49 |
| Letter | 35 | – | 50 | 67 | 45 |
| Telephone | 48 | – | 25 | – | 5 |
| No contact attempted | 1 | 44 | 1 | – | – |
| Total referrals (N) | (464) | (216) | (280) | (313) | (201) |
| Period sampled (in months) | 6 | 6 | 6 | 1 | 1 |
| Referral method (A=automatic S=selective) | S | S | S | A | A |

Scheme B's Co-ordinator, who worked on a part-time basis for about 20 hours a week, did not send letters because she had insufficient time and because the financial resources of the Scheme were stretched. There were insufficient volunteers to visit all the victims referred. Moreover, it was the policy of the Scheme not to telephone:

> 'We don't ask for victims' phone numbers. We feel that if a volunteer phones and the person is in a state of shock, that's more likely to put them off than a face-to-face presentation.'

The unfortunate result of these constraints was that 44 per cent of referred victims, who had been specially selected by the police as in need of assistance, were never contacted.

Scheme D, a large urban Scheme with high numbers of victims referred 'automatically', also followed the principle that 'It's better to have a wasted journey than to phone when someone is still in shock'.[11] Here the Co-ordinator selected her 'best guesses' of 'victims who most need help' and dispatched volunteers to visit them. The two-thirds of all victims who could not be visited were sent a letter, offering them a visit on request.

In complete contrast, at Scheme A, located in an inner city area, the Co-ordinator favoured a telephone contact wherever possible, explaining:

'We like the volunteers to phone first, and if possible to arrange a visit. This is partly because if the victim lives on one of the large estates, many don't open their doors after it gets dark.'

Scheme C was situated in an inner city area with a large Asian population. Visits at night were believed by female volunteers to be dangerous because of the general run-down state of the area, and although this problem had been overcome by some through hiring taxis, travel claim expenses were not encouraged. Consequently, although in such a poor area only a minority of victims had telephones, the telephone had become the first choice method of contact. Moreover, a bad shortage of volunteers meant that 50 per cent of all referrals had anyway to be dealt with by post. The Coordinator considered this highly unsatisfactory because:

'Letters aren't much use in this area because lots can't read or write English, or are not good on their feet to post back a reply, or the phones in the street don't work'.

(ii)    Information and criteria used in selecting those to be visited

Although they are constrained by limited resources and Scheme policies, many Co-ordinators still exercise important discretion in deciding which individual victims will be contacted in what way - or, indeed, will be contacted at all. Each one we interviewed who had this responsibility had developed his or her own 'rules of thumb' for such decisions, but some took very much more care over them than others, and some received (and demanded) much more information about cases from the police to help them decide. What was clear, however, was that the great majority were aiming, above all, to select from the information available those victims who would be most likely to benefit from a visit. In this, they were doing a job akin to that of the police link officer, although with the important difference that virtually all those 'filtered out' by the Co-ordinator as low priority cases would at least be contacted by letter or telephone. We found also that they were generally (though not entirely) free of prejudiced notions about victims who did and did not 'deserve' a visit.

Naturally, those who had to make the most decisions of this kind were Co-ordinators of Schemes with large numbers of cases referred automatically.[12] Unfortunately, these tended to receive the least information about individual cases. This was partly because of the time it took for details of perhaps twenty cases to be read out over the telephone and transcribed in longhand, but also because, when it became a routine administrative task, referral was more likely to be put in the hands of an officer working in an administrative capacity in a separate office (sometimes in Divisional HQ). Such officers had no regular contact with investigating officers, most if not all of their knowledge about the incidents coming from a pile of initial crime reports.[13]

The most frequent complaint by Co-ordinators who had to 'filter' cases was that the age of the victim was not always given. This was clearly the most important socio-demographic factor in the eyes of nearly all we interviewed: where there was a shortage of volunteers, pensioners - particularly those in their seventies or eighties - were almost always put among the priority cases. One Co-ordinator attached so much importance to the factor of age that in the absence of this information she selected for visits people with names such as 'Hilda', 'Ethel' or 'Albert'.[14]

A second common complaint was that specific details of offences - most often the type and value of property stolen or any damage caused in the course of burglaries - were inaccurate or incomplete. Several Co-ordinators (rightly, according to our findings - see Chapter 3) believed that burglaries involving untidy searches or vandalism were particularly distressing to victims, while others (again with some justification) picked out losses of jewellery or other articles of potential sentimental value. Where violent offences were concerned, it was pointed out to us more than once that knowing details of injuries helped the Co-ordinator to guess whether a CICB claim might be appropriate (a visit then becoming a priority).

While direct information about the social class of the victim was not passed to Schemes, most Co-ordinators knew their area well enough to infer this in many cases from the address given. However, they were divided in their opinions about its importance. Some were adamant that it was much more important to visit victims living in deprived estates - who were likely to have more practical and financial problems - than those in middle-class areas, but a roughly equal number felt that the effects of burglary were the same whatever one's financial circumstances. (This division

107

mirrors a difference we also noticed in volunteers we interviewed, between those whose main predilection was for practical advice and problem-solving and those who saw the VSS task first and foremost as to provide comfort and emotional support.)

Finally, of course, the one piece of information that is always given is the category of offence itself. This was used by some Co-ordinators as an almost automatic primary filter. For example, one said that, unless there were exceptional circumstances, she would not send volunteers to victims of theft of or from vehicles (these were sent a handwritten letter) and that, other factors such as age being equal, she would normally give priority to burglary and street robbery over everything but the most serious assaults. (A quick check of her records later showed that over half the victims of less serious assaults referred in the previous three months had been sent a letter.) Another said that she 'nearly always' sent a volunteer to cases involving handbag snatches as these were 'always upsetting and cause a lot of worry because the offender can find out from the contents where you live and he may have your keys, too'. The general position, however, seemed to be that while each Co-ordinator might have his or her own hobby-horse, it was a combination of the specific details of the offence and any known characteristics (particularly age) of the victim, rather than the offence type per se, which most influenced allocation decisions.

While all the abovementioned pieces of information were considered of some value, many Co-ordinators recognised that decisions based upon them were very much 'shots in the dark'. All they could hope to do was to increase slightly the statistical chances of finding a victim very much in need of support. Two Co-ordinators went further. Concerned at the amount of paperwork their task entailed, they argued that most of the offence details they were offered were unnecessary. One had actually asked the police to give fewer details in order to save time, and the other said she had

> 'stopped recording lists of what was stolen, because they are often inaccurate anyway and no guide to how upset the family will be'.

Another interviewee made the important point that police crime reports are not designed to record the kinds of information that a Victims Support Scheme most needs. She pointed out first of all that facts about the aggrieved person named on the report tell one nothing about others who might be affected:

'... If, say, a 30 year-old man reports an offence, does
he have a wife, or children, or aged mother, at home,
who may be more upset than he is?'

She also mentioned the important factor of <u>social isolation</u>:

'Ideally, I would like to know from the police whether
victims are well supported and whether they live alone.
But that's the kind of information they never have.'

Similarly, others said they wanted to know - but were not
always told - if a victim was <u>handicapped or disabled</u>, a
<u>single parent</u> or had <u>language difficulties</u>.  The latter
point was particularly important in areas with a high Asian
population, where it was recognised that sending letters to
some victims would be pointless if they could not understand
them:  one Scheme, in fact, did receive this information on
a fairly regular basis.  And, finally, a Co-ordinator in an
area with large numbers of automatic referrals made the
obvious, but fundamental, point that what she wanted above
all was some indication from the police of how badly
affected individuals were:

'I want them to refer as many cases as possible, but I
wish they'd steer me to the worst ones, so they can be
sure of an early visit.'

The strongest defender of selective referral we
interviewed would claim that much of what has been said in
this section gives support to her position.  She argued that
the most effective way of ensuring that those most in need
receive a visit, is to 'educate' all policemen to a
sufficient level of awareness of victims' problems and of
available VSS services, so that they will regularly and
effectively identify serious cases and pass them to the
local Scheme for assistance.  This kind of 'filter', she
felt, being based upon direct knowledge of the offence and
the victim, is potentially much more effective than any
filtering, however conscientious, undertaken by Co-
ordinators on the basis of a few bare facts about each case.
We would argue, however, that the ideal system is one which
takes the best features from each:  i.e. Co-ordinators
should receive cases on an automatic basis, but individual
officers should be trained to identify any among them with
particularly badly affected victims as <u>priority cases</u>,
passing on their reasons to the Scheme.  This would help Co-
ordinators with their allocation decisions while at the same
time guaranteeing a regular flow of cases and avoiding
serious cases 'slipping through the referral net' because of
individual officers' prejudices or forgetfulness.

(iii)     Choice of volunteer

With the exception of very serious offences (particularly rape) which might demand long-term support, most Co-ordinators we spoke to made little effort to 'match' the victim with a particularly 'suitable' volunteer.[15] This was partly because practical considerations - availability, proximity, access to transport, etc. - usually made such a system too difficult to operate, but also because they thought it unnecessary in most cases. Only one felt strongly enough about it to make the effort, as she quite often did, to ring the police station and seek out the investigating officer to acquire more information on which to base her choice of volunteer (a course of action, incidentally, which sometimes annoyed the police).

Where it did occur, 'matching' was usually based upon the perceived qualities or expertise of the volunteer rather than upon factors like age, sex, or race. Thus, for example, volunteers with experience in CICB claims would, where possible, be sent to cases of wounding, those with special knowledge about crime prevention to burglary cases, and those with experience of dealing with welfare agencies to burglaries or meter breaks in deprived areas. On the other hand, one Co-ordinator believed strongly that young male victims of violence responded best to male volunteers, and, if one was not immediately available, was inclined to send a letter rather than a female volunteer. Ironically, another Co-ordinator held the opposite opinion, saying that such victims 'opened up' better to a female volunteer!

Not surprisingly, sexual offences were unanimously considered to be the province of female volunteers,[16] although some Schemes believed that a male volunteer could be used as a second helper, primarily to support or counsel victims' husbands or boyfriends (see Chapter 7).

Race is perhaps the most sensitive factor on which volunteer and victim might be 'matched'. In fact, nearly all Co-ordinators interviewed in Schemes which had black volunteers had decided that the ethnic background of volunteers should not enter into their decisions, except where language was likely to be a problem (as, for instance, with Bengali women in one inner city area). Sending a black volunteer to a white victim who had been robbed by a black offender was not generally seen as problematic - indeed, it was believed by some to diminish the possible negative stereotype resulting from the offence. The only note of disagreement came at a Scheme we visited which had some newly trained black volunteers. The Management Committee discovered that the new volunteers were not being used in assault cases involving black offenders, because the Co-ordinator thought white victims would not wish it. The issue was debated at some length without a clear conclusion.

(iv)   Volunteers' efforts at contact

None of the Schemes we studied had managed to keep complete records of the outcome of all cases passed on to volunteers, and it was difficult for Co-ordinators to assess accurately what proportion of victims were eventually contacted either by visit or telephone, let alone how many were 'supported'.  There tended to be a general assumption that where a visit or telephone call had been suggested by the Co-ordinator, this was carried out soon after the referral, with contact normally achieved.  In interviews with 30 volunteers, however, we found wide variations in their ideas about when to telephone or visit, how many attempts at contact to make, and whether, if using the telephone, to attempt to 'convert' the call to a visit. Some, too, had much higher 'success rates' than others in establishing contact.  Such information was not available to many Co-ordinators, especially where close monitoring of volunteers' work was not considered important and the completion and return of volunteer forms not insisted upon (see Chapter 5).

When we asked volunteers how soon after receiving the victim's name and address they normally attempted to make contact, over half said within 24 hours, but a few - especially those receiving referrals on a haphazard (rather than rota) basis - reported attempted first contacts between 48 hours and one week later.  And at one Scheme where we traced the outcomes of a full set of referrals, we found that volunteers had made no attempt at contact in 12 per cent of the 136 cases passed on to them during a particularly busy period.

Schemes which encouraged volunteers to telephone victims did not all have definite policies on whether the aim should always be to 'convert' the call into a visit, and at one in particular this was reflected in major differences between volunteers.  In looking at this Scheme's records, we were struck by the fact that some rarely visited any victims at all, while others 'converted' high proportions of their calls.   Interviews with volunteers confirmed that these outcomes usually conformed with their individual views of the main objectives of telephoning.   In addition, as evidenced by victims' comments (see Chapter 6), some people undoubtedly had a better telephone manner than others, and it is likely that those conveying warmth, sincerity and understanding were more successful at 'conversion' (when

111

this was their aim).  Skill in communication by telephone, we suggest, is a largely neglected subject which deserves more attention in training.

We also noted major differences, both between and within Schemes, in the numbers of attempts volunteers typically made to achieve contact with a victim.  For example, at one Scheme where telephone calls to victims were not encouraged, a particular volunteer successfully contacted a higher proportion of victims than her colleagues, simply because she routinely made up to three visits and then tried the telephone, while they generally gave up after one visit.  Similarly in Schemes with a telephoning policy, some volunteers would try several times while others would give up quickly.

Such differences are explained partly by the pressure of time upon some volunteers.  However, they are also almost certainly due to differing beliefs about the distress patterns of victims.  There seemed to be a view, held quite widely among volunteers, that unless contact was established within 48 hours of the offence being reported, there was little point in offering emotional support.  We have already seen in Chapter 3, however, that a significant minority of all victims - and, in particular, victims of violence - experienced 'delayed reactions' several days after the event, and indeed that many still felt a desire to talk about their feelings several weeks later.

## Filtering systems in practice

In this final section, we give two examples of full 'filtering systems' in operation.  We trace the progress of sample sets of recorded offences as they passed through the referral and allocation systems in two Scheme areas.  Figure 4.1 represents diagramatically the progress of all recorded offences of burglary occurring in the sub-division covered by Scheme D over a one-month period.  In the month in question there were 363 burglaries recorded, of which 85 per cent were referred to the Scheme.  Such was the 'specialisation' of this Scheme in burglary that only 5 other cases altogether were referred, these being street robberies of elderly people.  The Scheme, located in a large city, had a part-time Co-ordinator.  The policy agreed by the Committee was that victims should not be telephoned, but as many as possible should be visited unannounced, the remainder being sent letters from the office.  Owing to the high referral rate and only an average number of volunteers, about twice as many letters were sent as visits made.  Moreover, volunteers were not encouraged to try again if victims were out, but to leave a card offering the Scheme's services.

112

**Figure 4.1:** 'Filtering' (burglary cases only) at Scheme D over a period of one month

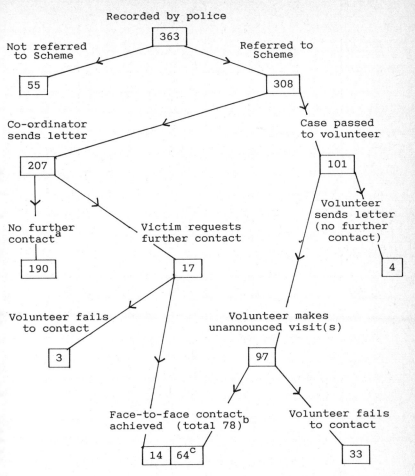

**Notes:**

a. Except perhaps a brief message from the victim, thanking the Scheme for its concern (no records kept).
b. With named victim or other household member.
c. Five of these 64 were contacted at the second or third attempt.

**Figure 4.2:** 'Filtering' of referrals (all cases) at Scheme F over a period of three months

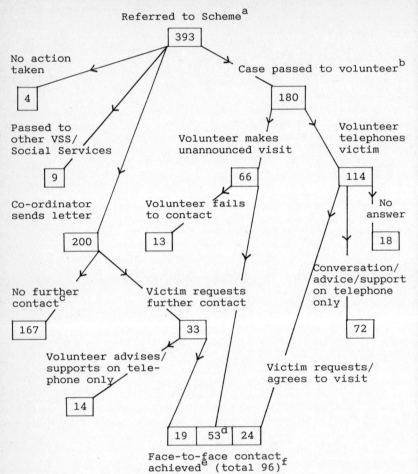

Notes:

a. Includes 282 burglaries (of 710 recorded by police over the period).
b. Including the Co-ordinator in her role of visitor.
c. Except perhaps a brief message from victim, thanking the Scheme for its concern (no records kept).
d. Seven of the 53 were contacted at the second or third attempt.
e. With named victim or other household member.
f. Fifty-two of the 96 were burglaries.

Scheme F (Figure 4.2) was situated in an inner city area with a high crime rate. Despite referral being on a selective basis, the Scheme received considerable numbers of victims of burglary and crimes of violence, as well as some sexual offences. Relationships with the police were particularly close, and few problems were experienced with referral practices. The Figure shows the progress of all cases referred to this Scheme over a three-month period. (282 of the 393 cases shown were burglaries. These constituted 28 per cent of all burglaries recorded in the division over the three months.) The accepted policy for making contact included telephoning victims (either as an end in itself or to arrange a visit), sending letters, and unannounced visits. Here almost as many victims were telephoned or visited as were sent letters, a fair proportion of these by the Co-ordinators themselves.

Despite the differences in approach, the outcome in terms of face-to-face contact was very similar in the two Schemes, about a quarter of each batch of referrals reaching the stage of a personal meeting between the victim and a volunteer. The main difference was that while in Scheme D, the 75 per cent of victims who did not meet a volunteer received no more than a standard letter offering the Scheme's services, in Scheme F, 30 per cent of the equivalent group at least had the chance to discuss their problems, if any, over the telephone. (In Chapter 6 we shall assess, from interviews with victims, to what extent this kind of contact is considered important by those receiving it.)

Two other points are worth noting from these diagrams. First, the eventual 'contact rate' (i.e. proportion of victims seen in person) from unannounced visits at Scheme D - which discouraged subsequent visits by volunteers if the victim was out - was 66 per cent, while at Scheme F, where further attempts were encouraged, it reached 80 per cent. Similar calculations we made at two other Schemes, neither of which normally expected volunteers to call a second time, produced final 'contact rates' of 61 and 72 per cent. Further analysis at all four Schemes revealed that (as far as could be discovered from volunteer records and the questioning of volunteers about unclear cases) victims were found at home on between 56 and 70 per cent of initial unannounced visits. Subsequent attempts at finding victims, while paying some dividends, did not increase the overall contact rate by more than 11 per cent. (See Appendix, Table R.)

Secondly, Scheme F also attracted more 'recalls' from victims than Scheme D (i.e. responses to letters, requesting further contact), namely 16 per cent, compared with 8 per

115

cent. This may be partly due to the selective referral
system, in that victims referred to Scheme F were more
likely to have major needs (and therefore to respond to the
offer of help), but it is also possible that the way that
letters were phrased made some difference. Letters at
Scheme F had a more 'informal' flavour to them.[17]

Tables 4.4 and 4.5 put some of the above points in a
broader context. Table 4.4, based upon a sample of 1,014
referrals to four of the Schemes studied, shows the eventual
results of cases dealt with by each of the three methods
used to try to contact victims. It should be noted first

### Table 4.4
Type of contact eventually achieved; by initial method of contact (attempted)[a]

| | Final outcome | | | | | | |
| | No personal contact achieved | | Telephone contact only | | Face-to-face contact achieved | | Total | |
| Initial (attempted) contact method | No. | (%) | No. | (%) | No. | (%) | No. | (%) |
|---|---|---|---|---|---|---|---|---|
| Unannounced visit | 119 | (31) | – | – | 265 | (69) | 284 | (100) |
| Letter | 457 | (90) | 13 | (3)[b] | 35 | (7) | 505 | (100) |
| Telephone | 18 | (14) | 83 | (66) | 24 | (19) | 125 | (100) |
| Total | 594 | (59) | 96 | (9) | 324 | (32) | 1,014 | (100) |

**Notes**

a. The samples were taken from four of the eight Schemes studied in
   depth, over periods of between one and six months. Schemes with
   incomplete or unreliable records were excluded from this analysis.
b. Others may have telephoned the Scheme to say 'thank you' but this
   was not always recorded.

that the percentage of victims, among all those referred,
who received unannounced visits - 38 per cent - was well
below the national figure of 57 per cent suggested by responses to our 1984 survey (see Chapter 2). Moreover, only
32 per cent were seen in person by volunteers, a 'personal
contact rate' also considerably lower than that claimed by
our survey respondents. It is true that two of the four

Schemes analysed here were dealing with referral totals well above the national average, so one would expect lower personal contact rates. Even so, Table 4.5 shows that these rates were not markedly greater even in the other three Schemes we studied which had referrals closer to the national average. Indeed, the best rate achieved was only 40 per cent (still 4 per cent below our survey-derived estimate in Chapter 2). Taking this evidence into account, we would suggest that a more accurate overall picture would show about 45 per cent (rather than 57 per cent) of referred victims receiving unannounced visits, and 35 per cent (rather than 44 per cent) of referred victims actually seeing a volunteer in person.

Table 4.5
'Unannounced visit' and 'personal contact' rates at five Schemes studied

|  | Scheme | | | | |
|---|---|---|---|---|---|
|  | A % | B % | D % | E % | F % |
| Percentage of referred victims who were visited unannounced | 16[*] | 56 | 33 | 49 | 17[*] |
| Percentage of referred victims who were spoken to in person | 23[*] | 40 | 25 | 30 | 24[*] |
| Overall referral rate | High | Medium | High | Medium | High |

[*] A high proportion in these Schemes were telephoned first.

The other major point to emerge from Table 4.4 is that if a Scheme's main aim was to see victims in their own homes, unannounced visits were far more likely to lead to this than were either letters or telephone calls. Only 10 per cent of those sent letters responded requesting further contact,[18] and only 19 per cent of telephone calls led to visits. On the other hand, the majority of telephone calls did result in a conversation with the victim and, indeed, some of these calls were lengthy and a surprising amount was achieved.

One final point to note is that a certain number of victims, although spoken to face-to-face, 'filtered themselves out' on the doorstep. Over the four Schemes analysed, 12 per cent of victims who had been found at home on an unannounced visit failed to invite the volunteer in.[19] (The proportion invited in varied between 82 per cent and 91 per cent at the four Schemes.)

117

In summary, what emerges above all from this chapter is, once again, the daunting nature of the task facing VSS if they wish to make personal contact with a high proportion of victims. The indications here (which suggest that the figures derived from our national survey were over-optimistic) are that not much more than a third of victims referred to Schemes actually see a volunteer, although most will at least receive a letter or telephone call. But even under 'automatic' referral systems, by no means all victims - even of burglary - are actually passed on to Schemes, and under 'selective' systems it is only a minority. Efforts to select those victims worst affected seemed to be successful to some degree (see Chapter 3, Table 3.2, which shows 79 per cent of people in visited households 'very much affected', compared with 60 per cent of those in a random sample of victims of the same offences). But the wide differences between areas in the categories 'filtered out' by the police or Co-ordinators show that many badly affected victims undoubtedly 'slip through the net'.

### Notes to Chapter 4

1. This was also admitted by most senior officers we interviewed, who claimed that constables were simply too busy to remember Victims Support on every occasion. The exception was a London Scheme where Home Beat Officers were specifically 'debriefed' daily by a sergeant very sympathetic to VSS, to identify any victims who might benefit from support. Individual officers we spoke to here were knowledgeable about VSS.

2. The main reason that virtually all Schemes exclude at least some categories is quite simply that they would be 'swamped' if they took everything. We also detected some feeling that, even if resources permitted, it would be a waste of time approaching many victims of petty crime. One Co-ordinator who (unusually) felt that the automatic system in his area had 'gone too far' remarked: 'I like to visit real victims. Some of the offences we get are absurd - like a lady who left her handbag in the park with nothing in it.'

3. We learn, however, from Carl Steinmetz of the Dutch Ministry of Justice (personal communication and unpublished papers), that 'victim support' in several Dutch towns arose initially from a conflict resolution perspective, domestic disputes constituting the bulk of referrals. This was strongly encouraged by the police, who are loath to become involved in domestic disputes (prosecutions are rare) and are greatly helped by being able to pass cases on to such an agency. Steinmetz, however, raises doubts about the success of the intervention, having found indications that it can sometimes exacerbate, rather than improve, the situation.

4. This tendency for people whose problems are not clearly the responsibility of any one agency to be 'shunted' from one to the other, has been noted in other contexts (cf. Carlen, 1983; Fairhead, 1981).

5. Of course, one of the pre-conditions for a CICB award is that the offence has been reported to the police, so this was either poor advice or a strong hint to these victims to report the matter.

6. One senior officer even made a sponsored parachute jump to raise money for the local Scheme.

7. NAVSS estimate that under one per cent of victims annually complain about breaches of confidentiality (Director's speech to the 1985 AGM). In the Schemes we studied, complaints averaged no more than three per year.

8. In a few areas, in fact, Co-ordinators visit the police station every day to gather referrals.

9. At another police station also, victims were not referred to the Scheme if a Home Beat Officer was involved.

10. Such a view implies, of course, that letters would be sent only to victims without needs, and relies totally on the investigating officer making an accurate assessment of need.

11. At this, and at other Schemes opposed in principle to telephoning victims, it was believed that telephoning would frighten some victims into thinking that it was the offender checking to see if the occupant was at home. The point was also put that misunderstanding can sometimes arise through the necessity for confidentiality. Since victims do not always tell other household members about their misfortunes, should someone other than the victim answer the telephone, the volunteer is theoretically supposed not to reveal the fact that it is a VSS calling until direct contact with the named person is made. Obviously, this procedure can cause suspicion. Victims' first reactions to telephone calls, as compared to visits and letters, are discussed in Chapter 6.

12. One Scheme studied was exceptional in that the Co-ordinator passed many of the filtering decisions on to the volunteers (who worked on a rota basis), dividing each day's referrals between them and allowing them to plan their own workload. She explained:

> 'It's ultimately up to the volunteer as long as the person is definitely contacted, but I do advise on whether I think there is a choice between phoning, lettering or visiting a particular person.'

13. Schemes relying upon referral with victim consent - particularly those where it was normally left to the investigating officers to suggest suitable cases for referral to the link officer - tended to get much fuller details about the victim's personal circumstances.

119

Ironically, these details were often of less use to such Schemes than they would have been to Schemes with automatic referral, because the referral rate tended to be low and nearly all victims could be visited, thus obviating the need for 'filtering' decisions by the Co-ordinator.

14. Only one Co-ordinator we interviewed said that she did not wish to know victims' ages. The reason given was that she wanted to prevent herself from 'acting on stereotypes of who might need a visit'

15. Indeed, two of the eight Schemes studied operated rota systems, with volunteers simply taking their turn and visiting whoever happened to be referred. This had several practical advantages, including spreading the visiting load, which could become unbalanced under other systems (see Chapter 5).

16. That is, until a Co-ordinator mentioned at a Regional meeting that he had been referred an adult male victim of a sexual offence. This provoked a lively discussion - and disagreement - on the topic of who should visit him.

17. A Co-ordinator elsewhere insisted that all letters should be individually hand-written and geared to the type of offence concerned. However, the 'recall rate' at this Scheme was not above average.

18. Although 90 per cent did not request further assistance, up to a fifth of these may have contacted the Schemes to thank them for their letters, to ask a few curious questions or even to offer their services as volunteers. Unfortunately, no Scheme logged every one of such responses although a quick check at one Scheme which did keep some records of this kind revealed that about 15 per cent of all those sent letters (over and above those requesting assistance) wrote or telephoned to say 'thank you'.

19. This includes 'rejections' by other members of the aggrieved's household when the person named on the crime report was not at home. As the great majority of cases analysed were burglaries, these other household members can also be generally regarded as 'victims'.

# 5 The internal structure of Schemes: management, co-ordination and supervision

In this chapter we assess the strengths and weaknesses of the systems of management, co-ordination, and supervision of volunteers in operation at the eight Schemes we studied in depth, and, with supplementary data from other sources, draw some general conclusions about the organisational structure which has come to characterise Victims Support. We shall suggest that this structure, while attractive in theory, requires exceptional individual and group qualities to make it work as it should. We are also concerned that it is not always capable of bearing the stresses of the rapid growth which many Schemes are experiencing.

## Introduction

The basic structure adopted by every member Scheme within NAVSS is the 'tripartite' system of Management Committee, Co-ordinator(s) and visitors already outlined in Chapter 1. In its ideal version, the Committee, which contains representatives from several other organisations, not only takes overall responsibility for the management of the Scheme, but acts as a focal point to mobilise community resources and make them available to victims. Meanwhile the Co-ordinator deals with the day-to-day business of the Scheme and supervises the work of the volunteer visitors.

From a national perspective, this formula has proved enormously successful. Its designers can point with pride to the ever-increasing numbers of Schemes, volunteers and referrals, the rarity of total collapses of Schemes (for financial or other reasons), the low turnover of volunteers, the widespread respect earned from the police, and the co-operation from other agencies represented on Management Committees. Yet despite its successes, when we came to look more closely at the day-to-day work of individual Schemes, we became increasingly conscious of ways in which the system could misfire. For some Schemes, the ideal of a smooth running, effective organisation seemed to remain continually elusive and the reality held numerous sources of dissatisfaction for members. In others, a period of great achievement was followed by a sudden slump. We shall draw attention to the main pitfalls of the basic tripartite model, showing how some Schemes were more successful than others in circumventing them. While not arguing that the model should be abandoned, we shall indicate ways in which it might beneficially be modified.

We shall argue that the major weakness of the standard structure is the excessive load which, in practice, almost inevitably falls upon the shoulders of the Co-ordinator. This is a serious problem, not only because of the resultant overwork and stress (and not infrequently illness or marital problems) experienced by many of these individuals, but because the overall performance of the Scheme often becomes over-dependent upon the personal qualities and commitment of one person. With the 'wrong person' in the job, morale, standards and activity can easily slip to low levels, while, as we witnessed more than once, if a dynamic and experienced Co-ordinator leaves without warning, the Scheme can be thrown suddenly into crisis. Five of the eight Schemes we studied in depth lost their Co-ordinator during or after our fieldwork period with them, and in nearly every case there was a virtual cessation of activity for some time. Two were still operating at a minimal level several months later, in one case with the busy Chairman trying to 'do two jobs'. Ironically, it was Schemes which had previously had Co-ordinators of high calibre which came nearest to collapse, because they had fallen into the habit of leaving everything to one person, and now found themselves bereft of both a willing workhorse and of expertise.

Other potential weaknesses of the tripartite system are less serious but if ignored can be damaging to morale or can lead to inefficiency. For example, there are in some Schemes few 'natural' opportunities for members of the three segments to meet, let alone exchange views, experiences and suggestions: lack of communication can easily lead to misunderstandings and resentment. The relatively little trouble it takes to identify and overcome such problems, we shall suggest, is an excellent investment for any Scheme.

122

## Workloads and division of labour: the Co-ordinator and the Committee

### (i) Excessive pressure on Co-ordinators

Since 1981, the National Association has issued several discussion papers and sets of guidelines concerning the respective roles and responsibilities of Management Committees and Co-ordinators.[1] While these have normally stressed that Management Committees should decide upon the division of labour according to local circumstances (individual abilities, time available, etc.), some general principles have also been formulated. The Committee, it is recommended (NAVSS, 1983), should be 'actively involved' in 'all aspects of the work which are essential to the Scheme's survival', especially the negotiation of referral policies with the police, recruiting and training volunteers, raising and managing funds, monitoring the effectiveness of the Scheme, publicly promoting the Scheme, and liaising with NAVSS both nationally and regionally. This, in theory, leaves the Co-ordinator free to concentrate upon the day-to-day operational tasks of receiving and allocating referrals, keeping records, supervising and advising volunteers, and dealing with cases which require follow-up work.

However, despite the obvious good intentions of all the committee members we met, we found at almost every Scheme we studied a tendency for Co-ordinators, by design or default, to become embroiled in work they should not have had to do. For example, one Co-ordinator had been left to organise most of her Scheme's fund-raising activities, and had personally set up and manned stalls at fetes at least three times a year for several years; another was expected to take, type up and distribute all the Minutes of meetings; another gave virtually all the Scheme's 'recruiting talks' to local organisations, and so on. These activities may not be greatly onerous on their own, but they should be seen within the context of the daunting amount of time and work it takes simply to carry out the 'core' tasks of a Co-ordinator in a busy Scheme. Indeed, to an outside observer this workload is probably the most striking single feature of the Victims Support movement as a whole, and it is difficult to over-state the degree of dedication and energy displayed by many of the Co-ordinators we met. Included among these were several unpaid[2] Co-ordinators whose homes were their Scheme's 'offices' and who were dealing with Scheme business for many hours every day, sometimes seven days a week. In addition to handling large numbers of referrals, supervising sizeable volunteer forces, and visiting regularly themselves, they were the prime movers and organisers of new initiatives to improve standards or develop their Scheme's

123

range and capacity. And any extra administrative tasks which arose seemed to fall almost as a matter of course upon their shoulders. As a volunteer in one such Scheme put it, 'X is the Scheme. Without her it would fold up'.

To be sure, in some cases Co-ordinators were partly responsible for creating their own excessive workload, deliberately becoming involved in areas which are generally considered the Committee's responsibility. More than one insisted, for instance, upon interviewing and selecting new volunteers and upon organising and running training courses, seeing these tasks as part of their overall job of supervising volunteers. Another was organising and carrying out most of the negotiations for the expansion of the Scheme into a new part of the county - primarily, it seemed, because she had clear ideas about how the new organisation should be structured and wanted to ensure that it was launched in a healthy state. Perhaps the clearest example of all was a woman who admitted to regularly working an 84-hour week (without payment) and to a foundering marriage. Her view of her own role was expressed in the words,

> 'I largely run it my way and the Committee don't interfere, but they're there to be called upon. Basically, I do everything.'

Committees, understandably, tended to be very happy to hand over more and more tasks to such willing volunteers. It can, however, be argued that they should review carefully the workload of any individual, and be prepared to refuse offers on occasion, not only to protect that person's health and to avoid the overall quality of his or her work from suffering through over-extension, but to avoid 'putting all their eggs in one basket' and thus lessen the chances of a crisis arising if the individual leaves the Scheme. As another Co-ordinator remarked, she was the only person who understood all the workings of the Scheme, and 'If I left tomorrow, the Scheme would have to start all over again'.

Moreover, although many Co-ordinators did seem to be 'workaholics', it should be stressed that this was less often through their own volition than as a result of short-sightedness or neglect on the part of their Committee. Over 80 per cent of the Co-ordinators we interviewed had at least a mild complaint about insufficient help or support from this quarter, and a few felt extremely isolated. For example, one who was herself very overworked stated:

> 'I think some of them see their role as attending meetings only, as a "yet-another-committee-we-sit-on" role, rather than doing anything.'

124

This comment is a frustrated criticism of individuals. However, we shall suggest that the problem should not be regarded simply as one of disinterest on the part of 'committee types', but as a consequence of fundamental confusions about the role of a Management Committee.

(ii)  Ambiguities in the composition and role of
      the Committee

VSS Management Committees are intended to perform two distinct roles which do not always sit easily together in practice.  One is to carry out the kinds of management tasks outlined in the previous section.  The other is to help mobilise local resources on behalf of victims, bringing together representatives of statutory and voluntary agencies which could play some part in assisting them:  in the words of Reeves (1985):

> 'Management Committees take responsibility for negotia-
> ting referral policies, recruiting and training volun-
> teers and volunteer Co-ordinators, and for raising and
> managing the necessary funds. Committees include such
> persons as the Police, Probation and Social Services,
> Solicitors and Magistrates, as well as a wide range of
> voluntary agencies and churches... Representatives of
> such agencies are able to arrange back-up resources and
> referral facilities with their own agencies.'

The problem, however, is that the first role requires people heavily committed to VSS, prepared to devote time and effort regularly to Scheme business outside Committee meetings, while the second role is often regarded as primarily a liaison task, requiring little direct involve- ment in the management of the Scheme.  As there are many local organisations which may at some time be useful to VSS, Committees tended, in our experience, to be overloaded with 'representatives' at the expense of active 'managers'.

The Management Committees of the Schemes we visited contained on average 17 members.  The largest at one point had 30 members (although an attendance of more than ten was unusual) and another had 25. As well as the three 'statu- tory' members who have to be appointed in order to conform with the Code of Practice (a police officer,[3] a probation officer or social worker, and a representative of an estab- lished voluntary organisation or Church), Committees tended to contain at least three or four - and in three cases, ten or more - others who had been appointed primarily as repre- sentatives of organisations with whom it was thought useful to maintain close contact (e.g. Citizen's Advice Bureaux, Rotary, Age Concern, FISH, Red Cross, Voluntary Service

Bureaux, WRVS, local Councils). It was also common to find a few individuals who had been invited to join for their specialist skills - e.g. psychiatrists, solicitors, locksmiths or builders. Valuable as all these people could be when asked to take up specific matters with their own agency or to provide a special service for a victim, few had sufficient time to become closely involved in the practical management of the Scheme. This latter task fell on a small number of shoulders, typically those of the Secretary, one or two non-'representative' members and the Co-ordinator.

Some illustrations of this division emerged from brief interviews we conducted (mainly by telephone) with 20 Management Committee members from four of the Schemes studied, in which we asked them about the extent of their commitment. Over half said that they devoted three hours or less per month, including committee meetings, to Scheme activity and only occasionally had contact with the Scheme between meetings. The great majority of these had originally joined the Scheme as 'representatives'. Those who were elected officers, by contrast, averaged about ten hours per month on Scheme business, and one Chairman said she gave over 24 hours of her time every month. At our prompting one Co-ordinator went through the names of her Committee members, picking out those who frequently helped the Scheme in some way between meetings. Excluding police officers and three visitors who had been co-opted on to the Committee, she singled out only four from a list of over twenty. And finally, one of the most telling illustrations of the division was provided by a Co-ordinator who pointed out that several of the 'representative' members of her Scheme had given only their work telephone number and could not be contacted at home.

Many Committee members were well aware that they were not 'pulling their weight', but regretted that, however much they wished to, they could not spare any more time. One admitted that she felt guilty about missing meetings, but was so busy that she was thinking of offering her place to another person within her statutory organisation, while another said, rather defiantly:

> 'I think the volunteers think we're not essential. I
> don't believe they can do it better, because most of
> them are in full-time jobs too. But I'd give them a
> chance, sure, if they'd like to have a try.'

Others pointed out that they had been told at the time of their appointment that little was expected of them beyond attendance at meetings. In fact, only a minority of those we spoke to had originally volunteered to take part or had

126

known anything about Victims Support - the most common means of appointment being a persuasive invitation 'out of the blue' from the Scheme or from their own organisation. This applied even to two Chairmen who had been pitched almost unprepared into their key positions. Both said that they had been told that chairing meetings was all that they would have to do. One had, in fact, done little else, but the other complained rather ruefully about her predecessor:

> 'What he told me was all wrong. He said the Chairman wouldn't do all the work - he would just chair the meetings. I soon found out that I would have to be a working Chairman.'

This, she explained, was because:

> 'Apart from the elected officers of the Scheme, the first commitment of nearly all the others on the committee is to other organisations. I'm very dissatisfied with this. We need people to represent us first, and I hope we shall be able to co-opt some individuals soon.'

(iii)   Activating Management Committees

We shall argue later in this chapter that, however well-intentioned the Management Committee, being a good Co-ordinator in an active and progressive urban Scheme is, at present, almost by definition associated with overwork. To avoid this, a basic reformulation of the Co-ordinator's role in such Schemes may be necessary. We begin, however, with examples of how some Co-ordinators were at least relieved of tasks which, it is generally agreed, should not be their responsibility.

The most obvious way, of course, was for the Co-ordinator to say point-blank to the Management Committee that certain tasks were necessary but that he or she would not do them. This occurred rarely in our experience, partly because few Schemes had arrived at a precise understanding of who should do what. Indeed, as far as those we spoke to knew, only two of the 21 Schemes we visited had drawn up written job descriptions for their Co-ordinators as recommended by NAVSS. Nevertheless, one voluntary Co-ordinator, who had no 'job description', had always been very firm with her Committee in drawing lines (e.g. by refusing to become involved with fund-raising), and had succeeded over time in 'educating' its members into providing regular help in several areas.

An interesting organisational feature of this Scheme was the appointment of an Executive Committee, which met once a

month and reported quarterly to the full Management Committee. This consisted mainly of the 'working' members of
the Management Committee, and was less unwieldy and better
geared to practical action. It seemed to us an improvement
over the normal system - although the Co-ordinator still
felt that some long-running problems were discussed and
postponed too often without anyone taking full responsibility for action. It may be, she speculated, that the
ideal way to deal with these was through another strategy
which only about half of the Schemes we visited seemed to
employ: the use of small sub-committees or working groups,
which can be given specific tasks and specific targets.

Of course, such organisational structures will only work
if there are sufficient people on the Committee willing and
able to spare the time to help. In this respect, some Co-
ordinators were keen to add more volunteer visitors with an
aptitude for committee or administrative work. Although
this may mean that they visit fewer victims, the experience
of Schemes which had three or four on the Committee was that
they can make a major contribution. They also have the
advantage of experience 'at the sharp end' and understand
the daily work of the Scheme. Such knowledge proved its
value at a Scheme which suddenly lost its Co-ordinator and
tried to keep a skeleton service in operation until she
could be replaced; the remainder of the Committee revealed
a surprising degree of ignorance about how referrals were
received and dealt with, and without the advice and
practical assistance of the volunteer members some fundamental errors would have been made.

The foregoing should not, it is stressed, be taken to
imply that there is anything essentially wrong with the idea
of including on VSS Committees representatives of several
local organisations. On the contrary, all the Co-ordinators
we spoke to recognised the value of maintaining good links
with these agencies. It was also pointed out more than once
that the representatives had been especially useful during
the first year of the Scheme's life in establishing it as a
known and credible local organisation and in facilitating
referrals of victims to others agencies. However, it was
felt that once the Scheme was properly established, there
was less necessity for them to come to regular meetings, or
even for all of them to remain on the Committee. In our
judgement, the objective of keeping the problems of victims
in front of the eyes of as many agencies as possible justi-
fies retaining a fair number of representatives, but as the
Scheme grows it also becomes desirable to increase the
number of active individuals on the Committee, especially
people with experience of visiting. We are thus most
attracted by the system described earlier, whereby a large

128

Management Committee meets three or four times annually and delegates much of its power to a smaller Executive Committee, which manages the Scheme from regular meetings.

(iv)  The Co-ordinator's role: a need for rethinking?

More active Management Committees may relieve a little of the pressure upon Co-ordinators, but in many busy urban Schemes even the <u>minimum</u> set of tasks generally agreed to form the basic job of the Co-ordinator is becoming too onerous for one person to carry out effectively.  Moreover, it is important to recognise that the unexpectedly rapid growth of the victim support movement has inevitably trans- formed many Schemes from small informal groups into sizeable, more impersonal, organisations.  As a result, the <u>nature</u> of the Co-ordinator's work, as well as its extent, has changed considerably.  The traditional 'core' tasks of a Co-ordinator have usually consisted of receiving and allocating referrals, supervising volunteers, dealing with other agencies on behalf of victims, and keeping records. But while in a small rural Scheme these may appear to form a compatible and unified set of tasks, in the context of a busy organisation it becomes clear that the Co-ordinator is performing in reality at least two quite different roles, each demanding different skills, abilities and predilec- tions.

This is most obvious in the most 'progressive' Schemes, which, in addition to increasing their referral rates and numbers of volunteers, are engaged in a drive to expand the range of services offered and to improve standards.  In such Schemes the skilful and sensitive supervision of the growing body of volunteers (especially those involved in long-term support - see Chapter 7) tends to be regarded as vital, as does the effective 'tapping' of other agencies on behalf of victims.  Yet while it is becoming ever more important for Co-ordinators to possess these quasi-professional abilities and skills, they are still expected to fulfil the other part of their traditional role and handle increasing volumes of routine paperwork.  In the commercial world, it would be seen as a gross misuse of skills for busy personnel managers to do all their own typing and filing.

Faced with such a daunting situation, Co-ordinators of large Schemes tended, in fact, to perform efficiently the types of task most suited to their character and abilities, and to neglect others.  Thus two Co-ordinators in our field- work areas were excellent managers and supporters of volunteers, holding regular volunteer meetings, keeping in close touch with the progress of difficult cases, and often visiting victims themselves;  yet both were poor record-

129

keepers and one quite often failed to keep up with routine
letter-writing. By contrast, another Scheme had a part-time
paid Co-ordinator who worked regular office hours, routinely
and efficiently receiving, allocating and posting letters to
large numbers of referred victims every day and keeping
immaculate records. Yet cases were rarely discussed with
volunteers (who worked very independently), there was little
atmosphere of 'progress' in the Scheme, and support was
generally limited to short, one-off visits to burglary
victims.

In our view, then, if Schemes as they grow larger are to
achieve the general aim of improving standards, the role of
the Co-ordinator has to be regarded in a new light. It
should lose all connotations of being a 'clerical' job. At
the very least, the Co-ordinator of a large Scheme should be
freed from the traditional tasks of ringing the police each
morning, writing down details of numerous offences and
victims, sending letters to victims not allocated to
volunteers, and copying the full list later into a referrals
book. In a busy Scheme with, say, 50 referrals per week,
this process alone can easily take up most of every morning.
It is a job tailor-made for a part-time clerical worker, or
if funds are not available, one or more volunteers (perhaps
on a rota basis), under the general supervision of the Co-
ordinator. This is already beginning to happen in some
areas, but in our experience too many Co-ordinators tended
to act as uncomplaining martyrs, and too many Committees
failed to realise how much they had to do.

Freedom from this kind of work - important as it is to the
efficiency of the Scheme - would give Co-ordinators more
time for tasks aimed at improving the 'front line' work of
the Scheme, such as those discussed in the next section. It
would also help to dispel the notion, still fairly prevalent
within some Schemes, that the Co-ordinator's 'job' consists
mainly of collecting and passing on names and addresses.


**Communication with volunteers: supervision, support
and 'involvement'**

A second major pitfall, which few Schemes we studied had
avoided entirely, was that of failing to maintain frequent
and productive communications with volunteer visitors. It
was all too easy in a busy Scheme for communications to
decline to the minimum level of simply transmitting names
and addresses or, equally, in a Scheme with a low referral
rate, for communications with some volunteers to lapse for
long periods.

There are three main purposes in maintaining good communications with volunteers: to give them support and confidence in what can be very stressful work with victims, to supervise and monitor their work, and to maintain their morale and satisfaction by making them feel 'fully involved' with the Scheme. As Schemes cannot operate at all without the commitment of a group of reliable volunteers, these aims can be fundamental to the success of the whole venture. We saw in Chapter 2 that, while the average turnover of volunteers across the country was not especially high (approximately 20 per cent over a one-year period), there were considerable variations in attrition rates. Indeed, 10 per cent of Schemes had reached the rather worrying position of having lost 50 per cent of their active volunteers within one year. If there is any truth in the opinion of one Regional Chairman that the main reason for volunteers resigning is that 'this is the most depressing, unrewarding type of voluntary work you can do', the challenge to those in supervisory positions is clear. The varying turnover rates between Schemes, although partly a function of the type of area, almost certainly also reflect the fact that some respond more positively to the needs of their volunteers than others.

We identified five aspects of communication between Schemes (mainly in the person of the Co-ordinator) and volunteer visitors, where even minor differences of practice or approach could have a significant effect upon volunteer satisfaction, as well as upon general levels of performance within the Scheme. These will be discussed in turn.

(i) Personal communications and relationships with
    the Co-ordinator

Virtually every volunteer visitor's main channel of communication with the Scheme is by telephone to the Co-ordinator. Indeed, for those who rarely attend meetings - and in three of the eight Schemes studied this applied to the majority - this may be the only normal means of communication with the Scheme. For others, the low frequency or irregularity with which some Schemes' volunteer meetings are held may not be sufficient to sustain motivation and interest during the ensuing gaps. And even for regular attenders at regular meetings, the individual support and encouragement received there may be minimal (see later). Thus the relationship with the Co-ordinator on the telephone can assume major importance for volunteer morale.

Three of the eight Co-ordinators at the Schemes we studied in depth stood out because of their appreciation of the importance of this channel of contact with volunteers. They were always careful to inform them by telephone about any developments in their past cases, in particular the results of any agency referrals made by the Co-ordinator on the volunteer's recommendation. Several volunteers in these Schemes expressed pleasure at receiving such 'feedback', a typical comment being:

> 'I haven't got time to do my own follow-up work, but I always tell the Co-ordinator what needs to be done, and I always hear what happened'.

(In one County Scheme we visited for a day, in fact, it was common practice to send a written memo to a volunteer if an agency referral had been made on his or her recommendation, or where there was a definite outcome to a line of action. According to the County Co-ordinator, this provided an important boost to volunteer morale. It also led to more feedback to victims, as volunteers were then more likely to re-contact them to pass on news of what was being done.)

The abovementioned three Co-ordinators also frequently offered general support and encouragement to volunteers over the telephone, and whenever a victim telephoned or wrote to thank the Scheme for their help or offer of help, this information would be passed on to the volunteer, underlining the fact that his or her efforts were valuable and appreciated. These Co-ordinators clearly made efforts to treat their volunteers as friends, regularly enquiring about their families or events in their lives. They also kept them well informed about developments and progress in the Scheme, all the time reinforcing their identity as part of a team.

The value of taking this kind of trouble - although it could be very heavy on telephone bills![4] - is illustrated indirectly by the comments of a volunteer at another Scheme, whose dissatisfaction at not knowing what had happened to her cases was evident:

> 'I'm getting despondent. Whenever I ring, the Ansafone is on. I leave my message about what I'm doing or what I think needs doing, and I put this down again in the report form, but I don't hear back from the Co-ordinator. I would like to know what happens in these cases, but I never do.'

When asked if she ever felt her time was wasted on visits, she replied:

> `My time is only wasted when I don't know the outcome. If nothing is done by the Co-ordinator, then my time might have been wasted.'

132

Monitoring volunteers' activities was less often seen by Co-ordinators as a function of telephone calls, although one of the three 'good communicators' said quite bluntly:

'I can see whether they're doing enough for victims and doing the right things.'

This Scheme had a policy - unusual elsewhere, except in regard to newly trained volunteers - of 'debriefing' volunteers after every set of cases allocated to them, insisting that they made at least a quick telephone call to report what had happened. At three other Schemes, by contrast, the Co-ordinators neither monitored volunteers' progress, nor made much effort to keep up their morale, and complaints about their inaccessibility were quite common. For example:

'It's difficult getting hold of her. I tried to phone her six times one day'.

'I've never had a long conversation with her on the phone, and she never asks me about the people I've been to see'.

'It's impossible to get hold of her during the day, and it's not always convenient for me at night'.

In several cases, we discovered, more than a few weeks had elapsed between the allocation of a case and the next conversation between volunteer and Co-ordinator; and the latter did not even know if the victim had been contacted, as no report form was returned.

The Co-ordinators at the remaining two Schemes studied were at least accessible, but again little monitoring took place. One of these Schemes had Co-ordinator paid under the MSC scheme and the other one who worked part-time. In the former case, the young Co-ordinator neither visited many victims, nor knew much about tapping community resources. She was not regarded by the volunteers (who were all older, and had considerable experience of the work) as of much help to them. In the second case, the sheer volume of cases made it difficult to find time, within the office hours worked, for detailed discussion of cases. In both these Schemes, telephone calls to volunteers usually only served the purpose of passing on the names of new victims to visit.

(ii)    Manageable, comfortable and regular workloads for volunteers

While the amount of time volunteers have available for visiting naturally varies a great deal, the majority of those we interviewed expressed a preference for one or two new referrals per week. When their preferred workload was either exceeded or not reached for long periods at a time, dissatisfaction tended to creep in. This could happen when the flow of referrals from the police changed significantly for any reason, as we observed at a Scheme where promises made to a group of new volunteers that they would be used regularly could not be kept, and the high motivation present during training appeared to founder rapidly. In our 1984 survey, too, respondents from nine Schemes reported that maintaining volunteers' interest and morale during periods when they were under-used was one of their major problems (see Appendix, Table A).

Similar problems could also occur when Co-ordinators failed to keep a careful eye on the distribution of cases. The volunteers who were easiest to contact, particularly if they accepted cases uncomplainingly, could become 'overloaded', while others could be forgotten entirely for lengthy periods. The resultant under-use of particular volunteers sometimes produced feelings of suspicion and of being undervalued. Thus one volunteer who was aware that others were still receiving regular referrals, stated:

> 'I would ideally like to see about three a week, but often now I get none. I feel a bit out of it and would like to know what's going on.'

Such situations also arose out of Co-ordinators' misapprehensions of the commitment volunteers were prepared to make. At a Scheme which had recently changed over to 'automatic' referral, two of the five volunteers we interviewed said that they felt under-used and would be happy to see more victims if asked, while at the same time the Co-ordinator herself was telephoning, writing to or visiting up to 20 victims per day. The latter commented to us that she did not wish to 'overburden' volunteers by giving them more than one per week. In fact, a perusal of Scheme records revealed that a number of volunteers were receiving hardly any referrals, while the Co-ordinator felt extremely overburdened herself.

Time pressure often prevented the Co-ordinator at another Scheme from making more than one attempt to telephone each volunteer, so that those immediately contactable were given four or five referrals each, and the others none. At volunteers' meetings, it was clear that this imbalance had caused dissatisfaction among both those receiving 'too many' and those receiving 'too few' (or in some cases none). And even at a Scheme with no particular pressure on the Co-ordinator, an analysis of Scheme records revealed that, of a total of 129 cases allocated over a three-month period, 64 (50 per cent) were dealt with by two volunteers, 27 (21 per cent) by another two, and the remaining 38 spread between ten others. This seemed to be partly explained by the experience of the four most active volunteers (who were 'trusted' with any kind of case) but also by their willingness to take cases and the ease of contacting them. As elsewhere, some volunteers felt dissatisfied at being 'left out'.

This situation highlights the advantages of the rota systems employed at two of the Schemes we studied. Here, volunteers chose, or were allocated, a set day a week on which they guaranteed that they would either be contactable and available for visiting, or else would let the Co-ordinator know in advance if they were not. Such a system, if used effectively, not only spreads the workload more evenly, but ensures at least one communication every week between Co-ordinator and volunteer.

(iii)   Report forms

Although all Schemes in the country are exhorted by NAVSS to use volunteer report forms, one of which should be completed and returned for each victim referred, some seemed to take this more seriously than others. At two of the eight Schemes, a reasonably high proportion of report forms were eventually returned, but the Co-ordinators often had no time to read them, and they were merely filed away in referral date order. At the other six, not much more than half the forms were returned, and many of these were extracted from volunteers weeks or months after the date of referral. The Co-ordinator of one of the latter Schemes commented:

'I can only ask them to return the forms, but they rarely do. Most dislike filling them in and there's nothing I can do. I don't push them too much'.

and a volunteer from another actually exclaimed, four months after completing training,

'I didn't realise there were report forms to fill in!'

Moreover, even among volunteers who returned forms regularly, some completed them whether or not contact was achieved, and some only if they saw the victim. The overall result was that there was no immediate way of telling what proportion of victims had actually been contacted. (A problem, incidentally, which involved us in a great deal of extra investigative work for Chapter 4!) As one of the Co-ordinators admitted:

'There are lots where the outcome is not known to me, there's just no time.'

Two Schemes we visited briefly were proud that they received all forms back, whether or not contact was achieved, and attributed this to their practice of instilling in volunteers from the beginning that one of their commitments would be to return a form for each victim referred. However, this had also been said to volunteers at some of the Schemes at which we found relatively few returned. The difference seemed to lie entirely in the degree of emphasis placed upon accurate record-keeping by individual Co-ordinators.

Volunteers themselves had differing views about the purposes served by report forms, many considering them a necessary evil or worse, and most believing they were for record purposes only. Only a small proportion claimed to complete and return them immediately following a visit so that their recommendations would be acted upon by the Co-ordinator without delay. For example, one volunteer commented that:

'The purpose I hope is that the Co-ordinator follows up any recommendations for further agency involvement.'

However, he, like several other volunteers, complained that he usually did not hear about the outcome and 'whether anything was done'. Indeed, he did not seem confident that these recommendations were noticed at all - a rather worrying situation, perhaps indicating a misunderstanding between volunteer and Co-ordinator. (The latter normally expected to be telephoned if any follow-up action was required and did not always read forms carefully.) The majority of volunteers we interviewed did not perceive any urgency about the return of forms, and few felt under a strong obligation to return them, believing that no real importance was attached to them by the Scheme. Another volunteer stated that:

'I've returned about half. I don't mind completing them, but there's no pressure to return them.'

Apart from the possibility that recommendations by volunteers for follow-up action remain unnoticed and are not acted upon, the neglect of report forms can be damaging to volunteer morale. If the return of forms or feed-back on referrals is not conveyed as important, this may be interpreted by volunteers to mean that the Scheme takes little interest in the quality of their work, and consequently they may feel undervalued.

(iv)    Volunteer meetings

The importance attached to volunteers' meetings by
different Schemes is partly reflected in the frequency and
regularity with which they are arranged and held.  In our
1984 survey, 10 to 12 meetings a year emerged as the most
popular arrangement, with 46 per cent of Schemes thus
averaging about one per month.  At the other end of the
scale, however, 15 Schemes (9 per cent) held three or fewer
meetings a year, four having arranged none at all within the
last year.  One Chairman commented forlornly,

> 'We have not held a meeting as yet, as we have not kept
> the same group of volunteers for more than two months at
> a time'.

Following the introduction of the revised (1985)
Code of Practice, Management Committees will in future be
under some obligation to 'hold regular meetings for volunteers and Co-ordinator(s)', and the new Training Manual also
stresses this, so the situation may by now have improved.

Average attendance at volunteer meetings also varied
considerably.  Fifty-two Schemes (32 per cent) claimed that
'all or nearly all' volunteers attended regularly and
another 61 (38 per cent) that 'most' attended.  However, 11
per cent of respondents admitted that 'less than half' or
'very few' tended to come to meetings.

Very low attendance levels were, in fact, associated with
infrequent meetings.[5]  For example, the Co-ordinator of one
Scheme we visited said:

> 'We usually have four to six meetings a year, top whack,
> but it's difficult to get them to come, they're very
> busy people.  Two came to the last meeting (out of a
> possible 18).  We also don't hold social evenings
> because the volunteers are too busy.'

Whether it was lack of interest that reduced the number of
meetings, or too few meetings that caused people not to
come, is not certain in every case.  However it is likely
that if Schemes fail to emphasise from the start the importance of attendance at volunteer meetings, and accept too
readily excuses for non-attendance, a downward spiral can be
set in motion.  In other words, low attendance causes a
reduction in the number of meetings held, the hope being
that with fewer commitments, more will attend;  but this
reduces attendance even more, since the Scheme loses its
sense of cohesion, the importance of meetings is further
devalued and volunteers feel even less obligation to attend.

At three of the Schemes studied, and at some others visited briefly, the main intended purpose of these meetings was to support the volunteers. Indeed, the meetings were explicitly called 'volunteers' support meetings'. These Schemes commanded the best attendances of those studied and all held a minimum of 12 meetings per year. On average, we calculated, between one half and two thirds of all volunteers attended regularly - which actually meant 60 to 80 per cent of all regularly active volunteer members. The meetings typically lasted about two hours, and at two of the Schemes they sometimes continued informally in a local pub.

The meetings at these three Schemes were conducted fairly formally, and were characterised by a sharing of experiences, a sense of cohesion, and a feeling that it was a safe place to bring problems, doubts and fears. (In fact, a main topic for discussion at one meeting we observed was feelings of fear aroused on visits.) Each meeting was led by the Co-ordinator or, in one Scheme, a probation officer or other experienced group leader. The importance of making a commitment to attend was stressed during the training courses, and this was re-emphasised during the early stages of visiting. One Co-ordinator exemplified these points as follows:

'It's very important for them to attend. They let me know if they can't. I know exactly who will be there, and nearly all turn up. The volunteers have a strong sense of cohesion. They're psychologically dynamic meetings. We're dealing with a lot of appalling things, and we need to face up to what we're going through, so there's much sharing of problems.'

Each volunteer would typically discuss victims he or she had dealt with over the last month (or was still seeing), and the Co-ordinator would bring up specific cases from which the group could learn. As another put it:

'We all discuss their cases together. They bring their triumphs and disasters, and they're encouraged and supported. The main aim is to make it a very safe place for them to bring their mistakes, so that they won't feel foolish and so that we can all learn from each other. Their caring, sensitive actions are reinforced, and this opens up the possibilities for others to follow.'

In stressing the importance of promoting group identity and cohesion, some Co-ordinators were careful to include identity with the Scheme and the Region as well as simply with other volunteers - thus implicitly recognising the

138

danger, under the 'tripartite' system, of the three 'parts' becoming isolated from each other:

'We're trying to promote a feeling of involvement with the Scheme, so that they don't feel isolated.'

'We want to make them feel an integral part of an organisation rather than a peripheral part, so regional information is given at these meetings.'

'We try to encourage contact and identity with the Scheme, because this is relevant to providing an efficient service. We help them to develop their skills, and practical and psychological issues are discussed, as well as matters of Scheme and Regional policy.'

Volunteers who attended these support meetings tended to confirm that the aims were achieved. For instance:

'I'm happy with the volunteer meetings, they're a good way of keeping in touch, and getting a kinship feeling with your fellow workers.'

The volunteer meetings at these three Schemes can be regarded as essentially an extension of training - particularly as they were sometimes given extra input by the invitation of an outside speaker. Indeed, one Scheme quite often held training workshops as supplementary sessions, when discussions and role-play centred on topics such as 'the manipulative victim', 'how to say no' and 'confidence and assertiveness training'. These sessions were conducted by members of the Scheme with relevant professional experience, and proved popular with volunteers. Experienced volunteers, particularly, tended to find them a welcome change from the usual 'case discussion' meetings, as the latter did not always keep them sufficiently stimulated and interested - a point recognised by one of the Co-ordinators:

'I now feel the meetings should be on different levels for volunteers with different types and amounts of experience, to keep experienced volunteers interested and not to overwhelm new volunteers.'

Indeed, this idea had already been put into practice at another of the three Schemes, where four separate monthly meetings were held, one for each of four 'intake' groups with different amounts of visiting experience. To counteract the possibility of each group feeling isolated from the others, all groups came together several times a year for special meetings.

Volunteer meetings at the other five Schemes studied were non-existent, irregular or badly attended. In one case, internal frictions and breakdowns in communication between all three levels of the Scheme took their toll, with the consequence that few volunteers turned up for the meetings - on one occasion none - and they were frequently cancelled. In another, there were only three active volunteers and no volunteer meetings were held during the period of our research. In the remainder, there seemed to be little plan or direction behind the meetings, which were badly attended and not infrequently turned into general conversation only marginally related to work with victims.[6] It was normally left to busy Co-ordinators to organise and run these meetings, and two of the Co-ordinators had little aptitude for group leadership of this kind. On the other hand, the meetings did have some value as 'social evenings', and not all volunteers were dissatisfied with them:

> 'I don't go as I haven't got the time. I attended a couple last year. I like the informality of them, and it's good to meet the others.'

> 'It's not really necessary to go, except to get new information, but it's nice for others to have a social evening out.'

> 'I would like general problems to be discussed more, but you can remotivate and recharge your batteries there. They're good for reinforcing the volunteers. I don't know why more don't attend.'

> 'It's good that the Co-ordinator doesn't make the volunteers' meetings obligatory. The meetings are fine for me - they're social primarily. The level and pace may not be what new volunteers are expecting - when they're all fired up and raring to go, because you hear bits of cases, chats, and names of people you've not heard of. What with the drinks it's all very laid back and social.'

Others, however, were openly critical:

> 'We need to discuss problem cases more, but instead there's a lot of chat which means nothing. I believe the main aim is to encourage newcomers, but in fact the meetings are not encouraging. They don't impress me at all, and I think they would actually discourage volunteers from joining.'

> 'I would like to talk about some of my cases, but I don't know the other volunteers, and the Co-ordinators

140

tend only to chat to those they know, and one has never
even spoken to me. I don't feel the meetings serve any
purpose for me, but I go because something might happen,
and we should show our faces. I feel I'm volunteering
in a vacuum without the support of any others. We
should all be introduced so we feel free to chat to each
other. It's like seeing strangers every time.'

Finally, if the style at the first three Schemes we
described may be called 'supportive', that detectable at one
of the latter Schemes was of the 'back-biting' variety. The
main purpose seemed to be the airing of the dissatisfactions
of the Co-ordinator and of the volunteers with the
Management Committee. There was a group identity and some
cohesion, but it was a cohesion based upon 'them' and 'us'.
It sometimes included cynical black humour suggesting that
the 'workers' in the Scheme were being deliberately
frustrated by the Management. Volunteers' dissatisfactions
were reinforced rather than tackled, as in 'It's a hard
life, love', spoken by the Co-ordinator in reply to a
comment from one volunteer that she felt under too much
pressure with an increased referral load. While this may
have sustained the spirits of the hard core of regular
attenders, it could hardly be said to be healthy for the
Scheme as a whole.

(v)   Volunteers and the Management Committee

Although Victims Support Schemes have relatively few
members, in several Schemes one 'half' did not seem to know
the other. A large minority of volunteers interviewed
expressed indifference as to how and by whom the Scheme was
managed, while most of those who said that they were
interested in Scheme policy felt that they were not kept
well informed about developments by the Committee. Indeed,
knowledge about the Management Committee itself tended to be
very sketchy. Few volunteers at any of the Schemes studied
could recall the names of more than one or two committee
members. Some typical comments bearing on these points
were:

'I know the Chairman's name but have forgotten the rest.
I would like the minutes (of the Management Committee
meetings) but I haven't received any.'

'I've asked for copies of the Management Committee
minutes, but we just haven't had them. We're largely
kept in the dark about developments, especially since
none of us are able to attend as the volunteers'
representative at the moment (through other commitments).'

'I don't know their names or who they are. In general volunteers should be able to attend their meetings as observers. I want to know what the issues are, why there's not more public support for VS, why we're still unknown, and what's happening about funding. At present we don't get enough information about these things.'

'I'm told incidentally what happens at MC meetings, but not formally. It would be nice to have more information, to have their Agenda, so the volunteers' viewpoint can be put. Volunteers have a right to put their point of view. For example, I would like a blanket referral system, because the police are slightly arrogant and have stereotypes.'

'As a volunteer, I would like more say in policy decisions that concern us. The volunteers should sit there with them.'

'I've never felt we've had enough say in policy decisions, but I suppose that's the Committee's job. However, we don't get enough feedback about what goes on at their meetings, and I really do wish they kept us better informed.'

One Committee had tried to solve the communication problem by sending a monthly newsletter to volunteers, but there was no noticeable difference between the responses of volunteers here and elsewhere. Comments like the following were made by several who received the newsletter:

'I've got no idea who they are. I don't know whether I have enough say in policy decisions, because I don't know what the policy is.'

The main reason for this low visibility of the Management Committee seems to be that, apart from occasional attendance by some members at volunteers' meetings, the only face-to-face contact that most members had with most volunteers was at the AGM or at occasional social evenings. Such events were generally mentioned favourably by volunteers, but three of the eight Schemes had not included, in their previous year's activities, a social occasion where committee members could meet volunteers informally.

The recommended 'official' avenue for communication between the Management Committee and the volunteers is through a 'volunteers' representative' on the Committee. However, not all Schemes had appointed such a representative (a situation that is now improving through the inclusion of a stipulation in the revised Code of Practice, 1985).

Moreover, the position was not taken very seriously in some Schemes, the 'rep' being self-selected without opposition, or falling into the role by default - no-one else being willing or able to attend Management Committee meetings, which are usually held during the day. There also did not seem to be a set limit on the period of time to be served, and one or two had held the position since the Scheme started. In fact, less than half of the volunteers we interviewed knew of the existence of a volunteers' representative, suggesting that little feedback was received at volunteers' meetings from their representative. (We never observed a 'report' being made.) The reverse side of this problem was that the representatives themselves were not often able to put the collective view of the volunteer group on any issue particularly concerning them to the Management Committee, since their opinions had not been canvassed. Thus at one meeting the volunteers' representative was heard to say, in relation to a long-running problem, 'I'm afraid I can't speak for the other volunteers'.

Only two of our eight Schemes had a regular item on the agenda calling for the volunteers' representative to speak. Without this, the 'reps' sometimes felt rather 'left out of the conversation'. Two complained:

'Even though I used to be the volunteers' representative, I wasn't ever introduced at the MC meetings.'

'It took me ages before I realised who they (the MC) all were. I wasn't introduced. There's a lot of talking but nothing is ever decided, they don't do much for the volunteers or the victims.'

The importance of maintaining a dialogue between volunteers and Committee lies largely in the dangers of misunderstandings, negative feelings and resentments building up. Certainly, a large minority of volunteers we interviewed expressed some such feelings, examples being:

'I couldn't name any MC members, but none of them should be allowed to come to volunteers' meetings because they are confidential.'

'Yes, I know the Chairman and his views. I don't think he's sincere. I don't need any support or help from the MC. Their role should be fund-raising, recruiting, developing and extending to other areas of the borough. I don't see any point in them attending the volunteer meetings, they should be fund-raising. I don't see what there is to manage. They've only failed if they haven't managed the fund-raising.'

143

'The MC are on an ego trip, where it suits their purposes to be on the committee of a voluntary organisation. They're not committed to Victims Support.'

'I don't think it would be advantageous to us if they attended the volunteer meetings, though it might be advantageous to them, because they can't know what an actual visit is like.'

That this can lead to more than simply 'background grumbling' is illustrated by incidents at a Scheme at which failures of communication over a period led to considerable mutual suspicion and ill-will. The main problem was over the payment of expenses, which was sometimes refused. The 'official' position, as explained by the Co-ordinator, was unclear to volunteers and seemed to change over time. Most were confused over whether they were entitled to claim, particularly for taking taxis at night, as they were receiving contradictory messages at volunteers' meetings from month to month. The upshot was that several volunteers felt increasingly disinclined to visit. The female volunteers also felt unhappy about visiting because they felt that going on foot on dark evenings (often the only time available to them) was dangerous in an inner-city area, and that the Management Committee did not care about them. One left the Scheme and another ceased visiting. In the end, they announced to the Committee, through the Co-ordinator, that they felt that their views were not being adequately heeded, and that they wished for 'proper' representation on the Committee. After discussions spanning several meetings, it was agreed that up to five volunteers could be elected.[7]

Interestingly, at another Scheme misunderstandings about travel expenses again contained the seeds of antagonism towards the Committee. Here, the claim forms included a space for volunteers to enter the amount they wished to donate to the Scheme. Two of the comments made were:

'I haven't been told I can claim for phone calls, and I haven't claimed for car mileage because I'm a volunteer. Anyway, there's a donation clause on the expenses form which stops me.'

'On the expense claim form it says "Amount claimed" and "Amount donated to VS". I think that may put some people off or may make them feel guilty if they don't donate their expenses incurred.'

The Committee, in fact, had no intention of embarrassing volunteers into not claiming, but there was no easy way for such concerns to be put to them by volunteers.

In sum, more positive communication with, and reinforcement of, the volunteer group by the Management Committee seemed clearly desirable in many of the Schemes we visited. This is largely a matter of manufacturing more opportunities for the two groups to meet. Certainly, more Committee members could attend volunteers' meetings, and more volunteers could sit on Committees. Another useful development might be the insertion of a formal volunteers' representative 'slot' on the agendas of both Management Committee and volunteers' meetings. And, as in some Schemes we visited, it seems wise to encourage Committee members to undergo training and to visit some victims (under 20 per cent of those in the Schemes we studied had been trained for this purpose).

We confess that it surprised us that such problems of communication could arise within what is still generally a small organisation locally. If Schemes grow larger without paying attention to the 'them and us' or 'I'm only a volunteer' feelings which already exist in many, they may weaken themselves unnecessarily for the future.


Notes to Chapter 5

1. For example, Codes of Practice (1981 and 1985); VSS - The UK Model (1984); Job Description for Co-ordinators (1983).

2. One of these was officially allocated an honorarium, but did not take it, she said, because 'the Scheme needs the money'.

3. Most Schemes, in fact, had more than one police officer on the Committee, and one had five.

4. At one Scheme, the Treasurer expressed mild concern at the increasing size of the telephone bills, by far the largest item on the accounts. However, the Co-ordinator, who laid a great deal of stress upon volunteer support, made no apology for spending hours talking to them over the telephone, and was supported in this by the Committee.

5. Of the 11 Schemes holding between one and three meetings annually, six said that 'very few' regularly turned up.

6. At one of these Schemes, this was partly accounted for by the fact that fund-raising tended to be left to the Co-ordinator, and group discussions often centred on ideas and plans for making money.

7. Even then, at the last minute some members brought forward constitutional reasons why such a number could not be elected, and after further discussion, a compromise solution was reached whereby two volunteers were elected and up to three more could become co-opted members.

# 6 Victims support in practice: does it work?

We turn now to the central questions of what volunteers actually do for victims, what victims think of the service offered or provided, and, ultimately, whether the organisation can be shown to 'work' in the sense of measurably affecting victims' recovery. A major assumption behind the importance placed by Victims Support upon contacting victims individually (sometimes referred to as 'outreach') is that even brief contact, demonstrating that 'someone cares', can mean a great deal to people suffering the aftermath of a crime (Reeves, 1985). We therefore examine the reactions of victims to letters and telephone calls, as well as to support offered in person.

We were unable to be present when volunteers were visiting victims, so our knowledge of what occurs comes only second-hand from the accounts of samples of both parties and from Scheme records. We begin by giving a 'victim's-eye' view of VSS and the services offered and given. We then look at the extent to which Schemes successfully 'tap' community resources already in existence in order to assist victims in a practical way. And finally, we consider whether there is any evidence that Victims Support actually 'works' - i.e. has a measurable effect upon victims' reactions to the offence committed against them.

146

# Victims' experiences of VSS

## (i)   Initial reactions to contact

   Responses to the British Crime Survey indicate that 32 per cent of victims had heard of Victims Support Schemes.  This is in line with the 29 per cent of our sample of victims drawn from police records - and the 28 per cent of victims who had only telephone or postal contact with Schemes - who told us that they had heard of VSS prior to the offence.[1] However, there was a different situation where <u>visited</u> victims were concerned:  under 15 per cent had heard previously of Victims Support.  The difference seems to be explained mainly by the policies used by Co-ordinators in deciding which victims should be visited:  as described in Chapter 4, those they selected for unannounced visits tended to be older, of lower socio-economic status, and more 'socially isolated' than victims as a whole.

   Although the majority had not heard of the service previously, the first reaction of victims on being approached by a Scheme was generally favourable.  We asked all interviewees who had been contacted by VSS to describe their very first reaction to the telephone call, letter or unannounced visit they had received, and whether their initial reaction had changed once the volunteer had had a chance to explain the purpose of the call (or once they had reflected upon the contents of the letter).  Table 6.1 summarises both initial and subsequent reactions to the approach made.[2]  Overall, 20 per cent said that their very first reaction had been one of great pleasure or 'delight', and 28 per cent that they had been quite pleased.  Fairly typical examples of each of these responses were:

   'Wonderful to find that there was an organisation who knew about how I'd feel.  It was a great balm.'

   'It was nice to find that somebody is there if you need them.'

   A further fifth had been 'surprised', 'intrigued', or had their curiosity aroused by the first Scheme approach (e.g. 'I thought to myself, who are these?'), but once they had some idea of what was being offered, most of these also took a favourable view of the idea.

   Finally, while 7 per cent, apparently, had had no reaction at all (e.g. 'I just ignored it.'), the remaining 22 per cent told us that their initial reaction had been a negative one.  More specifically, 5 per cent had felt 'embarrassed', 7 per cent 'irritated' or 'annoyed', and 10 per cent

## Table 6.1
**Victims' initial and subsequent reactions to contact from VSS; by method of contact used**

<u>Nature of reaction</u>

| Method of contact | Positive (delighted pleased) % | Negative (suspicious, embarrassed, annoyed) % | Other (surprised, curious, no reaction) % |
|---|---|---|---|
| **Unannounced visit:** | | | |
| initial reaction | 50 | 23 | 28 |
| later reaction | 87 | 6 | 7 |
| **Telephone:** | | | |
| initial reaction | 38 | 29 | 33 |
| later reaction | 71 | 17 | 13 |
| **Letter:** | | | |
| initial reaction | 50 | 11 | 39 |
| later reaction | 79 | 4 | 18 |
| **All:** | | | |
| initial reaction | 48 | 22 | 30 |
| later reaction | 83 | 7 | 11 |

Weighted data. Unweighted N = 207 victims of burglary, robbery, assault and theft from the person contacted by VSS.

'suspicious'. Again, it should be stressed, the majority of these reacted favourably once the purpose of the call had been properly explained. In the end, then, victims' reactions to being offered VSS services were overwhelmingly welcoming, with, after an early period of clarification, 83 per cent reacting positively and only 7 per cent negatively.

It is instructive, however, to look briefly at the initial negative reactions, in particular at their variation according to the type of contact first employed (see again Table 6.1). It was noticeable, for example, that a considerable minority of victims visited unannounced had reacted initially with suspicion. This was largely confined to victims of burglary, who, as has been pointed out in Chapter 3, often become less trusting of other people as a result of the offence. Over a quarter of these said that they had been suspicious of the volunteer when he or she first arrived on their doorstep. However, virtually all were reassured when the visitor produced an identity card - a point mentioned

148

specifically by many of our interviewees.  Comments of
burglary victims illustrating why it is important for volunteers to offer full proof that they are from a legitimate
organisation were:

> 'I felt a bit suspicious, as you know burglars dress up
> as officials.  But he showed me his card, and I let him
> in.'

> 'My first thought was "Who the hell's that?"  It was an
> elderly couple, and I didn't believe them at first.
> Even after she showed me her card I was very suspicious.
> I thought they were either casing the joint or had come
> back to see how I'd reacted, pretending to be Victim
> Supporters ... but I admit I've got a bit of a paranoid
> imagination.'

One other 'negative' reaction, mentioned by a few victims
who had been visited unannounced, was that of embarrassment
that the volunteer had taken so much trouble to visit when
it was 'not necessary'.  For example, a victim of 'snatch'
theft from the person said:

> 'I felt very embarrassed, as if I was a fraud, because
> she wanted  to help and I didn't need any, as if she had
> been invited on false pretences.'

However, most of these victims went on to say that the
volunteer had made some effort to reassure them that he or
she did not consider the visit a waste of time - i.e. that
the gesture was as important as actually giving support or
assistance.

Telephoning was the method most likely to produce an
immediate negative reaction - predominantly annoyance - with
over a quarter of those approached in this way making
comments such as:

> 'I was rather irritated that the police had passed on my
> information.'

> 'I was slightly put out to be approached over the phone
> without any preliminary correspondence.'

Moreover, even after volunteers' efforts to explain the
purpose of the call, one in six telephoned victims still
retained negative feelings about it.  The main cause of the
annoyance was the 'breach of confidentiality' by the police
in passing the victim's name and telephone number to another
organisation - a point much less likely,  for some reason,
to concern those visited unannounced.[3]

Information about reactions to <u>letters</u> is of particular interest to Victims Support Schemes, as, apart from the few victims who request a visit as a result (rarely more than 10 per cent - see Chapter 4) or who write or telephone to thank the Scheme for their interest (perhaps another 10 per cent), Schemes have no idea of how victims feel about receiving them. In fact, nearly 80 per cent our interviewees who had received letters were positively pleased to get them. And as we shall see later when discussing the possible influence of contact with VSS upon recovery from the effects of crime, a considerable minority also felt that it had made some difference to how they felt.

We also asked all victims which form of initial contact they would have preferred. About 30 per cent had no preference, and most of the others were quite happy with the method used in their own case. However, about a quarter of those telephoned would have preferred another method (or no contact at all), most of these naming a visit in person as the most satisfactory. And one in seven of those visited - mainly victims who had not been badly affected by the crime - would have preferred a letter. The overall picture of victims' responses to contact from VSS, then, is that while most are pleased to be contacted in any way at all, a small minority are annoyed or upset, most frequently by telephone calls. And while no one method is vastly preferred by all, unannounced visits are the most likely to be welcomed.

Finally, while it is important - in order to minimise complaints, as well as to encourage people to take up VSS services - to know whether victims react favourably to an offer of support, it is equally important to know whether they fully understand what is being offered. In fact, most victims said that, once introductions had been effected, they quickly understood the purpose of Victims Support. It was nevertheless of note that a significant minority - about 15 per cent of those contacted by telephone or post, but a much smaller minority of those visited - had retained only a vague, unclear or misconstrued idea of why they had been approached. One telephoned victim of robbery said, for example:

> 'He didn't explain particularly well what the Scheme was, and he wasn't receptive to the idea that I was all right. I felt that he wanted me to accept his services, but I had no clear idea of what his services were.'

Indeed, broad misunderstandings about what was being offered, coupled in some instances with pre-held images and impressions of Victims Support, seemed to account for at least some of the widespread reluctance of victims to take up offers of visits made over the telephone or by post. These misapprehensions tended to centre on three themes: that Victims Support was intended primarily for victims of serious violent crimes, that Victims Support had feminist connections and dealt mainly with rapes and domestic violence, and that the help on offer was primarily 'psychological' or 'psychiatric' in nature. Some examples may help to illustrate these points:

'I thought the letter was quite nice, but it didn't really apply to me as I wasn't hurt.' (burglary victim)

'I've got a vague idea. They're volunteers who help victims of violent crime.' (burglary victim, letter)

'They will help people if they've got psychological problems.' (assault victim, telephoned)

'I wondered why they'd called because I wasn't hurt.' (burglary victim, telephoned)

'I felt that Victims Support were feminist groups who dealt with rape victims mainly. I think I may have gained this impression from a newspaper article.' (victim of theft from the person, letter)

'I've heard the phrase, but haven't taken any notice. I've heard of them in connection with rape cases or serious muggings.' (burglary victim, letter)

'The letter was rather non-specific about what they do. I know it said or inferred they did counselling, but this implies a therapeutic setting, and I'm not ill.' (burglary victim)

In fact the particular Scheme letter referred to in the last comment made no reference to counselling at all, suggesting that this person's previous image of Victims Support (that it helped battered wives and rape victims) distorted her reading of the letter sent.

The confusions illustrated in the above remarks, together with the finding that only a minority of people had heard of Victims Support Schemes, not only suggest a need, where telephone or postal contact is used, for more efforts to make the nature of the service clear, but also for more national and local publicity to raise public awareness of the organisation and what it does. This might persuade more victims to take up offers of assistance, at the same time reducing the occurrence of annoyance or suspicion. As one victim said:

'The call made me feel irritated because it got off on the wrong foot. The phone service is so open to abuse these days - wrong numbers, salesmen, suspicious callers. Afterwards it felt nice to know that the Scheme existed. If its availability was more widely known I wouldn't have been so suspicious.'

## (ii) The service offered

### (a) Emotional support

In Chapter 3, we concluded that about 25 per cent of victims of recorded offences of burglary, assault, 'snatch' theft or robbery could be said to have a 'need' for emotional support from VSS volunteers, either by dint of failure by others around them to provide sufficient basic support, or because they were so badly upset that counselling from someone with experience of similar cases was necessary to supplement even very strong family support. Among victims of such offences visited by volunteers - who, owing to the 'filtering processes' described in Chapter 4, were somewhat more likely to be badly affected - about a third could be said to have a need for emotional support. One would not, therefore, by any means expect every visit to result in an intimate and painful 'talking through' of feelings between the  volunteer and the victim.  In fact, our interviews with victims indicate that only just over half of those who invited volunteers into their homes discussed their feelings about the offence with them in any depth.[4]

Very few victims 'blamed' the volunteer for any failure to talk about their emotions.  Indeed, in  most cases the omission was of their own volition.  Several of those visited unannounced said that, while appreciating the gesture from VSS, they preferred to discuss their feelings with friends or family rather than a stranger.  Others said that they had not been 'badly enough' upset, or simply wanted to forget the affair.

The minority who would have liked the conversation to have been more intimate than it was, tended to explain that the call had come at an inconvenient time, that they had felt inhibited because other people had been present,[5] or that they had not felt able to express their emotions despite the sympathetic manner of the volunteer.  For example:

'I felt choked as I was speaking to her.  She tried to make it easy but I wasn't able to respond very well.  I found it difficult to tell her how I was feeling.'

'I give the appearance that I'm self-reliant and not a tearful person, but underneath I'm not - I was affected. There is shock and stress there. You get self-contained and feel you don't need help but you do. Maybe, if I'd let her stay longer I'd have opened up.'

The few among this minority who thought the <u>volunteer</u> responsible for failure to express their feelings (about 5 per cent of all visited victims) referred most often to his or her 'wrong' type of character or general manner. For example:

'Her manner wasn't right, it didn't relax me. I was in the middle of washing up and I didn't stop. She was someone else to cope with. The way she presented herself was wrong. She didn't sit down and she was too tall. I felt bemused and a bit guilty for not being more sociable.'

'I can only describe it as a 'jolly hockey-sticks' approach. She just wasn't the sort of person I could talk to.'

It is worth emphasising that such lack of compatability was put down to the character, and not the age or gender, of the volunteers in question: in fact, only two of the 151 visited victims would have preferred a volunteer of the opposite sex to the one who arrived, and one would have preferred an older person. This suggests that (except in the case of sexual offences - see Chapter 7) there is no real necessity to 'match' victims to volunteers on the grounds of age or sex. Only one of the Schemes we studied did this to any large extent.

The other victims who thought the volunteer responsible for a failure to 'relate' emotionally said simply that the latter had not tried to talk about feelings at all. Two volunteers were said to have steered the conversation almost entirely towards advice about crime prevention or compensation, while one seemed to have provided little 'support' at all:

'We just had a chat. If he'd been more skilful, he would have made me realise why I was depressed.'

These few criticisms, however, are far outweighed by the number of people who made complimentary remarks about volunteers' sensitivity and understanding manner, and who had clearly felt better for the visit. Among those victims who had been willing (or had sufficient time available) to discuss their feelings, 71 per cent said that the volunteer had made it 'very easy' to talk about them. Moreover, the responses of all visited victims to our question, 'How did you feel after the volunteer had left?' show that, despite the number of short and relatively inconsequential conversations, the great majority still derived at least some short-term benefit from the visit:

| | |
|---|---|
| Very much better | 11% |
| Slightly better/mind eased | 71% |
| No different | 16% |
| Worse[6] | 2% |

Similarly, asked later to rate on a four-point scale how much difference the visit had made to how they or others in the household had 'coped with the emotional side of the situation', respondents replied as follows:

| | |
|---|---|
| Very big difference | 12% |
| Some difference | 50% |
| A little difference | 17% |
| No difference | 19% |
| Made worse | 2% |

In victims' comments about the degree of difference made, two themes in particular re-emerged frequently: the importance of having somebody to listen to them, and the value of talking to an outsider, rather than to someone they knew. While, as we have seen in Chapter 3, families and friends were often sympathetic, the particular value of a VSS volunteer seemed to lie in the special 'space' provided by a person who had come with the explicit purpose of listening, and whose very presence offered reassurance that others had undergone similar experiences and that somebody fully understood what the victim was feeling. Little as this may seem when examined in the cold light of day, it was clearly of great importance to some of the victims we interviewed, even among those who had not been injured and who had lost relatively little property. When when we come, in Chapter 7, to discuss the reactions to VSS support of victims of rape, it will be seen that nearly all those we interviewed attached central importance to the above factors, and some believed them vital to their efforts to cope with the damage done to their lives. But the following are more typical statements made by victims of burglary and assault, the first of whom stated that the visit had made 'a very big difference', and the remainder that it had made 'some difference'.

'The visit helped me look at it in a better light: I needed a two hour talk without feeling that I was boring a friend or a relative. It was helpful that it was an outsider.'

'It made me feel that an outsider cared about what had happened to me. I felt the volunteer understood what I'd been through, and it helped to know that others have felt like I did.'

'It relaxed me and I got over that nervous feeling, plus I had a phone number if needed.'

'It was lovely to have the moral support and someone to share my problems with. That's unusual nowadays.'

To sum up, the level of 'consumer satisfaction' is high as far as emotional support is concerned, and there is a considerable amount of subjective evidence that this aspect of Victims Support 'works'. Well over half the victims visited by VSS volunteers believed that the visit had ameliorated the emotional impact of the crime to some extent. Later in this chapter, we shall use a 'matching' exercise to see if there is any more objective evidence of victims who have been visited making a better or quicker recovery than victims who have had no contact with a Scheme.

(b)  Practical assistance

It was shown in Chapter 3 that the great majority of victims of burglary and crimes of violence have to deal with various practical problems arising from the offence, but that in most cases either they or others in their family deal with these problems quite quickly and satisfactorily. Even so, we concluded that about 25 per cent of all burglary victims, and 15 per cent of victims of violence, are left with at least one practical problem still not resolved to their satisfaction several weeks later - the most common being uncompleted repairs to property and dealings with agencies (DHSS, Council, Gas and Electricity Boards, rental firms, etc.). We identified these victims - many of whom also had emotional needs - as the minority as the proportion potentially in 'need' of some outside assistance with practical matters.

However, we also pointed out that if volunteers arrive early enough, they may help with practical problems which

the victim would soon have dealt with anyway. They may also
help victims to perceive 'needs' which the latter had not
recognised as such. Thus, it must be emphasised that, if
the practical assistance actually given by volunteers is to
be referred to (as it often is in VSS circles) as 'meeting
victims' needs', we have moved away from the strict definition of 'need' given above, towards a much looser one, based
primarily on demand. In this latter sense, any practical
problem mutually identified by (or, one might say, 'negotiated' between) the volunteer and the victim may be seen as a
'need', whether or not the victim is capable of dealing with
it alone.

We look now at victims' accounts of the 'practical needs'
they presented to VSS volunteers, and what the volunteers
did to assist. We shall concentrate here mainly upon
victims of burglary, who tended to mention a higher number
of (though not necessarily more serious) practical problems
than victims of violence.

We first asked all those who had been visited what
practical problems they had mentioned to the volunteer
during his or her first visit. Out of the 72 victims of
burglary who had been visited unannounced - mainly one or
two days after the offence - 38 (i.e. 53 per cent) said that
they had told the volunteer about at least one such problem
which had not yet been dealt with. In addition, 20 of the
26 who had requested a visit had mentioned one or more
problems.[7]

Altogether, these 58 victims recalled telling volunteers
about 75 different practical problems or tasks which had not
yet been attended to. Table 6.2 shows the nature of these
problems, and how the volunteers responded to them. Their
most common response was to offer advice: most of this was
couched in general terms, but in a large minority of cases
the volunteer left a specific telephone number or address
for the victim to contact. Secondly, one-third of the
problems mentioned produced a promise from the volunteer to
contact an agency on the victim's behalf. (The agencies
most frequently concerned were the local authority housing
department or repair yard, and the Gas or Electricity
Board.)

The advice to telephone or visit specific agencies was
followed by victims in most of the cases in which it was
given, and the problem was described as satisfactorily
resolved (albeit after considerable effort and inconvenience) in nine of the 16 cases shown. Similarly, the volunteers had largely kept promises to find out something or to
take action themselves: victims had had some 'feedback' in

156

relation to 20 of 25 problems in which volunteer action had been promised, and reported a satisfactory outcome in 15 of these. Satisfied customers included three victims for whom Schemes had obtained financial help in the form of a DHSS emergency payment or charity grant, and three on whose behalf Schemes had successfully persuaded Electricity Board officials to waive or reduce repayment of money stolen from meters.

By the time of our interview, satisfactory resolutions had been found to 39 of the 75 problems which had been mentioned to volunteers on their first (or only) visit. From what victims said, it appears that VSS intervention had made some contribution to the resolution of at least 24 of these problems (which concerned 18 victims, some having been helped with more than one).

Table 6.2

**Unresolved practical problems mentioned to volunteers by burglary victims; and type of action taken by volunteer**

| | | | Type of problem | | | |
|---|---|---|---|---|---|---|
| | Effecting repairs | Improving security | 'Meter break' problems, disputes | Insurance | Other | Total problems mentioned |
| Volunteer action | | | | | | |
| General advice | 3 | 15 | 4 | 9 | 2 | 32 |
| Advice to telephone/ visit specific agency | 5 | 2 | 5 | 1 | 3 | 16 |
| Promise to contact agency for victim | 11 | 1 | 5 | 1 | 7 | 25 |
| Offered help rejected | 1 | – | – | 1 | – | 2 |
| Total | 20 | 18 | 14 | 11 | 12 | 75 |

Notes

Total number of victims mentioning problem = 58
Total number of problems mentioned = 75
N = 98 victims of burglary visited by Scheme volunteers

In sum, then, helpful and productive practical advice or assistance was given to about a third of the burglary victims who mentioned a (thus far unresolved) practical problem to a volunteer. As these, in turn, constituted a little over half of our sample of burglary victims visited by volunteers,[8] it can be calculated that, altogether, Schemes had been of genuine practical help to at least 18 per cent of all those they visited. In a third of these cases, moreover (i.e. 6 per cent of all visited victims) the beneficiaries believed that the Scheme's help or advice had saved or acquired for them money they would not otherwise have received. And several others said that the process of repairing or securing their house had been speeded up by Scheme intervention with the local Council or by specific crime prevention advice.

On the other hand, it should be noted that, despite the VSS visit, almost half the problems mentioned to volunteers had not been resolved to the victim's satisfaction several weeks or months afterwards. In many of these cases, the victim felt that there was nothing <u>anybody</u> could do about them - particularly refusals of insurance companies to pay the full amount claimed, fuel boards' insistence on repayment of cash stolen from meters, or security improvements which the household could not afford. (Whether or not they were right is another question.) Yet there were also a small number of cases in which it was felt that the volunteer had raised hopes but had not 'delivered'. These included five incidences of volunteers having promised to contact an agency on a victim's behalf, only for the latter to hear from neither the Scheme nor the agency again.

The above pattern was reflected in burglary victims' more general statements about the practical assistance offered or given by VSS. The great majority who had mentioned practical problems to a volunteer were happy with the advice or service provided: asked to rate their satisfaction with the practical assistance given, 76 per cent of these said that they were 'very satisfied', while only 10 per cent - mainly those who had not been re-contacted as promised - pronounced themselves very or slightly dissatisfied. Similarly, when we asked all 98 burglary victims what more the visitor might have done to assist them at the time, only 15 could think of anything practical.[9] It seems then, that despite the fact that a number of practical problems did remain unresolved, most of these were regarded by victims as beyond the powers of Schemes to assist with - often because they involved financial expenditure. But what victims did see as problems with which the volunteer could be of help were generally dealt with in a way which fully satisfied them.

Finally, victims of offences of violence, as stated earlier, tended to consult volunteers about fewer, and a different set of, practical problems. Nevertheless, more 'follow-up' work was done on behalf of such victims than for burglary victims, mainly because of Schemes' help with claims to the Criminal Injuries Compensation Board. The possibility of a CICB claim also tended to be the major practical issue discussed on visits - the topic usually being introduced by the volunteer. Otherwise, victims were most likely to mention difficulties caused by pain or lack of mobility. Some, too, had to replace clothing, spectacles, keys and stolen documents; and a few were worried about financial loss caused by having to take time off work. Like Shapland et al. (1985), we found that self-employed people could lose a great deal of money by being temporarily incapacitated: one such victim estimated that a serious assault had cost him £1,000 in three months. Volunteers responded to problems other than CICB claims in a similar way to those mentioned by burglary victims - i.e. mainly by giving advice - although they did undertake a higher proportion of any suggested 'agency contacts' themselves, rather than leaving them for the victim to do. Again, most of the straightforward practical problems were satisfactorily resolved fairly quickly, and only four victims (8 per cent of the total visited), felt that the visitor could have done any more to assist them. Two of these had wanted the volunteer to arrange some immediate financial assistance and the other two would have liked better legal advice. The general level of satisfaction with the practical assistance provided was similar to that of the burglary victims, with only three of the 24 who had mentioned problems (excluding CICB claims) expressing any dissatisfaction.

Where CICB claims were concerned, it was as yet too early to know whether an award would be made. Nevertheless, as many as 43 per cent of victims who had discussed with the volunteer the possibility of compensation said that, if it was eventually forthcoming, the award would represent money that they would definitely not have obtained without the latter's help. Altogether, only a quarter of all victims of violence visited had even heard of the CICB prior to the first VSS visit, and several of these had not definitely decided to claim until encouraged to do so by the volunteer.

(c)   General views of visits

Following the basic principles of 'crisis intervention', the normal policy at every Victims Support Scheme we visited was to see victims as soon as possible after the offence. In fact, over two-thirds of the initial unannounced visits to victims in our sample took place within two days of the offence, and all but three per cent within a week. The majority of these visits were not repeated: only 13 per cent of burglary victims, and 34 per cent of victims of violence, received a further visit from the volunteer; and only just over a quarter of all those visited had any further contact at all with the Scheme.

The above practices seemed, superficially at least, to accord with the wishes of most victims. As mentioned in Chapter 3, BCS respondents who would have liked a visit from a Scheme volunteer were asked at what point in time after the offence this would have been most welcome, and about 80 per cent stipulated the day of the offence or the next day. Similarly, our interviewees were generally in favour of an early visit. While a third (predominantly those least affected) had no preference, nearly all the remainder thought that the first visit should occur within three days of the offence. In most cases, the simple reason given was that this was the period during which they had felt worst (cf. Chapter 3). The highest number named the day after the offence as the optimum time, many saying that by then the 'hustle and bustle' of visits from police or neighbours had ceased and the realisation of what had happened was beginning to 'sink in'.

Victims were generally content with only one visit, although one in five of those who had had no further contact with the Scheme would have liked to see the volunteer again. These were fairly evenly divided between people who said they would have liked a 'social chat' because they had liked the volunteer personally, and those who thought he or she could have helped them with problems or feelings related to the crime. More specifically, we asked those interviewed three to six weeks after the offence whether, if it had been a volunteer rather than we who had contacted them this time, the Scheme might have been able to 'help you with anything else connected with the crime now'. Sixteen per cent replied in the affirmative. Although a few of these mentioned legal advice or help in disputes with gas or electricity boards, the general tendency of victims of burglary and violence to be more concerned about their feelings than about practical problems was again in evidence: for the majority the main 'service' which could have been provided was a fresh chance to talk over the event and its consequences. Several of these victims were among the small proportion (6 per cent of all, but 14 per cent of victims of violent crime) who would have preferred the first VSS visit a week or more after the offence. The main reason given for this, too, was that they had needed time to 'digest' what had happened before they were ready to talk about it.

These findings raise the question of whether Schemes should routinely re-contact certain victims a few weeks later in order to see if they need further support. If they are to do this, the indications from findings presented in both this chapter and Chapter 3 are that those who would most benefit from a follow-up visit are victims of serious assault, although a relatively high proportion of female victims of burglary also stated that they would have found a follow-up visit helpful.

Another striking feature of most visits made to victims in our sample was their short duration. As far as respondents could recall, only 32 per cent had lasted more than half an hour, the most common length being 15-30 minutes. This, together with the infrequency of follow-up visits and the finding that in only half of all visits were feelings talked about in any depth, suggests that terms such as 'crisis intervention' or 'counselling' are inappropriate to describe what happens in the majority of cases. The reality is more often a brief talk about the offence and its effects, and some simple crime prevention advice.

The fact that most victims, although rating themselves very much affected by the offence, were perfectly happy with these short, 'one-off' visits - and, indeed, felt that they made a difference to how they had coped with the effects - suggests that it is the gesture, as much as the content of the visit, which they find important. This is confirmed by an examination of answers to the question, 'What was the most important aspect of the help they gave you?' Fifty-three per cent stated, unprompted, that it was 'the offer', 'the fact that someone cared', or a 'restoration of faith in society'. Answers referring to elements of 'support' in a more concrete sense - e.g. the opportunity to express feelings (23 per cent), comfort or emotional reassurance (5 per cent), or practical assistance or advice (13 per cent) - were given by considerably fewer respondents.

Again, it is worth stressing in this context that victims found very little fault with the type or level of support they had been given. Pressed to name any criticisms at all of the service provided, only 7 per cent mentioned insufficient practical assistance and a mere 3 per cent failure to help them express their feelings. It should, however, be remembered that 15 per cent were able to think of other things the Scheme could have done to assist them at the time of their visit, and about the same proportion thought they might have benefited from another visit at a later stage.

Having established from victims' accounts that the 'typical' relationship between a VSS volunteer and a crime

161

victim consists simply of one short, friendly, sympathetic, much appreciated, but not necessarily 'deep' or 'emotional', conversation (quite often with more than one member of the household present), we must redress the balance by referring to some of the very different patterns to be found in an important minority of cases. The most obviously different sort of VSS work is that with rape victims, which almost always involves difficult and stressful long-term support. This is left for discussion in Chapter 7. There were also, however, a number of other cases in our sample in which volunteers spent a great deal of time with victims, sometimes spanning several visits and involving communication with other voluntary or statutory agencies. We give only three brief examples below, but it is worth stressing that these are by no means uncommon. We came across comparable cases in most of the Schemes in which we carried out fieldwork, and in some of them it was normal for several such cases to be 'live' at any one time.

(a) A woman badly beaten by her boyfriend was visited numerous times, during which the Scheme first persuaded the DHSS to pay for redecoration to her home, then successfully bullied the local council into rehousing her and persuaded the local Probation Service to provide a full set of new furniture.

(b) An elderly couple, both attacked and badly injured by their mentally disturbed neighbour, received visits and telephone calls from a volunteer intermittently for almost a year. The Scheme mediated between the couple and the CICB, requested an interim compensation award for them, and put them in touch with an elderly persons' welfare agency. In addition, moral support was given by the volunteer during several meetings between the victims, their landlord and people representing the offender's interests.

(c) An elderly man suffered a heart attack and broken bones as a result of being robbed in the street, and then his home was burgled while he was recovering in hospital. The volunteer purchased a vacuum cleaner on his behalf (with his permission) and personally cleaned up his house. She then organised a home help for his return and arranged a free local transport service for him twice a week. His shopping was done for a few weeks and she accompanied him to his doctor on several occasions. Community Services were brought in to mend his fence and do some gardening, and the volunteer engineered a reconciliation with his daughter, with whom he had previously been on bad terms. Finally, she liaised with the DVLC in Swansea about the victim's stolen driver's licence.

Crimes of violence were much more likely than burglaries to lead to this more intensive work. Nine per cent of first visits made to victims of violence (compared with 4 per cent of those to burglary victims) lasted for at least an hour and a half. And 17 per cent of victims of violence (compared with 3 per cent of burglary victims) had received at least three visits from volunteers by the time we interviewed them. Some of these differences are explained by complications arising from CICB claims, but certain types of victim appeared to have received particular attention owing to the severity of their problems - especially some old people who had been very violently attacked, and some younger victims from deprived areas who had serious financial or social problems which had been exacerbated by the offence.

(d) Letters and telephone calls: Do they help?

As shown in Chapter 4, the great majority of letters sent to victims meet with no response, and Schemes have no way of knowing whether receiving them is of any value to these victims. In fact, our interviews with victims who failed to reply to Scheme letters showed that the great majority had appreciated the gesture, and, moreover, when asked whether receiving the letter had 'made you feel better in any way', 18 (69 per cent) of 26 interviewees replied that it had. The majority of these said that they had felt slightly better, typical remarks being 'It helped to put my mind at rest' and 'It was reassuring', while five said that it had made them feel very much better. Similarly, when asked (unprompted) what was 'the most important thing it did for you or your family', seven (27 per cent) mentioned 'the gesture' or 'the fact that someone cared', six (23 per cent) 'the fact that the service exists if you need it' and another six the general reassurance or moral support. One other said that it had given him back his 'faith in people'.

When asked why they had not taken up the offer of help, ten (38 per cent) replied that they had 'had no problems', four (9 per cent) that they had been 'too busy', and - as mentioned earlier, a finding that deserves VSS attention - six (23 per cent) replied that they had misunderstood the letter or the service that was being offered. However, when asked whether, in retrospect, they thought that they might have benefited from a visit by a Scheme volunteer, as many as seven of the 26 - i.e. 27 per cent - replied in the affirmative. Finally, a small number of victims - four of the 26 - said that receiving the letter had made a positive difference to how they felt about the police, giving the latter some credit for having referred them to the Scheme. Three, however, expressed some reservations about their names and addresses having been passed on.

All the above responses may be compared briefly with those of victims who had been telephoned, but not visited, by Scheme volunteers or Co-ordinators. A slightly lower proportion (48 per cent) of telephoned victims than victims who had been sent letters said that the contact had made them feel better. Unfortunately, too, three of the 21 said that it had made them feel worse, mainly because of a perceived intrusion upon their privacy. The 'most important' aspects of the contact were, again, mainly 'the gesture' or the 'fact that someone cared', although two victims mentioned practical advice given over the telephone (re CICB and insurance claims). The reasons for not asking for a visit were more diverse, including four victims who said that no visit had been offered. Others said that they had been too confused at the time or did not have time to think about it properly. Moreover, with the benefit of hindsight, eight (38 per cent) of 21 said that a visit might have been of some use to them. Finally, while two said that the call had improved their image of the police, three said that it had worsened it, owing to the fact that the latter had given 'confidential' information to the Scheme. Overall, then, telephone calls were not appreciated by victims as frequently as visits or letters, although about half still found that they made them feel better.

## The effectiveness of Victims Support

(i)   Schemes' identification of needs and use of other agencies

One of the keystones of the VSS model as presented by Reeves (1984, 1985) is that Schemes should act as referral agents themselves, identifying victims' needs and channelling them towards particular agencies already existing in the community which are able to provide relevant services. We have seen that volunteers did this job to the satisfaction of a fair proportion of the victims they visited: in about 30 per cent of all burglary cases dealt with, the volunteer either advised the victim to contact one or more specific agencies or else promised that the Scheme would do so - advice or actions which led to a satisfactory outcome in over half of these cases.

However, to get a fuller picture of the nature and extent of VSS dealings with other agencies, it is necessary to look at the records of individual Schemes. We examined a total of 448 volunteers' report forms concerning visits made to victims by members of five different Schemes. These showed what needs had been identified in each case and what follow-up actions had been taken by volunteer or Co-ordinator.

164

Where unannounced visits in areas with automatic referral were concerned, volunteers identified a clear need for emotional support or practical assistance[10] in 41 per cent of all cases - a figure a little higher than our estimate of 'needs' based upon interviews with victims (Chapter 3). Most of these cases involved both practical and emotional needs, and 23 per cent altogether involved the volunteer or Co-ordinator in some form of 'follow-up' action, such as telephoning another agency.[11] We show in Table 6.3, for each Scheme, the proportion of cases in which other agencies were contacted on behalf of the victim concerned.

Table 6.3
Numbers of cases in which agencies were contacted by volunteers or Co-ordinators on behalf of victims

|  | Scheme | | | | | |
|---|---|---|---|---|---|---|
|  | A | B | C | F | H | All |
| % of cases where another agency contacted on behalf of victim | 20% | 28% | 16% | 33% | 13% | 28% |
| Average number of agencies contacted | 1.1 | 1.5 | 1.3 | 1.7 | 1.0 | 1.2 |
| Average number of agencies contacted per visited victim | 0.2 | 0.4 | 0.2 | 0.6 | 0.1 | 0.3 |
| (Number of victims visited) | (110) | (86) | (57) | (95) | (100) | (448) |

This exercise confirms the finding from interviews with victims, that Schemes wrote to or telephoned other agencies in connection with about a quarter of all cases in which the victim was visited. However, it also indicates certain differences between Schemes in the amount of 'follow-up work' they carry out. The proportion varied between 13 per cent (in a small Scheme with a young and inexperienced Co-ordinator) and 33 per cent (in a large urban Scheme with a full-time paid Co-ordinator with her own office).

The type of agency contacted also varied widely, as will be illustrated below. First, however, it is useful to gain a more general picture from responses to our 1984 survey of all Schemes. Respondents were asked to state, to the best of their knowledge, which five agencies their volunteers or Co-ordinators contacted most frequently on behalf of

165

victims. Table 6.4 shows the results. <u>Social Services</u> <u>Departments</u> emerge as the agency most frequently called upon, with several other agencies, including Housing Departments, the DHSS, Gas and Electricity Boards, and old people's welfare agencies, vying for second place.

### Table 6.4
#### Agencies most frequently contacted by Schemes on behalf of victims

| Agency | Percentage of Schemes mentioning | Percentage of Schemes selecting as the most frequently contacted agency |
|---|---|---|
| Social Services | 78 | 22 |
| DHSS | 65 | 9 |
| Housing Departments (repairs) | 54 | 11 |
| Gas/Electricity Boards | 47 | 12 |
| Crime Prevention Officers | 46 | 10 |
| Age Concern/other old people's·agencies | 42 | 14 |
| Housing Departments (other services) | 31 | 6 |
| Citizens' Advice Bureaux | 25 | 6 |
| Insurance companies | 23 | 3 |
| Other repair agencies | 19 | 2 |
| CICB | 13 | - |
| GPs/hospitals | 12 | 2 |
| Legal advice centres | 9 | 2 |
| TV/video rental firms | 4 | - |
| | | 100 (N=159) |

Source: Questionnaire to all Schemes and districts, Summer 1984

In the Schemes we studied, the types of agency most often contacted varied to some extent according to the types of victim most often dealt with. For example, at Scheme F, where about a quarter of those visited had been victims of violent offences, nine of the 54 'agency contacts' made were inquiries in connection with CICB claims. The remainder, however, show what a rich field of resources can be mined on behalf of victims by an experienced Co-ordinator in a large city. They included calls to Social Services departments (to arrange, among other things, meals-on-wheels services, a visit from a deaf worker, and from an Asian language worker), to the Council's Housing Department (to speed up repairs, or, in several cases, to argue for urgent rehousing), to the local welfare association for elderly people (to arrange long-term visiting), to charities (for emergency funds), to a local ethnic community group, and to a number of individuals including two private landlords, a psychotherapist, and an insurance assessor.

Scheme B, which was geared primarily to assisting victims of burglary, was most often in touch with the local Housing Department, but among other services, it managed to help one victim to move urgently into sheltered housing accommodation, contacted the Community Service Scheme (for free repairs, gardening and decorating), the Probation Department (to provide free furniture) and the local Crime Prevention Officer (who supplied free bolts and chains).

Finally, while we may safely conclude that some Schemes were both proficient and effective at contacting other agencies on behalf of victims, this should not be confused with what is often called the 'referring on' of victims - i.e. where another agency takes on the responsibility of resolving the victim's problems. The latter is often talked about in Victims Support literature as though it were a common occurrence, but in fact we found it to be comparatively rare. This seems to be mainly because other agencies are not geared up to deal with the special problems of crime victims, and statutory agencies in particular tend to be reluctant to take on new clients without a very clear duty to do so. Mawby and Gill (forthcoming) also point out the enormous difficulties inherent in the notion of a voluntary agency like a Victims Support Scheme attempting to coordinate the efforts of statutory agencies - not renowned for mutual cooperation - on behalf of a particular client group. Moreover, especially where the assistance of victims of serious crime is concerned, VSS members are increasingly coming to realise that there are anyway virtually no other 'experts' to take responsibility: with accumulating knowledge and experience, they are becoming the experts themselves.

(ii)    Comparisons of 'supported' and 'non-supported' victims

We conclude this chapter with our own very modest contribution towards filling what is surely the most gaping gap in the existing research knowledge about victims and victim support. Quite simply, it is not known for certain whether intervention - be it in the form of a short visit by a volunteer, intensive 'crisis intervention', or even regular counselling or therapy by professionals - actually aids, speeds or enhances recovery from the effects of crime. For example, as Stein (1981) rightly points out:

> 'We have available to us precious little evidence to support our case for crisis intervention for crime victims ... Although crisis intervention has proven its

167

efficacy to the mental health profession, there are no evaluation studies showing the benefits of crisis intervention to crime victims as a particular group in need of its services.'

Of course, one means of evaluation is to examine clients' own perceptions of the effectiveness of the service provided. We have already cited examples of the generally warm response of victims and have noted that 12 per cent of those visited thought that the support given had made 'a very big difference' to the way they coped with the emotional effects of the offence. Unfortunately, victims' comments of this kind are insufficient to prove the point, as neither we nor they know for certain what would have happened had there been no intervention.

An alternative research strategy for testing the effectiveness of VSS intervention is to compare the recuperation of a group of victims who have received support with that of a 'matched' control group who have not. It has to be stressed that the difficulties of ensuring that two such groups are strictly comparable, and of isolating the effect of the intervention from that of any other factor, are daunting.[12] We do not pretend that the small exercise of this kind we were able to carry out in the limited time available avoids these difficulties: indeed, it will almost certainly take a full-scale and highly sophisticated clinical study to produce any authoritative results in this area. Equally, differences between small groups are unlikely to reach levels of statistical significance unless some extraordinary changes take place, and when it is remembered that most visits by VSS volunteers are brief and simple, it would be astonishing to find these making a difference of this magnitude. Nevertheless, while our results clearly must not be taken as firm evidence of the effectiveness of support by volunteers, it is interesting to find that they do give a number of indications all tending in the same direction.

We sought, among our samples of victims visited by VSS volunteers, the closest possible 'twin' for each of the 26 non-VSS-contacted victims of burglary, snatch theft or assault who rated themselves initially 'very much' or 'quite a lot' affected by the offence. We succeeded eventually in finding 26 VSS-visited victims, each of whom had also rated themselves initially very much or quite a lot affected, and who 'matched' their chosen twin fully in terms of simple binary categories of offence type (burglary or violence), age (under or over 60), sex, marital status (married or single as opposed to separated, widowed or divorced) and whether or not living alone. The pairs were also matched as

168

closely as possible in terms of social class, whether
previously a victim, and whether or not friends and
relatives had provided a 'listening ear'. Although the
match was not perfect in every case, we could find no
personal or offence-related variables on which the two
groups of 26 cases differed at a statistically significant
level.

Table 6.5 compares various measures of the extent to which
the two groups were affected both immediately after the
offence and at the time of interview (three to six weeks
after the offence). It emerges that, on all our measures of
effects, the VSS-visited group had been slightly more

Table 6.5

**A comparison of two groups of individually matched victims, visited by
VSS and having had no VSS contact, showing indicators of how badly
affected each group remained after three to six weeks**

|  | Visited by VSS (N = 26) | No contact with VSS (N = 26) |
|---|---|---|
| Number 'very much' affected: |  |  |
|   initially | 22 | 20 |
|   after 3-6 weeks | 1 | 8 |
|  |  |  |
| Number naming three or more strong effects:[a] |  |  |
|   initially | 20 | 17 |
|   after 3-6 weeks | 6 | 9 |
|  |  |  |
| Measures of effects after 3-6 weeks: |  |  |
|   Average GHQ.60 score[b] | 10.3 | 13.3 |
|   Number with score above 12 | 7 | 11 |
|  |  |  |
| Number 'very frightened': |  |  |
|   initially | 19 | 17 |
|   after 3-6 weeks | 8 | 10 |
|  |  |  |
| Felt at 'lowest point': |  |  |
|   first day | 20 | 9 |
|   five or more days later | 0 | 8 |
|  |  |  |
| Wanted to talk more about the offence | 4 | 9 |

**Notes**
a. From the list of 22 shown in Table 3.8
b. For notes on GHQ scores, see Appendix, Table P.

affected at the time of the offence, but by three to six weeks later the position was reversed. Thus, for example, the number of visited victims naming three or more strong emotional effects fell from 20 at the time of the offence to six a few weeks later, while the equivalent fall for non-VSS supported victims was from 17 to nine. A similar pattern occurred in the numbers reporting themselves 'very frightened' at the time of the offence and 3-6 weeks later. Moreover, scores on the GHQ, and a comparison of the numbers of victims still feeling a need to talk about the offence, indicate that the 'supported' group had recovered more fully than the others. Such findings, while not at all conclusive, are certainly encouraging. The fact that there was even the degree of consistency in one direction demonstrated in Table 6.5, suggests that VSS support could possibly be shown in a large-scale study, to make a statistically significant difference to the speed of recovery. Further research along these lines might well pay dividends.

Finally, whether or not it can be shown to ameliorate the effects of crime, there are signs (Table 6.6) that a visit from a VSS volunteer may have some effect in reducing anger and, in particular, in altering attitudes towards the offender. The clearest difference of all between

Table 6.6

A comparison of two groups of individually matched victims, visited by VSS and having had no VSS contact, showing changes in levels of anger, and attitudes to offenders and mediation

|  | Visited by VSS (N = 26) | No contact with VSS (N = 26) |
|---|---|---|
| Number feeling more punitive towards offenders generally | 2 | 12 |
| Number who would accept mediation | 11 | 3 |
| Number 'very angry': | | |
| initially | 19 | 17 |
| after 3-6 weeks | 8 | 9 |

the two groups was in response to the question, 'Do you feel differently than before the offence about what should be done to offenders?' While 12 of the group who had had no contact with VSS said that they felt more punitive, only two of those who had been visited felt this way. Similarly, a much larger proportion of the VSS-visited group said they would be prepared to meet the offender under one of the new 'mediation' schemes (cf. Appendix) if he or she were caught.

Notes to Chapter 6

1. Shapland et al. (1985) found that 30 per cent of victims of violence in Coventry (where there was a Scheme in existence) and 17 per cent in Northampton (where there was no Scheme) had heard of Victims Support Schemes. There had been considerable local publicity in Coventry about the Scheme at the time of the study.

2. Rape victims are excluded. The data are weighted to take account of our over-sampling of telephone calls and letters which were 'converted' into visits, as opposed to remaining the only form of contact. The former were given a weight of 0.2.

3. Similar results emerged from the question we asked later in the interview: 'Did you mind the police giving your name and address to the Scheme?' Only 5 per cent overall, but 12 per cent of those initially telephoned, said that they had 'minded'. The only explanations we find plausible are (a) that the professional and executive classes - who formed a higher proportion of those telephoned than of those visited unannounced - are more likely than others to take a strong view on the issue of confidentiality, and (b) that it is much easier to put someone's mind at rest about one's bona fides in person (where an official card can be produced), than over the telephone.

4. This figure was much higher (around 80 per cent) in the case of victims who had requested a visit in response to a Scheme letter or telephone call, but for unannounced visits - by far the most common source of invitations into victims' homes - it was slightly below 50 per cent. In this chapter, when presenting findings from which we wish to make general statements about the reactions of victims visited in their own homes, we have weighted responses to compensate for the oversampling of visits arising from telephone calls and letters, as opposed to from unannounced calls at the victim's home.

5. More than one person (apart from the volunteer and the 'official' victim) was present during over 30 per cent of all visits.

6. The three victims who had felt 'worse' explained that the visit had only served to remind them of an incident they had been trying to forget.

7. Another 12 of the whole 98 had still had problems to deal with, but did not mention them to the volunteer, either because the volunteer did not ask or because they did not think he or she could help.

8. With the sample weighted to compensate for oversampling of visits requested by victims in response to letters and telephone calls, the proportion mentioning practical problems emerges at 55 per cent.

9. Over half of this group (8 per cent of the total) would have liked more effective support in disputes with gas or electricity boards, local

authorities or other agencies; and a few others would have liked the Scheme to produce some direct financial help or information about the progress of the case (each 3 per cent).

10. Excluding general crime prevention advice. We are referring here to clear signs of emotional distress, or to practical problems requiring some considerable effort on the part of victim or volunteer - often involving 'follow-up' work.

11. Where more 'selection' had preceded the visit (i.e. in areas with selective referral or where the victim had requested a visit), over 60 per cent of victims had been identified as in need of assistance, and 'follow-up' work had been carried out on behalf of nearly 30 per cent.

12. See again Stein (1981). A good example of the kind of potentially important factor which is very hard to control for is the pre-victimisation psychological state of the victim. (It seems quite likely that people already in a state of stress or anxiety, for example, will not recover so quickly from the effects of a crime as people who were previously more stable.) The only way to control for this effectively would be to interview a very large random sample of individuals (using a variety of psychological measures) and then wait for some of them to be victimised!

# 7 A special case: victims of rape and serious sexual assault

## Introduction

In this chapter we focus on official and community responses to rape, and in particular on the services offered to rape victims by Victims Support Schemes. We shall cite ample evidence from our own study and elsewhere that rape leads, in a high proportion of cases, to serious and lasting trauma. This evidence suggests that professional help, if needed, should be available to all victims at any stage after the attack. Yet the medical profession in Great Britain has paid scant attention to the effects of rape or to the support of rape victims, and few women ever see a professional counsellor or psychiatrist. What help and support has been given has come almost entirely from the voluntary rather than the statutory sector, and from concerned individuals rather than the professions.

This discomforting situation raises some thorny issues. It is possible to argue that in many cases the psychological effects are so damaging that it is wrong to entrust victims to the support of volunteers at all. Yet it has also been suggested that well-trained and experienced volunteers are as capable of giving support as professionals. Indeed, Durlak (1979), in his review of American studies comparing the effectiveness of professional and 'paraprofessional' (trained voluntary) helpers, concluded that the latter obtained clinical outcomes equal to or better than professionals.

A second question, which is related to the first, is less easy to answer. If it is accepted that volunteers are to be used for this task, what standards, if any, should be adhered to? It might be argued that 'some support (whatever the standard) is better than none'. But the danger is that a victim's recovery could actually be adversely affected by the intervention of an unsuitable or untrained volunteer. Moreover, in such a sensitive area, any hint of poor standards could discourage further referrals, so depriving other victims of the support of more able volunteers.

We begin this chapter by illustrating, from previous studies and responses to our interviews, the short and long-term effects experienced by rape victims. We shall then examine the systems used to refer rape victims to Schemes, the selection and training of volunteers who wish to undertake this specialist work, and the kinds of help, services and support that are offered. As Rape Crisis Centres provide the other main service available in the United Kingdom, a brief comparison will be made between the two agencies in the types of support and practical help offered. Finally, we shall consider the views of raped women about the support offered by VSS, and how this differs from that given by friends, family and other agencies.

## The subjects of our study

The interviews with rape victims - all carried out by Dr. Corbett - were always time-consuming and sometimes emotionally demanding upon victim and interviewer alike. Moreover, owing to the sensitivity of the subject, potential interviewees had to be approached carefully (usually through a Scheme Co-ordinator) and we had to take VSS advice to avoid approaching a few who, it was felt, might have been upset by questioning. Thus the number interviewed was small and cannot be assumed to be representative of all rape victims. It consisted of 18 'supported' victims with whom four Schemes were still in at least intermittent contact; and five 'unsupported' victims from four areas which did not have a local VSS service for rape victims.[1] All 23 had been raped more than two months previously, and all but six within the past year. The 'oldest' offence had occurred 30 months previously.

In terms of age, marital status and social class, the group was very diverse, illustrating the fact that women who are raped come from all sections of the community. Although just over half were in their twenties, their ages ranged from 18 to 76. Five were married, twelve single, six separated, divorced or widowed. Thirteen had children (five

174

being single parents), and four were also grandmothers.  The
group included students, a company director, a publishing
editor, two catering assistants, three women on disability
pensions, and an ex-prostitute (who had given up her work as
a consequence of the rape).

Of the 23 rapes, 17 were committed by total strangers and
six by acquaintances.  The fact that other studies of both
recorded and self-reported rape show much higher proportions
than this committed by acquaintances (e.g. LRCC, 1984;
Hall, 1984), suggests that 'acquaintance' cases are less
likely than 'stranger rapes' to be referred to VSS by the
police.  This is a tendency that we have already noted in
relation to other offences (see Chapter 3).  Finally, 14 of
the 23 rapes took place in the victim's own home, nine of
these by strangers and all except one during the night.  The
other victims were attacked in vehicles, in the street, in
an underground station, and on a towpath while jogging -
mainly in daylight by strangers.  Other studies similarly
indicate that women are more likely to be raped indoors than
outside (e.g. LRCC, 1984).


## Emotional, psychological and behavioural effects

As studies of rape - particularly in the United States -
have multiplied and become more sophisticated over the last
15 years, a fuller realisation has gradually come about of
the devastating psychological, behavioural, physical and
financial problems which may be experienced by rape victims,
in the long as well as the short term.  We summarise below
some of the main findings from previous research about the
effects of rape, in particular those relevant to the
question of what kind of help should be provided if women
are to escape some of the worst psychological consequences.

(i)  Short and long-term effects

Each woman responds in her own way to being raped, but two
contrasting patterns of initial response have been
frequently identified.  Some women respond immediately in
an emotionally expressed, upset and tearful manner.  Others
react in a more controlled and calm way with little
expressed emotion, as if nothing dramatic has happened,
often claiming that they feel distanced from the attack or
that the whole thing seems unreal (e.g. Resick, 1984).

The threat of being killed, mutilated or injured doubtless
underpins many of the ensuing symptoms and effects, which
may last for months or even years, whatever the initial
response may have been.  The most frequently reported

175

reaction is that of fear (e.g. Kilpatrick et al., 1984). This may be accompanied by exhaustion, anger and anxiety (Veronen et al., 1979), lethargy, irritability, and feelings of guilt, shame and loss (King and Webb, 1981). The latter effects may stem from the experience of loss of control over one's body, and the sense of helplessness associated with the shattering of former beliefs in the 'safeness' of the world (Silver and Wortman, 1980). In addition, victims may become unable to cope with normal daily activities for either a short or long period, or alternatively, these difficulties may disappear for a while only to keep recurring (Peters, 1975). In the weeks that follow a rape, it is not unusual for women to experience elevated levels of fear, panic, anxiety and depression, mood swings and intrusive thoughts and feelings (Kilpatrick et al., 1979; McCahill et al., 1979).

Women may also suffer the pain of physical injury, although findings on this point vary very much - from 9 to 63 per cent - according to the sample under investigation. Fortunately, the risks of pregnancy or venereal disease appear to be quite low, but are of obvious concern to victims (see Katz and Mazur, 1979).

Physiological changes frequently follow a rape. Victims may experience changes in sleep patterns (insomnia, early awakening and nightmares), changes in eating patterns (with acute weight loss or gain), or disturbances in the gastro-intestinal and genito-urinary systems. Reports of reduced sexual satisfaction and sexual activity are not uncommon, and in the weeks and months that follow, many women report withdrawing from any sexual contact (Ellis et al., 1980; Ellis, 1983).

Many behavioural responses and changes following a rape are avoidance-oriented. In order to feel safe again, women may avoid situations in which they feel insecure, and this may involve severe restrictions on their normal routines. For instance, if the rape occurred outside the home, they may not go out unless accompanied or in a vehicle. If it took place inside their home, they may engage in elaborate, time-consuming security rituals or obsessive 'checking' behaviours before entering or leaving (Miller and Williams, 1984). Most need to take some time off from their employment, but some women may leave their jobs permanently. Burgess and Holmstrom (1976) found that 45 per cent of their sample left or changed their jobs within six weeks, and another study showed that work adjustment, for some women, continued to be a persistent problem for up to eight months (Resick et al., 1981).

Another frequent consequence is the decision to move home, usually to a different neighbourhood (e.g. Veronen and Kilpatrick, 1983). This may be to avoid conditioned fear responses arising from the rape which are associated with particular places, but in some instances it may stem from a fear of retaliation or a repeat attack by the offender.

The financial consequences of rape victimisation have received little attention, but these can be quite considerable. Taking time off work (to assist the police in the investigation as well as for personal reasons), leaving a job, moving house, changing one's telephone number, improving home security and taking taxis whenever one goes out, are all expensive consequences of the offence. As Shapland et al (1985) and others have pointed out, while a reasonable amount of compensation may be forthcoming eventually from the CICB, it is often in the early stages that victims are in the greatest need of financial help.

The psychological effects and problems described by our interviewees largely concur with these findings from other studies. Fear, sleep pattern disturbances and weight loss were experienced by almost all our group. For instance, half lost over a stone in weight. Among several extreme examples of sleep disturbance was one woman who was unable to sleep at all for the first week and then went to the opposite extreme, sleeping or dozing almost continuously for three weeks. There was a higher incidence of disruption to normal sexual activity than that reported elsewhere, all but two of those with regular partners reporting that they had had no intercourse for at least a month following the attack. Two-thirds wished to move after the rape, and all those in employment found work adjustment a considerable ordeal, complaining mostly of loss of concentration and memory. One, a graphic artist, who took five months off work, remarked that this was the worst of the effects she suffered.

Table 7.1 shows more specifically the proportions of rape victims who experienced a range of reactions, either intensely or moderately, at different periods of time following the attack. The proportions experiencing anger, depression, and feelings of weakness and loss of strength actually increased over the three-week period post-rape. Three months later the proportion experiencing intense or moderate anger had risen even further. The third column in the Table represents those who reported various effects and reactions at the time of our interview - this was usually between 4 and 12 months after the rape. It was striking to find therefore that, at this later stage, ten of the 22 effects were each being experienced to a considerable extent

# Table 7.1
## Types of reaction to rape at different time periods after the event

Percentages of women experiencing reaction:

| Types of reaction | First day or so after attack: intensely % | (moderately) (%) | Two to three weeks after: intensely % | (moderately) (%) | Three months or more after: intensely % | (moderately) (%) |
|---|---|---|---|---|---|---|
| Unsettled, uneasy | 87 | (9) | 78 | (13) | 36 | (14) |
| Frightened, nervous | 91 | (4) | 70 | (13) | 40 | (27) |
| Shaking, shivering | 96 | (0) | – | – | – | – |
| Loss of trust in others | – | – | 61 | (26) | 45 | (32) |
| Dazed, confused | 87 | (9) | – | – | – | – |
| Loss of interest in work/hobbies | 83 | (4) | 61 | (13) | 14 | (23) |
| Unable to do ordinary daily tasks | 78 | (9) | 48 | (26) | 14 | (18) |
| Feeling helpless or vulnerable | 74 | (9) | 52 | (30) | 19 | (32) |
| Loss of appetite | 65 | (30) | 48 | (30) | 14 | (10) |
| Afraid to go out | 65 | (9) | 48 | (26) | 27 | (23) |
| Feeling depressed | 57 | (17) | 61 | (30) | 19 | (44) |
| Difficulty sleeping | 57 | (26) | 44 | (22) | 10 | (27) |
| Not wanting to be alone | 57 | (13) | 35 | (9) | 14 | (6) |
| Feeling contaminated | 57 | (17) | 35 | (9) | 14 | (6) |
| Afraid to stay in | 57 | (26) | 22 | (26) | 5 | (23) |
| Crying, tearful | 52 | (35) | 35 | (39) | – | – |
| Persistent thoughts of the attack | – | – | 30 | (9) | 27 | (32) |
| Sad about loss | – | – | 26 | (26) | 19 | (31) |
| Headaches/feeling ill generally | 39 | (9) | 39 | (13) | 19 | (27) |
| Afraid to enter room/house | 35 | (26) | 9 | (26) | 0 | (19) |
| Feeling angry | 26 | (9) | 52 | (4) | 36 | (31) |
| Feeling weak, loss of strength | 13 | (13) | 44 | (30) | 27 | (23) |
| Feeling or being sick | 9 | (35) | – | – | – | – |
| Feeling guilty, 'your fault' | 9 | (13) | 0 | (4) | 0 | (0) |
| Loss of memory of what happened | 0 | (4) | 0 | (0) | 0 | (0) |

by at least half of our interviewees. The effect experienced intensely by the greatest number was 'loss of trust in other people', but high levels were also reported of fear, anger, unease, depression, and persistent thoughts about the

attack.  Indeed, most of those we interviewed more than a
year after the attack were still frightened and angry,
unable to trust others, and troubled by persistent thoughts
of the rape.  Thus, notwithstanding the help given by
Victims Support, we found strong evidence that rape produces
long-lasting trauma in a significant proportion of victims.

(ii)    Recovery from rape

It is now well established that women vary a great deal in
the length of time they take to recover from rape.  Some may
be symptom-free after a few months, while others may still
feel distress several years later.  Burgess and Holmstrom
(1979) found that of their sample of 81 women seen at four
to six years post-rape, 37 per cent had felt recovered
'within months', 37 per cent 'within years', and 26 per cent
still felt unrecovered.  More recent controlled studies
(e.g. Calhoun et al., 1982) also show disturbances in
behaviour and 'clinical symptomatology' in rape victims
several years after the event.  It should be noted, finally,
that a few women report functioning better one year after
the attack than before it, having used the experience in a
positive way to make major changes in their lives (Notman
and Nadelson, 1984;  Veronen and Kilpatrick, 1983).

   Studies which have sought to identify factors associated
with slower or faster rates of 'recovery' (variously
defined) have produced confusing and contradictory results.
Those identified by different American researchers have
included:  the existence of pre-rape psychological problems,
a bereavement or a major change in life-style;  the nature
of the attack, in particular the degree of violence used and
whether or not the attacker was a stranger;  demographic
variables, including age, race, class and marital status;
initial levels of distress and self-esteem;  and personality
style and coping mechanisms.  (For useful summaries, see
Burt and Katz, 1985;  Kilpatrick, 1985.)  However, one set
of findings may be of particular interest to Victims Support
Schemes.  This concerns the degree of support received by
victims following the offence.  For example, Sales et al.
(1984) found that, while early symptom levels were
associated with other factors, the speed of recovery in the
longer term was best predicted by the quality of personal
relationships, family experiences and self-image.  They use
their own and others' findings to state that:

      'diverse streams of inquiry converge on the conclusion
      that the general quality of a victim's life, especially
      her relationships with others, centrally affects
      reactions to victimization'.

Burgess and Holmstrom (1979) also found the response of formal and informal helping institutions to be a significant variable in long-term recovery. And Atkeson et al. (1982) found that poor support by others was associated with long-term depression. They comment:

'Crisis counselling that focuses on reducing the amount of disruption experienced by the victim and on increasing the quality of the victim's social support may directly affect the duration and severity of a victim's depressive symptoms'.

Several of the women we interviewed said that their partners, close friends and relatives had been of only limited help to them in the immediate aftermath of the rape, since they were often coping with their own intense feelings. This suggests that an outsider, like a VSS volunteer, may prove more beneficial to a rape victim in the short term. However, in the longer term, voluntary helpers can be no substitute for close friends or partners, and because volunteers primarily support the victim only, 'poor' post-rape relationships may remain relatively untouched. Thus, extrapolating from Sales' and Atkeson's findings, the slow recovery made by some victims might be accelerated by family or 'marriage guidance' therapy, which is not at present, nor likely to be in the near future, a service offered by VSS volunteers themselves. Nevertheless, provided that such lasting difficulties are identified by volunteers, back-up counsellors, therapists or psychiatrists associated with local Schemes could be introduced to give professional help where appropriate.

Although not a proven factor associated with recovery, testifying in court is still one of the most fearful consequences for many rape victims (Calhoun et al., 1982), and most of our interviewees due to appear as witnesses felt they could not begin to recover until the trial was over. Anticipation of this event can be traumatic for various reasons. The victim is again at close quarters with the assailant, re-living the experience in all its embarrassing detail to an audience who may attack her credibility. She may feel that she, rather than the defendant, is on trial. Moreover, Resick (1984) reports that even a finding of 'guilty' will not always diminish a woman's fear and anxiety. This can be because the victim and others close to her expect that her problems will now be behind her, but 'it is upsetting to discover that conditioned fears and avoidance problems continue even after a successful prosecution'. An acquittal, if taken by the woman to mean that nobody believes her story, can be devastating and may, of course, be exacerbated by another form of 'secondary victimisation' - media coverage, with headlines such as occurred in her local paper about one of our interviewees: 'Woman invited man into home'.

Only one of our 23 interviewees considered herself fully recovered. Among the remainder, the older women tended to feel the effects lingering on at a more intense level than those in their twenties or thirties. This seemed to be associated with their poorer physical health and greater restriction on their social activities. Perceived and actual responses of 'significant others' also seemed to influence recovery patterns, with older victims more likely to experience shame and guilt. Finally, few found the court case a source of relief: where defendants were acquitted the victims naturally felt hurt and angry, while several of those whose cases resulted in a 'guilty' finding found themselves feeling no less depressed than before.

(iii)    Explanations for the patterns of effects shown

In the early 1970's, several models were put forward to describe the stages of responses to rape. One of the best known, which draws upon 'crisis theory' (Caplan, 1964), is called the Rape Trauma Syndrome (Burgess and Holmstrom, 1974). This posits that there is an initial acute stage of 'crisis and disorganisation', usually lasting for between two and three weeks, in which disruption occurs in all areas of normal functioning. After this stage there follows a period of 'reorganisation', where the woman comes to terms with the assault and integrates it into her life. Another popular model, proposed by Sutherland and Scherl (1970), interposes a middle stage of outward or 'pseudo-adjustment' to the event, which may involve denial of the rape or 'blocking', before beginning the phase of long-term resolution.

A major postulation of crisis theory is that most victims will make steady progress towards full recovery in a relatively predictable pattern. Depending upon the level of the initial trauma, full recovery is expected within a matter of months. However, as we have seen, in recent years ample evidence - not least that of Burgess and Holmstrom (1979) themselves - has accumulated to show that many victims retain serious symptoms several years later. Moreover, the steadiness and predictability of the pattern of recovery, which would be expected from crisis theory, has also come into question. Sales et al. (1984) found evidence of a 'second peak' of symptoms in many victims more than six months after the event. In the light of this increased knowledge, Resick (1984), among others, has suggested that a cognitive-behavioural theory may explain the data better.

The _behavioural_ element first involves classical conditioning. This is the pairing of previously neutral 'cues' with reflexes and emotions, so that in a life threatening and terrifying experience like rape, all of the cues that are associated with the attack automatically become paired with the feelings of terror and imminent danger. Common fears that are classically conditioned include fear of the dark, of strangers, of being alone, and of being indoors or outdoors. Women may find that, when other cues more specific to their own attack are present in the environment, these are also associated to produce flashbacks of panic and fear. While the victim usually learns to avoid situations in which these cues are likely to be present, avoidance prolongs and feeds the fears, so they have no opportunity to fade and may, in time, develop into phobias.

The _cognitive_ element involves beliefs about rape that the victim brings to the situation, and the perceived and actual beliefs and behaviour of others towards her. Many people believe 'rape myths' - prejudiced, stereotyped or false beliefs about rape, rape victims and rapists. For instance, Burt (1980) found that over 50 per cent of a sample of the population in Minnesota agreed with the statement: 'In the majority of rapes the victim was promiscuous or had a bad reputation'. If the victim shares common attitudes about who gets raped and why ('Nice girls don't get raped'), her feelings of guilt and shame may be exacerbated and fail to diminish over time. The victim, in order to regain some sense that the behaviour of others is predictable and not random, may find it preferable to accept the perceived or actual blame of others. By doing so she may feel that she has gained some control over the event and can avoid the occurrence of a similar situation in future. While this may serve a useful purpose in the initial stages following a rape (Resick, 1984), such self-blame may be detrimental in the long term. Thus persistent feelings of worthlessness, low self-esteem and hopelessness about recovery were reported in Atkeson et al.'s (1982) long-term study.

Our data tend on the whole to support the cognitive-behavioural model better than the 'stage' model. None of our interviewees could clearly recall passing through 'stages' in the aftermath of rape. Moreover, many serious effects had lasted for periods well beyond that predicted by crisis theory, even among victims who had received considerable support. By contrast, as predicted by the cognitive-behavioural model, stimuli associated with the rape were feared and avoided by many victims. Some of these had 'generalised' and even developed into phobias. For example, one woman, 18 months post-rape, was distressed that she could no longer go to her hairdresser because of the hood that would be placed over her head. Others in our sample reported being terrified of hearing rustling trees, seeing scarves, seeing anybody wearing a hood or anorak, and smelling particular body odours or alcohol.

It seems, too, that such cues can be linked to particular times, as again experienced by one of our interviewees 12 months post-rape, who reported still being unable to sleep and feeling very ill every Thursday night without fail. Another said that she always woke up at exactly the time of her attack every month. In addition, the majority needed to justify to the interviewer why they did what they did, or where they went, and six freely admitted, unprompted, that they never expected that this could happen to them, since they had previously shared common attitudes about who gets raped. Two victims who believed that close friends and family were 'ashamed of them' many months after the attack seemed particularly far away from recovery.

## Services to rape victims

In this section we consider the work of Victims Support Schemes with rape victims, looking specifically at referral policy, the selection and training of specialist volunteers, and the kinds of support given to raped women in practice. First, however, we say a few words about what is virtually the only alternative source of help and support for rape victims, the Rape Crisis Centres. These are well-established and better known that Victims Support Schemes, and obviously specialise to a much greater extent. If this is the case, why, it may be asked, is there a need for a second organisation to become involved in this area at all?

(i)    Rape Crisis Centres

The first Rape Crisis Centre was set up in London in 1976 and was granted charity status. Since then 25 other centres have been established in the UK, but unlike VSS, there is no national association to which they all belong. All RCCs are dependent on external funding, which is raised mainly through grants and donations from trusts, organisations and individuals. Some have also obtained local authority funds. There is a high demand for their support and assistance. The range of services available is broadly similar to that of Victims Support, but considerable differences in approach between the two organisations suggest that there need be no competition for clients. Indeed, we shall argue that they should be seen as complementary services, each suitable for some types of women with different sorts of need.

As each Centre is autonomous, services offered may vary. However, as an example, we shall discuss the largest Rape Crisis Centre, situated in London. In 1986 the London RCC employed four full-time and one part-time paid workers, and used the services of 28 unpaid volunteers. The Centre is located in a private house, purchased by means of a specific donation. The London RCC operates a 24-hour telephone service, manned by the paid workers during weekdays, and by the volunteers overnight and at weekends. All workers are involved in the administrative and day-to-day running of the Centre.

A large number of women apply to become 'counsellors', and of these some are selected for training after an 'extensive interview' (LRCC, 1979). Basic counselling skills form an important part of training, whether or not the person has previous counselling experience. Other topics include medical issues, the law, public speaking, the media and role play. Trainees receive personal back-up support throughout training and in the initial stages of the work.

The offence does not have to have been reported to the police before assistance is offered. Indeed, in 1984, 75 per cent of telephone callers to the London RCC had not reported the rape. Moreover, women may ring up shortly after being raped, or months or even years later: the Centre estimates that only about half of all callers contact them within a week of the attack (LRCC, 1982). Consequently, the range of services offered is fairly broad. Primarily, according to a spokeswoman for the LRCC, their aim is to 'respond to what the caller is saying, to listen, offer space, and to believe.' At the same time, the LRCC offers a full information service, offers to arrange appointments at special clinics with female doctors known to them, and is willing to accompany women to the police station to report a rape, or to go with them to a court hearing. If a woman rings up with a query about criminal injuries compensation this can be answered, although the London RCC say they are unlikely to mention the CICB unless asked. Besides these practical services, they can arrange one-to-one counselling sessions. Yet, in fact, most of the emotional support provided is given on the telephone. In 1982, the LRCC reported that half their contacts with women comprised a single telephone call (LRCC, 1982).

Should women decide to call again, continuity with the same worker is not encouraged (although it can be arranged if specifically requested by the caller). There seem to be two reasons for this. Firstly, the London RCC say that workers all hold a collective view, so all will say similar things to the caller. Secondly, its members hold strongly to the principle that women should not come to rely upon the Centre, and encourages them to take the initiative to regain control over their own lives. Callers are exhorted to find someone they can trust in their daily lives. 'We can offer counselling but not friendship' said the spokeswoman for the London Rape Crisis Centre.

The great strengths of RCCs are that most women know of their existence and that some degree of help and support is available to anyone who calls, at any time of the day or night, wherever they live, whenever the offence occurred and whether or not they chose to report the offence. The basic services offered by RCCs (telephone information, advice and support) may help women to understand the event and their feelings about it better, and to take positive steps towards recovery. These services seem particularly well suited to those women who are determined to 'cope' with the aftermath of rape. Some, indeed, may prefer the relatively impersonal relationship of a telephone conversation to that of face-to-face contact.

On the other hand, the RCC model and philosophy may be less suited to other women, and five potential disadvantages need to be considered. First, victims with particular needs and problems are not always able or willing to ask for help (Reeves, 1985), and many may not take the first step of telephoning the RCC at all. Second, if they do ring, they may fail to ask for specific services they need (e.g. face-to-face counselling, accompaniment to special clinic or to court), and as these are not always offered spontaneously over the telephone, they may never receive them. This, possibly, partly explains why many callers make only one call. Third, some rape victims may find it easier to talk to the same person about their feelings than to different people. Fourth, not all women can identify their own 'personal support network', and some may not have or cannot find anyone to whom they can entrust their feelings and problems. And finally, RCCs are unashamedly feminist organisations and some women might be put off contacting them because of this. Moreover, there is, in any case, a question-mark over how far they can help a 'non-feminist' woman towards recovery, even though the spokeswoman for the LRCC said that women can still be helped to deal with feelings of self-blame without realising that feminist views are being offered.

Victims Support services, which will be discussed in detail later, are at present available only to a limited number of women in a limited number of areas, and then only to the minority who report an offence. However, in our view, the major advantage of the VS model for some women is

185

that the Scheme takes the first initiative in offering support. We say this despite the theory held by American rape support groups, and the RCCs to some extent, that everything should be initiated by the victim in order to reassert her control over events. Several women among our interviewees - including two of the five who had received no VSS support - stated that they had felt unable to take the step of telephoning a Rape Crisis Centre, nor were they likely to do so in the future. It is better, we would argue to 'reach out' to such women with an offer of support (and help them to regain control and independence as soon as they are able), rather than to leave them with no assistance at all. Furthermore, the immediacy, frequency and duration of VSS support is potentially more beneficial to many women than the usually short-term nature of contact with a Rape Crisis Centre. Lastly, we would argue, frequent personal contact by an individual volunteer over the first few weeks may be helpful in preventing avoidance behaviour from becoming set into a pattern, a task difficult to assist with purely by telephone. In other words, there seems to be a place for both VSS and RCCs, who may both attract, and be better suited to, different types of people.

(ii)    The referral of rape victims to VSS

We saw in Chapter 2 that only about half of the Schemes and districts existing in mid-1984 ever received referrals of rape cases. One reason for this is that not all Schemes are willing, or have sufficient resources, to take on the considerable amount of work and responsibility involved. Rape victims are likely to need longer-term support than other victims, and the difficult and sensitive nature of the work means that special training and close supervision of volunteers are highly desirable, if not essential. Thus, even though one large, well-established London Scheme had a paid Co-ordinator with the kind of experience and training necessary, the Management Committee did not allow her to accept rape referrals because it feared that her time would then be spent disproportionately with these victims at the expense of others.

In addition to the attitude of Schemes themselves, police confidence in each local Scheme is a crucial factor. In the Metropolitan Police District (one of the forces keenest to see Victims Support involved with rape cases), the force-wide policy now is that the local Detective Chief Inspector must be satisfied that volunteers are 'willing, capable and trained' and have sufficient back-up support to handle these difficult cases. Elsewhere, we found that the referral of rape cases more frequently depended upon the general attitudes of individual senior (and occasionally more junior) officers towards Victims Support. Thus, one Scheme received occasional rape cases on an <u>ad hoc</u> basis through an informal arrangement between the rape squad and the Co-ordinator, and another was given cases unofficially by the referral officer although this had not been formally approved at a higher level. Others were denied <u>any</u> cases (despite requesting them) because the local Chief Inspector feared that it might be alleged in court that volunteers had 'interfered with evidence' by putting ideas into the victim's mind.

In most areas which did refer rape cases, the consent of the rape victim was required before the police would pass on her name to the Scheme. However, not all women were asked if they would like support, it being said by several officers that they were reluctant to refer cases where they doubted the veracity of the reported rape. It is also not known what proportion of women refuse an introduction. This will partly depend on what the police say about the Schemes, and how the victim perceives her treatment by the police. If she has unfavourable views, she may refuse the offer of assistance from a Scheme thought to be closely linked to the police.

The stage at which referral is made to a Scheme tends to be at the discretion of the investigating officer, although in the MPD it is recommended that this should be at the 'earliest possible' appropriate moment. However, while most of the 18 'supported' women we interviewed had been told of the Scheme's existence during their first attendance at the police station, none was visited at the station by a volunteer. And some were not told about the Scheme until up to three days later. Few victims can welcome spending long periods of time at a police station unaccompanied and if a rape victim has no-one with her, we believe that the existence of VSS should be made known to her immediately on arrival. If she wishes (and if the local Scheme is prepared to provide such a service), a volunteer should be asked to attend - not necessarily to be present during questioning, but as a companion during the waiting periods between medical examinations, interviews, etc.[2]

(iii)    Criteria for selecting volunteers

The criteria according to which volunteers are accepted as suitable to support raped women vary widely. Past experience in professions such as social work, the mental health services or nursing, is usually considered desirable although not compulsory. Alternatively, relevant voluntary experience such as bereavement or marriage guidance counselling, or work with Samaritans is regarded as helpful.

Of the large group of participants who attended the London Metropolitan Region's approved training course for rape counsellors, in February 1985, all had this sort of relevant experience, and all had had at least one year's experience of other types of Victims Support work. Nevertheless, some volunteers elsewhere have been dealing with rape cases with relatively little experience or training.

At all the Schemes we visited which accepted rape referrals, the decision whether to accept a volunteer as suitable to undertake the support of rape victims rested with the Co-ordinator. One Co-ordinator said that it was based on a 'gut reaction', depending on whether 'they have seen a bit of life before'. Another said she always had

> 'a long discussion with each intending volunteer to talk about whether the person really wants to be so committed, and whether they are harbouring any of the rape myths which may prejudice and impair the type of service they give'.

This is an important point. During a one-day training conference for potential volunteers for sexual assault support, several participants admitted that they could be shocked by (and even would not understand) the words used by victims in describing details of the rape. Another Co-ordinator reported that the Scheme's only trained volunteer had said about one rape victim 'Well, what did she expect?'. These comments may say more about these volunteers' views on who gets raped, and their suitability as non-judgmental helpers, than they realised. In order to counteract and help with victims' frequently expressed self-blame and guilt, it is essential that volunteers should be supportive and not attribute blame. Thus careful selection of volunteers is imperative, however strong a volunteer's commitment and willingness to get involved may be.

(iv)    Specialist training

Up to mid-1985, VSS-organised specialist training courses for volunteers intending to deal with rape cases were the exception rather than the rule. Our 1984 survey showed that at that time 45 per cent of Schemes had volunteers with some form of special training relevant to the long-term support of victims of serious crime, but most of these had been trained as part of their own profession or in another voluntary organisation. However, there are signs of a growing interest in training for work with rape victims, and Schemes and Regions are now requested to submit proposed training programmes to the National Association for approval.

188

The most common meetings so far have been day conferences, which usually cover fairly preliminary ground and do not pretend to constitute full training in themselves. Even by the end of 1985, few Schemes or Regions had arranged longer programmes (comprising several weekly sessions), though one - Region 10 - had organised a series of weekend training conferences. These are worth examining more closely.

As a prelude to Region 10's weekend course, a Working Party was set up comprising Co-ordinators and volunteers who were already assisting in sexual assault cases, medical professionals specialising in counselling victims of rape, and senior police officers from the MPD Working Party on Sexual Assault. The first (three-day) training conference was held at Hendon Police College. All participants came with the assurance from their respective Management Committees that sufficient back-up support would be provided for specialist trained volunteers after the conference. One of the main topics covered was women's reactions during and following a rape, which emphasised how a breakdown of all learned behaviour often occurs. The audience was warned of the dangers of 'doing too much' for the rape victim since this can take away the control and independence the woman wishes to regain. This is clearly a crucial issue in crisis intervention by any agency and we shall return to it later. Police responses to rape victims were discussed next, and further talks were given on the physical after-effects of rape, and the court ordeal. Participants were prepared for the possibility that in addition to accompanying a woman to court, they might eventually have to appear in the witness box to state their relationship to the chief witness (the rape victim). This has already happened to one VS volunteer, and to several Rape Crisis Centre counsellors.

During the closing stages of the conference, it was empha- sised that the role of Management Committees was going to be crucial in ensuring the provision of sufficient and contin- uing support for volunteers. The Chairman of the Region told the delegates 'You have a right to this support'. However, given the varying degrees of involvement of Manage- ment Committees in the day-to-day work of Schemes (see Chapter 5), it is unlikely that this will be forthcoming in all Schemes. For example, after the conference, one Co- ordinator, when asked who would provide the back-up support for the specialist trained volunteer, gave the alarming response: 'probably no-one, but she's very self-sufficient'. Some are more fortunate. Already three Schemes in North London have collaborated to provide a rape counselling support group, which meets every few months and where prob- lems, current developments, the latest research and their own observations are brought together and discussed.

While these weekend conferences, like three full-morning workshops we attended at a Scheme in a medium-sized town, provided excellent background information about both the effects of rape and the details of police procedures, and helped to sensitise volunteers to the special difficulties of work with rape victims, they continually left in our minds the question of how much training is 'enough'. Does a weekend conference or a short course of weekly sessions provide sufficient preparation? Where should the line be drawn? Certainly, courses of this length leave little space for the development of counselling skills, which are arguably as important as information and knowledge about the consequences and problems of rape. And as far as we are aware, only one Scheme and one Region are devoting further training time to the systematic acquisition of counselling skills.

(v)     The types of support offered to raped women in practice

Rape victims who were supported by VSS volunteers were seen at differing intervals, depending on their family circumstances, the nature of the case and their initial reactions and expressed needs. Most were seen several times in the first week, some every day, and one woman was telephoned hourly at one stage when she was in an extreme state of distress. Some women were also encouraged to telephone the volunteer whenever they needed to talk or wanted some other kind of help. In fact, frequent contact over the first few days was as often occasioned by practical problems as by emotional support.

While the lowest number of visits made by a volunteer to any one victim was four, others typically received between 10 and 20 visits, with several being seen more than 20 times, in addition to numerous conversations on the telephone. The period of support also varied quite a lot. Several volunteers had been encouraged to delineate boundaries with rape victims, advising them how often they would be in contact and until which point support would be given. Quite often, for example, the existence of a court case would be seen as a natural point after which to break contact. However, others were far less rigid about this. One Co-ordinator commented: 'We just can't fix boundaries because we don't know what is going to be thrown up'. In fact, the majority of the women we interviewed had been seeing volunteers for a period of several months.

The kind of emotional help offered usually required at least some basic skills in counselling:

190

'It's got to be a safe enough place for women to pass it
all on, to deposit it in a safe, quiet receptacle.  If
VSS weren't around they'd find someone else probably,
but they may not be as suitable.  Relatives or friends
may not be able to handle the intensity of the feelings
and emotions brought up, and may not have enough time
when needed.  A trained volunteer has undertaken to give
time and to accept the intensity of her emotions, and is
anonymous - where friends or relatives might not be.'

'I say I'm here to use as you want, whatever your needs,
and I try and hear what people want.'

'We must strike a balance between directing their lives
towards restoration and listening.  We must not take
over their lives and must not be directive.  I would
never tell a woman what her decision should be.  I might
encourage her in that direction if she expressed the
wish, but I would not give her my thoughts.'

'We try and rebuild the shattered ego and self-
confidence, and the blame is laid firmly at the rapist's
feet ... There's also a colossal need to talk about it,
but families tire or get bored, and the fact of VS
coming in and going out sometimes helps dispel the myths
and sort of legitimates the experience.'

This last comment underlines the fact that relatives do
not always believe the victim's story in full, and VSS
attention may add credibility to her experience.  We learned
this in a vivid manner when one woman interviewed, who had
not been contacted by a Scheme, said on the day of our
interview ten months after the rape:

'I was talking to my mother this morning about it [i.e.
the facts of the rape], and she implied that until today
she's never really believed me.'

Types of practical help offered by Schemes included
arranging and accompanying women on visits to special
clinics, accompanying them to see their GPs when they felt
too embarrassed or unable to discuss the problem, help with
shopping or other household jobs when the woman was unable
to cope herself, providing support and advice to family and
partners, help with completing compensation forms, liaising
between the victim and the police, assistance with
rehousing, occasionally contacting charities for monetary
help, and accompaniment to court.  Each case raised its own
particular problems, and different agencies were contacted
to suit individual needs.

On average, approximately five external agencies or organisations including the CICB and the police were contacted for each woman supported. Critics might argue that this figure indicates that the volunteers were trying to direct the lives of these women or doing too much for them, rather than helping them regain control over their own lives. However, nearly all of the supported women said they were encouraged to make their own decisions and to play a part in resolving some of the problems arising from the rape. The volunteers also talked sometimes of making 'contracts' with the women or setting 'targets', couched in terms like 'You go and see X or phone Y, while I do Z'. In this way, women were helped to regain their equilibrium, perhaps halting avoidance patterns, such as not wishing to go out, and further loss of confidence or self-esteem. Nevertheless, less experienced volunteers, without adequate support and supervision, could quite easily be tempted to do more for the woman than might be of true benefit to her. Although we had no direct evidence of this, one interviewee said she felt very dependent on the volunteer and did not know 'how they're going to wean me off this'.

## The experiences of rape victims: police, VSS and other sources of support

We have so far examined the ranges of reactions to rape and the kinds of services offered to victims. In this section we turn to the sample of 23 victims whom we interviewed, and examine from their perspective the treatment they received from the police and the support given by VSS, family and other agencies.

### (i)   Treatment by the police

Most of the raped women we interviewed had come into contact with several different police officers, some of whom they felt had treated them very well, others much less so. Ten of the 23 were fully satisfied with the responses of the first officer they had spoken to - usually a PC or WPC responding to a '999' call. The other 13 (i.e. almost 60 per cent), however, expressed some dissatisfaction with the way the responding officer had behaved. Two officers were said to have been 'tactless', one 'inefficient', five 'unsympathetic and inconsiderate' - including two pairs of officers who would not allow the women time to drink the cup of tea that had just been poured for them by relatives - and five had caused the victims to feel that they had been disbelieved. Two of the more critical comments from our interviewees were:

'A WPC came on her own. She said I had got to go to hospital because a lot of people make it up that they've been raped. I was still bleeding from my forehead, and my wrists still had the ties on them. She really was no help at all.'

'Two male PCs came. They were rather tactless and were clearly embarrassed and didn't know really what to say. I was in a terrible state, in pain, and all muddy, and they said "You do know what a rape is, don't you?" '

It seems that responding officers sometimes took it upon themselves to decide if the complaint was 'genuine', acting as the first filter, rather than allowing the investigation to be made by officers more able and trained to deal with such allegations. An example in point:

'One WPC and a PC arrived. The WPC asked very brusquely, "OK, what happened?" I said, "I can't tell you in front of these people", and they were quite hostile to me. Then they rang the station and said "OK, it is rape", as if they'd seen forty cases that day. I was sobbing my heart out at the time, and I was amazed that they didn't believe me to begin with. Later they told me, "We get so many false accusations." '

The officers who took down victims' statements seem to have been generally more sympathetic, with seven victims positively praising their tact or 'considerate' attitude. Even so, six had some criticisms: two had felt disbelieved, three had felt that they were being blamed for the rape, and one had found the officer 'tactless'. Only about half of the officers taking statements had been female, but, contrary to our expectations, by no means all women preferred to see a female officer. Similarly, most of the (usually more senior) officers responsible for the investigation, who had questioned them at length, were regarded as reasonably courteous and sympathetic, although there were three major exceptions.

The overall diversity of police responses and attitudes - often within the same police station - is reflected in some of the following statements by victims:

'I felt all along that I was on trial and I said so three times during the statement. She had no compassion and made me feel a lot worse.'

'The police were smashing, they couldn't do enough for me.'

'They were lovely, I can't find fault with them at all. They got British Telecom round straightaway to reconnect the phone wires, stayed with me for a couple of hours, and rang one of my sons to come and look after me.'

'At the first police station, two CID officers questioned me in a corridor. One was nice, but the other one wasn't. He said "Has enough time passed for you to make a joke about it yet?", and told me I was wearing a provocative red T-shirt and shorts. It was a hot August night, and I'd been raped in my flat by strangers.'

'I was shaking all the time and couldn't stop, and wanted to cry but couldn't. The police offered me breakfast and coffee and gave me four glasses of brandy. I really appreciated that gesture and didn't get drunk.'

'After seven hours she was getting tired and wanted to go home. She kept saying "Did you resist?" over and over again. That puts you very much on the defensive, and it's outrageous that you're made to feel guilty, when you've been a total victim.'

'An arrogant DS interviewed me. I wanted to say 'vagina' and 'penis' and he said "No, no, no, just use your normal language." '

'They were really nice. The WPC was more choked than me and later the DI dropped me at my mum's place. He spoke to mum about the effects (of rape) and told her I should go for VD tests. He was brilliant.'

'Before I started talking there were several male officers sitting around casually on window-sills. I felt they just wanted to listen to a juicy story, so I protested and they left then.'

'They treated me with great understanding and accepted what I said. They didn't make me feel as if they thought I was lying, which is almost what I expected. I had plenty of coffee while I was there, it was really relaxing. In fact, X [the DS involved] together with Y of VS, helped to get me moved within three weeks of it happening.'
(This last statement came from a prostitute.)

The police surgeon's forensic examination was recalled as an unpleasant experience by six of our interviewees, who variously described the surgeon as 'cold', 'nasty' or having 'no compassion'. An equal number, however, thought the

194

surgeons were 'sensitive', 'warm', 'reassuring' or 'informative'. An improvement suggested by several was that more information imparted in a warmer manner would ease the necessary unpleasantness of this examination. Many were upset and distressed at not being able to wash afterwards, and thought that such facilities should be routinely provided. One woman lamented:

> 'I felt terribly bedraggled. I wanted to wash and comb my hair and freshen up, and all these different people were looking at me. It was very distressing to be on show, but not ready for it.'

Over half of the women were seen by a male police surgeon, and few of these had been asked if they had a preference for a female. (And most of those that were asked were warned that there would be a long delay waiting for a female.) Eleven examinations took place in a police station cell or office, ten in a GP's surgery, and one in the victim's home. Of those examined in a police station, five expressed discontent. In two instances, uniformed police officers walked into the unlocked office, in another two, the door was 'ajar', and in the other case the woman was examined in a police cell by torchlight! Clearly, recent efforts to provide proper examination suites for rape victims are both very welcome and overdue.

Our research clearly supports the findings of Chambers and Millar (1984) in Scotland regarding the necessity for more attention to be paid to the prevalence of 'rape myths' and unsympathetic attitudes to victims among police officers of all ranks, as well as to the treatment of women in police stations after they have reported a rape. It is, of course, recognised that most of the women we interviewed had been raped in 1984, and that considerable efforts have been made to improve matters since then. Perhaps the main point to emerge from this section is that our interviewees were more critical of the officers responding to their calls than of the investigating officers later - a finding which helps justify the involvement (as occurs in several areas) of VSS members in the training of ordinary PCs, as well as of officers likely to be deeply involved in rape investigations. For instance, several London Co-ordinators give regular talks at Hendon Police Training College. Finally, we would emphasise again the value of mentioning VSS to victims early and allowing volunteers, if wished by the victim, to be present at the police station early on. While a few of our supported rape victims did have a personal friend or partner to wait for them, four of the 14 who were unaccompanied said that they would have liked a volunteer to have been at the station with them.

(ii)   VSS support and assistance

(a)   The extent of help given

   Seventeen of the 18 rape victims we interviewed who had
received VSS support had nothing but praise for the
volunteer and the Scheme. Some, indeed, felt that without
the help they would have been in a seriously disturbed
psychological state. (The only dissenting voice came from a
woman who said she 'had a feeling that I was seeing her to
satisfy her rather than me'.) The main help given, they
felt, was in terms of friendship, advice, and above all the
ability to discuss the offence and its aftermath without any
embarrassment or blame. However, the practical help given
was also mentioned by many as extensive.

   Practical assistance was most important over the first few
days or weeks, when it was said by several victims to have
eased their emotional distress and helped them regain some
'equilibrium'. The following are fairly typical stories,
illustrating how much was done for a large proportion of
these victims.

   One woman, a 67 year-old grandmother, burgled and raped in
her bedroom by a group of youths, said:

> 'X came the same day. She gave me £10 because
> everything had been stolen. She came regularly in the
> first three weeks because so  much needed sorting out.
> Then Y started coming, and I've seen her every second
> Tuesday since then, in an informal way now though
> [eighteen months later]. They contacted the DHSS to
> sort out my next pension payment, and got the DHSS to
> give me some money for a new bed [because of her
> physical disabilities]. They wrote to the Gas Board
> about the meter, but eventually they arranged for Social
> Services to pay the bill. They got in touch with a
> locksmith recommended by the Crime Prevention Officer,
> and got a charity to pay the locksmith, helped with a
> compensation  claim and got in touch with the Housing
> Welfare Officer for me, and eventually helped me with
> the move.'

A 47 year-old divorcee, raped in her bedroom, reported:

> 'I just hit it off with her from the word go. The thing
> is she knows about rape, which is terribly important.
> She came and 'phoned frequently over the first weeks,
> and I sometimes called her. She sometimes came with her
> husband and I could talk to him too, probably because he
> was an older man, so I wasn't embarrassed. They got a

bed for me, so that I could sleep in a neighbour's flat for a while, and she came with me to tell my boss what had happened. I just couldn't face that on my own, but I'm glad I did it, because my memory was letting me down at work and it was being noticed. She certainly speeded up my rehousing and she and the police actually helped to move me. She eventually recommended I see a psychiatrist, so I decided to take a crash course of six sessions, and this helped me a lot in weighing up the essence of my problems and getting things into perspective. Finally, she came with me to court, which I found a great help.'

A young, separated wife and mother, who was raped at knifepoint in her bed, recalled:

'The following week she took me to the Housing Department and they offered me a flat. We went to see it together but I thought it was horrible. Since then I've been going myself to the Council every week and now I've been to see my MP. In the meantime, X has come with me to a local housing association office and we're keeping in close touch about the move I want. She's also helped me over the compensation claim.'

This woman successfully achieved her move soon afterwards, and her comment illustrates the way that VS can encourage women to help themselves, through sharing the load and offering reinforcement for their own efforts.

A 49 year-old wife commented:

'X was colossal, she came with me to my GP to get some medication, she brought me three handbags to choose from to replace the one stolen, she helped sort out the compensation claim for me, and she got me some money from a charity. I decided not to press charges because I couldn't face a court trial, but she still kept coming to see me and we still speak on the phone now and again.'

A 19 year-old single woman remembered:

'She told my mother about the VD appointment. It didn't sound so bad coming from her. I wouldn't have made the appointment myself, I was petrified. I'm glad now that I went with her, it wasn't a bad experience. She offered to clear up the mess in my flat, but I wanted to do this myself. She came with me to look at the photos [of suspects] and kept in touch with the police for me, and I'm sure she got more information than I would have got. She later advised me over the complaint I wanted to make against the police treatment I received, and wrote a covering letter for me.'

(This latter point is interesting since it illustrates the willingness of some volunteers to demonstrate their independence from the police, despite their frequently close relationships with them.)

As noted, some women were accompanied to court by a volunteer. Indeed, all seven supported women who appeared as witnesses accepted this offer made by the Schemes, and there was among them some preference for accompaniment by VS members rather than by family or friends. For example, one woman (accompanied by a volunteer) still partly blamed the presence of her boyfriend for the acquittal of the defendant, since she reported:

'I didn't want him to be there, but he insisted on coming, and I don't think I did as well as I could have done, because I felt awkward at him listening.'

Most women said the experience had been worse than they had anticipated, and attached great importance to the presence of the volunteer:

'I definitely wouldn't have gone to court if it hadn't been for her.'

'The most important thing they did for me was having someone to sit in court with me. I don't think I could have faced it on my own and I had no-one else to come with me. I felt much more confident because she had had experience of other cases.'

'I'm not looking forward to this, and can only handle it because X will be there.'

'She was like a sister to me, I'm so glad she was there, sitting next to me.'

These not untypical stories illustrate the immense amount of trouble taken to assist rape victims with practical problems - a level far beyond what is normally carried out for victims of other crimes, including quite serious non-sexual assaults (see Chapter 6). This raises the possibility that Schemes are falling into the trap of 'doing too much' for rape victims. Certainly, several told us how they had telephoned the volunteer frequently during the first month or so - even in the middle of the night - and how the volunteer had immediately come to see them. On the other hand, there was little evidence of this continuing for long periods, and hence of 'overdependence'. We did, however, note warning signs in a few instances. One point that we did find striking was the depth of the relationships achieved between some women and their supporters, illustrating how contact might be severely missed once formal support ends:

'I felt we had a genuine friendship. She never let me down and came regularly and was so supportive.'

'Her emotional counselling was the best, and I would have liked her as a friend rather than as a counsellor.'

These comments make the case for delineating boundaries of the contact much stronger in order to prevent any further feelings of loss to the victim, but as noted earlier not all volunteers and Schemes agreed that the parameters of victim-volunteer contact should be agreed in advance.

(b)    A substitute for family support?

Rape may not only represent a crisis for the victim; it may also be a crisis for those around her, particularly a partner. Families can feel at a loss to cope with the intensity of the woman's feelings, and may be struggling to cope with their own. Frequently, they will be too embarrassed to talk about it, particularly when there is a generation gap, like a son to his mother. And they may hide behind the misconception that if they do not talk about the rape she may get over it faster or the problem will go away. Recovery frequently takes longer than many people believe, and friends, families and employers may get impatient when that recovery seems slow.

Interviewees reported that volunteers supplemented whatever kind of support was given by families and friends, but, sadly, there was often no-one else but the volunteer to give the sort of help really needed:

'I had lots of moral support, but not a listening ear as such. My family were very embarrassed. It's not really something you talk to your daughter about, and my son-in-law has never mentioned it. I don't know how I would have survived without X.'

'I want my family to come and see me, so I don't want to bore them with my troubles. I couldn't talk to my family about it and after the first day they never mentioned it again, for fear of upsetting me so I never referred to it again either. One son told me not to mention my "little bit of trouble" to my sister. This still bothers me and I wonder if he, and are all of them, ashamed of me? On the other hand, I can't speak too highly of X. She's so understanding and sensitive and has been very helpful, and she's been the only person I could confide in.'

'My family and friends weren't much help. To begin with my parents didn't know what to say, and then my mother said "don't let the neighbours know". Later she said "It's eight months now, what's the matter with you?". The girlfriend of the guy who attacked me has threatened to get me, and even one of my other friends said "Come on, I bet you enjoyed it". X pushed me through the worst time like trying to get me enthusiastic about decorating my flat, which she helped me get. It was a great comfort, knowing I could call on her any time of day or night, especially since I'd been turned away by everybody else.'

'It's a big weight to carry around, and I've had enough of people avoiding the topic. I keep saying oblique things like "Oh, the police said this and this to me" and they neatly sidestep. What annoys me is that when I want to talk about it, they don't respond to my cues. That makes me feel guilty about it ..... it's for their sakes they don't want to talk about it, not mine. It's as if they're saying "Don't bring that in here". With X, it's so different, I feel I can say exactly what I want.'

'I phoned my mother a few days later and that was terrible. I gave her X's number, and she rang and spoke to X for one and a half hours. I was so pleased because my mother wanted to help but it was so embarrassing and X gave her advice and told her how I was feeling.'

The reactions of male partners to the rape were especially diverse, and not always helpful to the woman. One woman, happily married prior to the rape two years previously, said:

'We were very close before, now we seem to be miles apart. We still love each other very much, but now that love has changed. The physical side of things has disappeared now. He doesn't complain, but then we don't talk about it, you're frightened to ask.'

Another (who was eventually able to ask VS for professional help for her partner's problem) recalled:

200

'At the time I was expecting support from him, but knew
he couldn't give it, and I felt he needed help and I
couldn't give it. VS were potentially there, and X
[from VS] was aware of the situation, but I was trying
to cope with it on my own.'

Anger and upset towards wives and girlfriends for having
allowed it to happen is another type of male response, and
the victim may feel as if she is being blamed for the
offence. Male guilt and responsibility may also be demonstrated occasionally in remarks such as, 'If only I hadn't
allowed you to go to your mother's, this wouldn't have
happened'. This supports the 'wife as property' thesis (see
for example, Stanko, 1984) where the male feels his goods
have been devalued and that it is a crime against him not
her. As a result men may even take to the streets to search
for the rapist, and three interviewees stated that their
partners or close male relations had responded in this way.

The following stories exemplify some of these male
reactions.

'He was more interested in his own feelings and with
getting his own revenge. He wasn't very concerned for
my feelings and what I'd been through. He didn't
understand really and wasn't much support to me, so we
agreed to split up for a couple of months. Afterwards,
whenever we argued, it always came back to the rape.
I'm sure it was because of that we eventually broke up
eighteen months later.'

'I rather wish I hadn't had my family's support. My
husband didn't understand, he has male attitudes, which
are different from mine. He often got very angry and
upset and locked me out at night, and my son went
berserk and ended up in hospital with a broken arm ... I
never blamed myself, but my husband did, he told me the
court would have said I'd arranged a secret assignation
with our neighbour, the rapist, because of the problems
in our marriage ... He said he'd clobber me if I took it
further, so I dropped charges.'

Return to normal functioning for the rape victim may often
be contingent on the recovery of close partners in her life.
Supporters can and do listen to and advise relations about
their own likely responses and how they can help the woman,
but male partners and relatives may find it easier and more
beneficial to talk to a man. However, there are few males
trained for this kind of work in the ranks of VSS
volunteers, and we feel that programmes for male volunteers
should become more widely established.

Finally, one woman succinctly summed up the differences between the support she had received from VS and the support of her family, and she probably speaks for others:

> 'The differences are that Victims Support are not embarrassed, they're quite objective, and aren't shocked or disgusted. They're well informed in their knowledge while friends and family aren't. I'm nothing to them because there was no relationship before, which helps. They don't take things personally, so I know I'm not losing a friend if I'm irritable and moody with them. When I say how I'm feeling they say "I'm not surprised", which is most important to me. It means "I recognise that" and is much better than the alternative approach of some of my friends of "Oh, don't be silly". Lastly, VS aren't like normal people - they don't talk about themselves. It's not like a friend where you have 50-50 each of the conversation. They just grunt every so often. I asked them why and they said so that I don't lose the thread of what I'm trying to say or express, which I frequently do with my friends.'

(iii)    Victims without VSS support

The five victims who had not been referred to Schemes all had problems which would almost certainly have been dealt with successfully if they had received VSS assistance. For example, three of them wished to move house, but one had not felt able to organise a move herself and another had been waiting two months for the Detective Inspector to write a letter on her behalf 'which they said they would do', and was distressed about the apparent lack of action. The other woman had eventually found a friend who offered her a room, six months after a letter to the local Council had yielded no positive response. Yet no fewer than nine (half) of the group referred to VSS had moved house with active assistance from Schemes.

Few of the VSS-supported women had been informed of their right to apply for criminal injuries compensation by the police, but all but one had applied after information or assistance was given by VSS volunteers. Among the five victims not contacted by a Scheme, the police had helped one with the completion of the form, and another had made a claim with the assistance of a solicitor, after learning of the CICB 'purely by chance'. The other three had not even realised that there was a possibility of a successful claim.

The court experience is invariably feared, but the terror in the faces and in the words of the three 'unsupported' women waiting to be witnesses was almost palpable, and was

202

far more intense than in those who were to be accompanied by a volunteer. Although their families intended to come and give them 'moral support' at court, this was not seen as particularly soothing: indeed, one had even asked the police to make sure her family were not allowed in. Another said:

> 'I'm terrified of going alone, and also not knowing about all the procedures and so forth, and while I want their moral support, I get into a panic every time I think about it because I don't think I shall give very good evidence what with my mother, brothers, sisters and daughter sitting there, but I don't think I can face going on my own.'

When at the end of our interview the non-supported group (only one of whom had heard of the organisation before that point) were asked if they would have liked Victims Support, the three facing being witnesses at a trial all said they would have liked advice from a Scheme about what to expect and to be accompanied to court.

For those not given emotional support by a VSS volunteer, one alternative source of help could be a Rape Crisis Centre. All five women not supported by a VSS knew of the latter's existence and three had been offered their telephone number by the police. Only one actually contacted a Centre. This victim insisted on speaking to the same person for the first three telephone calls and said 'she was wonderful'. She then asked about counselling and went to see them:

> 'The counsellor didn't suit me so well as the first woman I spoke to so I didn't bother going back, and got myself a professional counsellor elsewhere. They had such a fortress attitude to the world and reinforced my own fearfulness. The women there seemed to feel that the whole world was a threat to them, but you need help and hope, not to think that everyone's out to get you.'

Two other non-supported women felt daunted by the prospect of asking for help, a 24 year-old remarking that:

> 'I really wanted support to be on my doorstep. I didn't want to go and look for it. Rape Crisis leave it to your initiative to contact them, but I didn't have any to begin with. I was like a zombie. It would have been more helpful if they'd come to me ... I was also scared to get in touch with them, they seem like a big organisation and a bit formal.'

About a month after the rape this same woman plucked up courage to go and see a counsellor she knew at the Brook Advisory Centre for Young People, who was found to be very sympathetic. But she added:

> 'I only saw her once because she hasn't got much time and the gap between appointments had to be two weeks, and that was too long for me. I wanted to talk for two weekends consecutively ... I needed some continuity, someone with some time regularly.'

Only three women from the VSS-supported group had contacted Rape Crisis Centres - all before seeing the VSS volunteer. Two reported negative phone calls, saying 'they were totally useless' and 'I didn't like people telling me what emotional reaction I should have', while the other reported that she was very pleased and comforted by the call, saying 'I talked to her for hours, and she really calmed me down.'

## Discussion

At the beginning of this chapter we asked whether, in view of the serious and lasting psychological effects experienced by many rape victims, the support of raped women should be entrusted to volunteers, or whether instead there should be a fully-fledged professional service readily available to all victims at any stage post-rape. Duddle (1985), for example, advocates the incorporation within major hospitals of a network of 'sexual assault centres', with both medical and counselling services available to any woman who requests them. In an era of less financial stringency, we would have no hesitation in strongly supporting this: after all, why should people who are seriously damaged by rape have to rely upon the public-spiritedness of individual volunteers? Unfortunately, a realistic appraisal of current policies and attitudes suggests that, for the foreseeable future, there will be little choice: put crudely, it is volunteers or nothing. This being the case, the first priorities are (a) to ensure that the voluntary service offered is of the highest quality possible, and (b) that some professional help is available as a 'back up', at least for the most serious cases.

In fact, our research with Victims Support Schemes leads us to conclude that voluntary help can be both of a high standard and beneficial to victims. While we cannot tell for certain whether the VSS intervention actually speeded recovery from rape, the accounts of all the supported women strongly suggested that it had considerably eased their distress. In addition, most felt that they had begun to regain the control over their lives that they lost through being raped: volunteers had encouraged them to take an active role in dealing with their problems and in some cases to set themselves behavioural targets to achieve by specific dates, in order to prevent avoidance behaviours from becoming firmly established. Thus, Victims Support appeared to make a normal recovery more likely within a reasonable period than if no assistance had been available.

It is also possible that, for some victims, the informality of the VSS service may be preferable to the kind of centre suggested by Duddle. Reluctance actively to seek professional help has been documented elsewhere (King and Webb, 1981; Kilpatrick, 1983) and it is known that for some the idea has the connotation of being 'thought to be mad'. If such victims do eventually need professional counselling, they are more likely to accept it (and to have the chance of locating it) after a period with a volunteer We therefore conclude that, providing other groups of volunteers adopt the same kinds of scrupulous and self-critical attitudes towards the maintenance of standards that were displayed by those we studied, the expansion of Victims Support services to more rape victims would be a valuable and welcome development.

In saying this, we would argue firmly that, whatever the pressure from Management Committees or local police for supporters to offer help to rape victims, scrutiny in selecting volunteers must not be relaxed. Not all, even if willing, are suitable for this type of work. It is most important that intending supporters do not hold any 'rape myths' and common stereotyped attitudes, which may cause further damage to the victim. They must also have explored and come to feel comfortable with their own feelings and attitudes towards sex. Judging by the statements of victims, we found that these standards had been met by the Schemes in the areas in which we carried out fieldwork.

Further, we are in no doubt that the support of rape victims requires skills beyond those normally imparted in basic training for Victims Support work. The sorts of skills required in many cases are of the kind used by trained counsellors. In particular, supporters must be fully aware of the dangers of inadvertently encouraging dependency in the raped women, and of being tempted to 'do too much' for victims - as illustrated by the interviewee who said, 'I don't know how they're going to wean me off this'. Acquisition of these skills also helps supporters to select and set 'targets' or to make 'contracts' with the raped women, so that they can progress - and see themselves progressing - steadily towards a return to normal functioning. And, most important of all, a fundamental training in counselling skills enables volunteers to understand the limits of what they themselves can and should do. We feel particularly that non-professional counsellors should not attempt to resolve serious sexual and other difficulties between husbands and wives. Here, professionals are called for.

So far - and understandably, considering the relatively short time for which VSS have been involved in rape cases - the level of training has been inadequate in most areas. We found ten Schemes whose volunteers had taken on rape cases with no special training at all. Even weekend conferences and workshops, we are certain, although very useful for imparting general knowledge about the subject, do not in themselves equip a volunteer to support rape victims. Although we recognise that, with mutual support and sharing of experience, several groups of volunteers with little formal training have gradually accumulated considerable expertise in supporting rape victims, this carries too many risks to be recommended as a model to be followed universally. It seems to us imperative that, unless volunteers have experience of counselling from work in other fields, they should receive extra training in counselling skills. Ideally, this would be supplied in properly planned courses with qualified trainers, and would last <u>at least</u> ten weeks. It is recognised that, at present, it is difficult to find the resources and the personnel to set up such courses, but by pooling resources, groups of neighbouring Schemes, with help from the Region, should be able to develop them over time. Indeed, we understand that one has already been successfully concluded in Sussex.

In addition to more intensive training, close supervision and support of specialist volunteers is essential. First, this reduces the risk of volunteers becoming too deeply entangled with victims' problems or becoming too 'directive' in giving advice. Secondly, it gives Schemes more chance of monitoring effectively the progress of a victim's recovery. Warning signs of an abnormal response or very slow recovery may not always be heeded by volunteers, and it can be difficult to judge at what stage a woman might require professional help. This is one of the reasons why we consider that back-up medical advice by a professional consultant linked with the Scheme should always be available. At some Schemes visited, the qualified supervisor or Co-ordinator usually met the victim first in order to assess the likelihood of serious problems arising, and so that she gained an idea of the difficulties the volunteer would be likely to experience in giving support.

She also made occasional follow-up visits to women she was particularly concerned about. These practices seem particularly sensible, as they enable supervisors to monitor cases directly rather than at second hand. And thirdly, like other professionals engaged in emotionally demanding, distressing and painful work, volunteers need support in order both to protect their own emotional well-being and to help them give of their best in helping the victim. It is vital for them to have regular 'unburdening' sessions with a supporter or support group themselves: no volunteer should be left in the position of the one mentioned earlier, whose Co-ordinator, when asked what support had been arranged for the volunteer, was heard to reply that 'she's very self-sufficient.'

Of course, all this raises the sticky problem of who should carry out the supervision. All the Schemes from which we drew our sample of rape victims had Co-ordinators with either relevant professional experience and/or with accredited counselling qualifications. It is not known to what extent this accounts for the overwhelmingly favourable picture of the VSS service which emerged from the interviews, although we suspect it had some influence. It is known, however, that not all Schemes which accept rape cases have a suitably experienced or qualified person in the role of overseer or supporter of volunteers, and here the quality of the supervision is almost certainly lower. Both the importance of the work and the dangers of doing damage to vulnerable people lead us strongly to the conclusion that in any Scheme handling rape cases, the regular supervisor should have an appropriate counselling qualification or relevant professional experience. Where this is not presently so, we feel that government funds should be made available to enable such people to acquire an accredited counselling qualification.

It should be noted, finally, that this supervising role need not go to 'the Co-ordinator'. At present, already over-pressed Co-ordinators usually take on the highly demanding role of main supporter and supervisor of specialist volunteers. Clearly, there is a real danger of other victims and other volunteers suffering relative neglect as a consequence. The obvious - though possibly more expensive - alternative is for large Schemes which accept significant numbers of rape referrals to divide duties between two Co-ordinators - one to supervise the support of rape victims (and other cases needing long-term support), the other with responsibility for all other referrals. Again, some neighbouring Schemes could co-operate and perhaps work under one supervisor of rape cases. In similar vein, there is no reason, too, why some volunteers could not be permanently deployed assisting rape victims. We believe that this is essential work, of the highest priority for VSS, and deserving, above all else, of financial and other assistance from central and local government.


## Notes to Chapter 7

1. This latter group consisted of the victims of five of the seven rape cases dealt with by four different senior police officers during the previous year (the other two victims had moved and could not be contacted).

2. Following the suggestion of Blair (1985), some police divisions in London have altered the traditional practice of keeping victims at the police station for many hours on their first visit, and now allow them to go home quite early for a rest period and to return the next day for fuller questioning about the event. In this case, the need for a volunteer on the first visit is reduced, but the second visit affords a good occasion for the victim to be introduced to a volunteer. We understand that this already occurs in some areas. We also understand that at some other stations, at the victim's request, volunteers have been present during medical examinations and even during questioning. The latter, however, does raise questions about the relationship between the police and VSS, and seems to demand careful thought.

# 8 Discussion, conclusions and summary of findings

## Problems of evaluation

One of our primary objectives in embarking upon this project was to 'evaluate the work of Victims Support Schemes'. However, this has turned out to be a very difficult and complex task. First of all, Schemes are not branches of NAVSS working to a 'blueprint', but independent units, whose aims, ideas and practices vary enormously. Secondly, the Victims Support movement is growing and changing rapidly, and almost any general statement one makes about it is liable to be out of date by the time it is published. And thirdly, as with all voluntary organisations, it is difficult to decide by what standards to judge a Scheme's 'performance'.

Underlying this last point are fundamental questions about the extent to which victims of crime are entitled to expect assistance, and how far the state has any responsibility for ensuring that they receive it. The kinds and quality of services provided for victims, the numbers of victims who receive them, and the criteria by which the performance of those delivering them should be assessed, all depend crucially upon the answers to these questions. Broadly speaking, there are three alternative approaches that can be adopted, as follows:

(i) The support of victims may be seen purely as a charitable act - a humanitarian response to people in trouble. Under this view, there is no obligation on anyone to provide services and the work of VSS may be regarded as a 'bonus', a 'nice surprise'. The idea of 'evaluating performance' is itself fairly foreign to this conception, and it might be seen as inappropriate to measure performance in terms of, for example, how close a Scheme comes to meeting all the needs in its area. Evaluation might instead be limited to issues such as the efficiency with which the organisation uses whatever resources it happens to have, and whether or not those supported appreciate the service and make a speedy recovery.

(ii) The support of victims may alternatively be regarded as the satisfaction of an important 'social need', a necessary service on a par with those provided either statutorily or by major voluntary agencies such as Marriage Guidance Councils or Citizens' Advice Bureaux. In this case, the criteria for evaluation have to include more demanding questions about the level and standards of the service provided. It becomes important to look at, for example, the capacity of the relevant agency for identifying and reaching those who need its services; its standards of training, organisation, supervision and record-keeping; and the general quality and efficiency of its service delivery. This, however, is complicated by the question of available resources - in the case of VSS often an uncertain and fluctuating situation - and it can be argued that it is the responsibility of the government to ensure that sufficient funds are granted to make it possible to deliver at least a minimum level of service to all those deemed to have a certain level of 'need' (however defined).

(iii) It is also possible to adopt a 'rights'-based approach and argue that it is incumbent upon the state to ensure that certain responses are made to all victims, regardless of needs. Some of these responses could be put on a statutory basis, such as making it a duty of the police or courts to inform victims of relevant arrests or court appearances (Mawby, 1984; Shapland, 1986), although it is difficult to imagine statutory entitlements to most 'VSS-type' services.[1] Nevertheless, it can be argued that a victims' services agency should act as if such entitlements did exist, and, indeed, should play a part in campaigning for 'victims' rights' in general. Thus, the view is held by some in the Victims Support organisation that, with or without state assistance, the objective of the movement should be to contact every victim with an expression of sympathy and an offer of services if required. Evaluation based on such a view would have to include the question of whether Schemes can realistically hope ever to achieve such an ambitious task. It might also be asked whether NAVSS has been playing a sufficiently active role in promoting victims' rights vis-a-vis the criminal justice system as a whole (e.g. in matters of compensation, treatment by the courts, etc).

At present, the Victims Support movement seems to be in a period of transition - and to some extent, conflict - between the first and second approaches above. There is still a strong 'charitable' tradition at grass-roots level, which, many would argue, provides a great deal of the strength and appeal of the movement to ordinary people. At the same time, NAVSS, in company with many of the more 'professionally' organised Schemes, is continually pushing for expansion of services and the attainment of higher and more consistent standards, aimed ultimately at effectively meeting all the serious needs existing countrywide. An integral part of this drive is the effort to persuade the government to provide adequate funds to give each Scheme an organisational base - mainly in the person of a paid Co-ordinator - capable of taking on the task.

However, as the government has not taken on special responsibility for the welfare needs of victims (beyond, that is, the CICB scheme and small grants to NAVSS), many Schemes which have become convinced of the need to achieve particular standards or to provide a comprehensive service have been trying to do a 'semi-professional' job with an 'amateur's' resources. Any assessment of their achievement cannot be separated from the fundamental stresses and limitations imposed by this problem.

In the face of these complications, our main task in this final chapter is to produce some broad evaluations of the work of Victims Support Schemes from a number of different perspectives.

## Broad assessments

Evaluated purely in terms of the results of visits by volunteers to individual victims, there is no doubt that the Schemes we studied achieved their aims successfully. The great majority of victims we interviewed had welcomed the gesture, and a substantial minority believed that the support or assistance provided had significantly affected their recovery. This belief was supported to some extent by the results of our 'matching' exercise (Chapter 6).

The success of letters or telephone calls, either as expressions of 'caring' or as ways of persuading seriously affected victims to ask for a follow-up visit, was more limited, but in both cases, at very little cost, at least some victims were reached who would otherwise have received no attention at all. Telephone calls annoyed a number of victims, and both telephone calls and letters left some misunderstandings about what the Scheme was and what it was offering.  It is possible that attention both to 'telephone manner' and to the wording of letters might reduce these problems a little.

Evaluated in terms of their use of resources, Schemes can be said to perform very effectively in some areas, but not in others.  First, there is little doubt that they provide 'value for money'.  Responses to an NAVSS questionnaire in December 1984 revealed that Schemes had spent on average only £2,000 on running costs during the previous year, excluding any salaries or rent, and that those with paid Co-ordinators had spent an additional £10,000 each on salaries and/or rent.  We calculate from these figures that at that time, over all Schemes, and including all salaries and overheads, the average cost per referral was somewhere in the region of £8.  (Or, alternatively, the average cost per victim seen in person by a volunteer was about £20.)[2]  The 'cheapest' Schemes in these terms were those based in large urban areas which had voluntary Co-ordinators working from home:  here, high numbers of referrals were dealt with at apparently minimal cost.  However, this ignores the unquantified costs of the stress and disruption to such Co-ordinators' lives (Chapter 5).  Moreover, costs in most Schemes in our experience were considerably reduced by supporting agencies (such as the Probation Service) or by the generosity of sympathetic to individuals: some were given the use of offices at nominal rent[3], had photocopying done for nothing, trainers' fees waived, and so on, while (less desirably) it was common for volunteers to forego travel expenses and one Co-ordinator had not taken her honorarium.  In fact, it was calculated from a small NAVSS survey in 1982 that 43 per cent of Schemes' administrative costs were absorbed by supporting agencies or individual members (NAVSS, 1985).

Secondly, however, use of the other major 'resource' - volunteers - was less efficient than it might have been. Several we interviewed stated that they were not being given as many cases as they would have liked, and some felt they had been either 'forgotten' or 'deliberately ignored' for long periods.  This was true even in Schemes with large numbers of referrals.  Some Co-ordinators - understandably, given their own workload - tended to give cases perceived to be urgent to those volunteers most easily contactable, to those who 'always said yes', or to those thought to be most capable, and then to write letters to many of the remaining victims.  The result was sometimes a wide imbalance in volunteer workload and dissatisfaction among those under-used.  The most successful use of volunteers was observed in Schemes which used rota systems, so that everybody knew when to expect to be called out and made themselves readily contactable and available at those times (or, if not, let the Co-ordinator know so that a 'reserve' could take their place).

On average, the volunteers we interviewed put their 'ideal' workload at about one new case per week, while our survey revealed that volunteers across the country averaged one new case per fortnight. This suggests that there is considerable scope for more efficient use of the existing manpower.

A related problem, found particularly in large Schemes based in inner city areas, was a high turnover of volunteers. This seemed to be partly due to a lack of recognition, among Management Committees and Co-ordinators, of the importance of maintaining morale among people working in a difficult area, and of encouraging a sense of identity with the Scheme. Many volunteers were simply given names and addresses at irregular intervals and left to work on their own. Few Schemes insisted that they report back on every case, and some either held volunteer support meetings only infrequently or did not 'sell' them to volunteers as important to attend. Moreover, several such meetings we observed were run somewhat aimlessly, with nobody quite sure of their purpose. The most successful were those in which a leader (not necessarily the Co-ordinator) systematically encouraged each volunteer to discuss his or her recent cases, as well as to raise any fears, anxieties or problems connected with the work; in some Schemes, too, volunteer meetings often constituted 'further training', with guest speakers and special topics for discussion. Finally, only a few Schemes used suitable volunteers to help Co-ordinators with 'paperwork' or to join the Management Committee and assist with, for example, recruitment, training or fund-raising. Such mixing of roles could do much to bring together the three elements of the 'tri-partite' structure, reducing mutual misunderstanding and leading to better knowledge of the part that each 'section' plays.

Evaluated more strictly in terms of organisational efficiency, record-keeping, monitoring of their own activities, etc., Schemes varied enormously. One of the most common weaknesses was the failure of volunteers to return forms describing visits made to victims. In some cases, more than 50 per cent of such forms were not returned. In others, volunteers kept them at home for long periods, returning a batch perhaps three months old when they next attended a Scheme meeting. And almost everywhere, some volunteers did not bother to record the fact that they had not managed to contact particular victims assigned to them. These omissions arose mainly from a failure of Scheme

213

organisers to make clear to volunteers either the purpose or the importance of completing forms and, indeed, a widespread failure to use them to monitor the work of the Scheme. Most Schemes measured their performance in terms of numbers of referrals received: it was far more difficult -indeed, normally impossible without 'chasing' volunteers - for them to produce the more important measures of how many victims had been visited, what problems had been found, and what the Scheme had done for those it had seen. Moreover, few Co-ordinators used report forms to monitor and supervise the work of individual volunteers - for example, to note patterns in how they dealt with cases (as with one volunteer we noticed who almost invariably gave 'security advice', but rarely made any mention of victims' emotional reactions) or to suggest that they go back and see victims with particular problems.

However, the major organisational weakness, in our experience, was reflected in the tendency of Management Committees to leave far too much of the work of the Scheme to their Co-ordinator. As described in Chapter 5, a large proportion of Committee members saw their role primarily as that of attending meetings to represent another organisation, and many had only superficial knowledge of the day-to-day work of the Scheme. Apart from the Officers (Chairman, Secretary and Treasurer), Co-ordinators normally had little contact with Committee members between meetings, and some Co-ordinators were left to organise recruitment, fund-raising, training and other activities which were not in theory their responsibility. Indeed, in some cases nobody seemed quite clear about what tasks were whose responsibility. As Schemes become larger and more complex organisations, consideration may have to be given to whether the present management structure is the most effective way of dividing up tasks and responsibilities. At the very least, Schemes will need to draw clearer lines between the tasks of the Co-ordinator and others, and they may also come to re-think even the current role of the Co-ordinator as recommended by NAVSS. As pointed out in Chapter 5, in a large Scheme this post can require a number of very diverse skills (e.g. knowledge of office management, secretarial work, supervisory skills, counselling, public relations), and it may be that these tasks should be divided between more than one person.

Evaluation in terms of the extent to which Schemes as a whole 'meet victims' needs' is a complex matter, but our overall conclusion must be that, as yet, they fall far short of the aim of sending volunteers to see all victims badly affected by crime (even if we include only victims of recorded crime). From interviews with victims, and from BCS data (Chapter 3), it can be calculated that at least 500,000 victims of recorded offences in England and Wales annually consider themselves 'very much' affected by the offence. Scheme volunteers have recently seen perhaps 50,000 victims annually face-to-face, of whom fewer than 40,000 would describe themselves as 'very much' affected: so, despite all their efforts, they are as yet only scraping the surface of the problem.

Even so, the indications are that, with some exceptions, Schemes are increasingly concentrating their efforts upon victims of the crimes most likely to have serious consequences. Residential burglary, particularly where aggravated by theft of sentimentally valuable objects or by vandalism, is certainly one of these, and has for a long time been the offence most commonly referred to Schemes. Assaults, robbery and 'snatch' theft from the person are equally likely to have psychologically damaging effects, and while a surprisingly large minority of Schemes still do not deal with offences of this kind, they also receive fairly high priority in many areas. On the other hand, if it is their aim to meet the most serious needs, most Schemes still need to invest more effort in developing the capacity to handle the consequences of very serious crime, including rape and murder. As we have pointed out in Chapter 7, special training and careful supervision of volunteers are almost essential for Schemes taking on the support of such victims over several weeks or months (which is often necessary), and neighbouring Schemes may need to pool expertise and other resources in order to provide a satisfactory service.

While the above 'gap' can be explained by a lack of resources, others cannot. For example, many young male victims of serious assault were not being referred to Schemes because of police officers' attachment of blame to their behaviour prior to the assault. In many cases, no doubt, injuries followed an argument or provocation ('six of one and half a dozen of the other'), but this does not alter the fact that people with serious injuries need support and assistance - a point stressed by many people within Schemes. Nonetheless, Committees rarely pressed for the referral of such cases, even when aware that they were not being passed to the Scheme. This was one of the signs of a fairly widespread contentment among Schemes to 'take what they were given', rather than to make conscious decisions, based upon a knowledge of local crime rates, about precisely what cases they wished the police to refer.

A further gap in services to victims of violence (as opposed to burglary, for which most Schemes were well

215

'geared' with advice about repairs etc.) was indicated by the revelation, in responses to our questionnaire in 1984, that under 60 per cent of all Schemes had ever advised about a CICB claim, and only 16 per cent had advised on more than three. This reflects not only the generally low numbers of violent offences referred, but suggests that volunteers may not always be aware of the low threshold in terms of injury for which an award may be given, despite the apparently high lower limit for awards of £400. Certainly, in training sessions we observed, this was not made clear to volunteers, and, moreover, some of those we interviewed believed that it was the police who decided whether a claim should be made, rather than the victim.

We also pointed out in Chapter 3, two types of criminal (or near criminal) behaviour which quite frequently fail to reach police records as notifiable criminal offences, but which are nevertheless very distressing for large numbers of victims. These are threats and ('minor') vandalism. Such offences are made more disturbing by the fact that, particularly in inner city areas, they tend to be repeated upon the same victims, and are also the type of behaviour associated with racial harrassment (cf. Maclean et.al. 1986). At present, few Schemes are referred more than a handful of these kinds of incident annually. There seems a good case for Schemes at least to ask for the referral of more recorded cases of criminal damage, and beyond this it may be possible to persuade the police to refer 'harrassment' type cases (with or without racial overtones), with victims' permission, even if no notifiable offence has been referred.

Finally, if we evaluate Schemes according to the aim of conveying a message of sympathy, or an offer of help, to all victims, regardless of need, it is clear that they have a very long way to go. This is partly a matter of referral policy, but even in Schemes with 'automatic' referral, large numbers of 'ordinary' thefts are excluded because with present resources it would be virtually impossible for most Schemes to deal with them all, even by post. (It would also be an exceedingly tedious task for police liaison officers to read them all out over the telephone). If Schemes wish to advertise the fact they they 'care', as well as to offer their services, the most obvious way to reach all victims is for police officers to leave a Scheme card with every victim they visit. Unfortunately, this idea met resistance from most senior officers we interviewed, mainly on the grounds that their officers are already 'loaded down' with other material. However, if police thinking about priorities - aided by pressure from the Home Office - moves in the direction of according more serious attention to the needs

216

of victims, this hurdle could be easily overcome.  It would
be possible, for instance, to attach to initial crime report
forms carried by constables a tear-off strip containing
brief details on VSS.

We now summarise what we consider to be the most important
points made in each chapter, some of which were not alluded
to in the foregoing 'evaluations'.  This is followed by a
very brief set of concluding remarks.

## Summary

In Chapter 2, we presented the results of a survey of all
Schemes in mid-1984, to which over 90 per cent responded.
The general picture to emerge was of a fast-expanding
movement, with strong growth in terms of numbers of Schemes,
size of areas covered, numbers of volunteers, and numbers of
referrals received.  There were healthy signs in the claims
that, overall, 80 per cent of volunteers were regularly
active, and that the turnover in volunteers was only about
20 per cent per year.  On the other hand, Schemes in inner
city areas clearly had greater problems than most, both in
recruiting and keeping volunteers.

It was calculated that, by 1985, almost 60 per cent of the
population of England and Wales lived in an area nominally
covered by a Victims Support Scheme.  However, only a small
proportion of victims were actually referred to Schemes in
these areas, and even where residential burglary was
concerned (the offence most often dealt with), on average
only one in three cases known to the police was passed on.
Moreover, shortages of volunteers contributed to the fact
that not many more than a third of all victims referred to
Schemes were seen face-to-face by volunteers.  Even so, it
is still a remarkable achievement for a voluntary
organisation only a few years old, already to be visiting
the homes of (according to our calculations) at least seven
per cent of all burglary victims in the country.

Over a third of respondents named financial difficulties
as the worst problem facing their Scheme (shortage of
volunteers being the second most often mentioned problem).
This applied to Schemes with and without paid Co-ordinators.
The latter were found mainly in large urban Schemes - almost
a third of Schemes in cities of over 250,000 population
having a paid Co-ordinator.  While Schemes with paid Co-
ordinators tended overall to have more volunteers, receive
more referrals, and to be both more 'productive' (e.g. to
visit more victims _per_ volunteer) and more 'progressive'
(e.g. to take on victims of very serious crime) than other

Schemes, there was also a sub-set of Schemes with voluntary
Co-ordinators which matched them in every respect.  As we
saw during fieldwork, many of the Co-ordinators in such
Schemes regularly worked a full week without any financial
reward.

At the time of our survey, the police in 57 per cent of
Scheme areas had agreed to refer victims of at least one
category of offence (most often burglary) on an 'automatic'
basis.  It was clear that this produced both considerably
higher numbers, and more consistent numbers, of referrals
than the 'selective' systems employed elsewhere.  On the
whole, Schemes were satisfied with the operation of their
referral system, although a minority complained of fairly
frequent 'hiccups' as police personnel changed, or
misunderstandings arose.  Burglaries dominated the referrals
at most Schemes, and a significant minority never dealt with
assaults, vandalism or other theft.  Almost half had dealt
with rape cases at some point, although ten Schemes had done
so without any special training for their volunteers.
Surprisingly, under 60 per cent had ever helped with CICB
claims.

In Chapter 3 we used data from our interviews with victims
and from the 1984 British Crime Survey to tackle the complex
subject of the impact of different types of crime on
different categories of victim over different periods of
time.  It was shown that survey and 'in-depth' interviews
produce somewhat different results, and that the degree of
'prompting' used also considerably affects victims'
statements about both the effects of the crime and any
'needs' arising from it.

The common wisdom among Scheme members was found to be
generally correct as far as the relative effects of
different types of offence are concerned.  Burglary in a
dwelling-house, wounding, 'snatch' theft from the person and
robbery, all among the types of offence most frequently
referred to Schemes, are more likely than most other
offences to have a serious emotional impact upon victims.
Rape, however, (see Chapter 7), is virtually always deeply
damaging, and in our view demands priority attention,
whatever the cost in terms of special training, etc.
Moreover, two other categories of offence - criminal damage
(vandalism) and threats (by telephone or in person) - which
are less commonly passed to Schemes, were also found to have
a serious impact, as well as being likely to be repeated,
and seem to deserve more attention.  The difficulty with
threats is that they are frequently not recorded as offences
by the police, but it is still possible for victims to be
asked whether they would like referral to a Scheme.

Finally, offences committed by people known to the victim were found more likely to have strong effects than those committed by strangers.

Among different social categories of victim, widows over 60 who lived alone were significantly more likely than others to report a serious emotional impact. However, the initial emotional effects of the offences mentioned above were strong on sufficiently high proportions of victims of all ages and both sexes to make it unwise for Schemes to concentrate only upon the highest risk groups. Moreover, 70 per cent of victims with children reported that the latter had been frightened or disturbed.

It was calculated that in a putative 'average-sized' Scheme area (130,000 population) with an average crime rate, about 1,500 victims of recorded crime would describe themselves as badly affected over a period of a year - i.e. about three times the average number of victims currently referred. Rather more than this would be badly affected by non-recorded or non-reported criminal incidents, raising the question of whether Schemes should make 'self-referral' easier. It seems unlikely that more than a small percentage would come forward to request assistance, but ideas such as 'hot-lines' might be worth pursuing in large urban areas, perhaps as joint ventures between neighbouring Schemes.

Specific emotional and practical effects were examined at some length. Fear, worry and anger were the most frequently reported emotional effects, the first two particularly common after crimes of violence and burglary, and the last after theft and vandalism. The emotional effects were described as worse than the practical effects for burglary, robbery and assault - this being true for young male victims as well as all other categories - but the reverse was the case for 'ordinary' types of theft. The BCS results suggested that less than half of all reported offences cause practical problems for the victims, but our 'in-depth' interviews revealed considerably higher proportions for comparable offence types. The two sources, however, agree that property offences tend to cause more such problems than offences against the person. The offence causing serious inconvenience to the highest proportion of victims, it seems, is car theft.

Our interviews with victims of burglary, robbery, 'snatch' theft and assault, conducted mainly three weeks after the offence, indicated that the majority had recovered substantially by that point. Even so, 15 per cent rated themselves still 'very much' affected, and only 20 per cent 'not at all' affected. Again, the majority reported feeling at their 'lowest point' within the first 24 hours, but delayed reactions of some kind were reported by a third of all victims, and by 45 per cent of assault victims. Victims of violence were likely to report fear of another attack (and fear of returning to the scene) and burglary victims to report a general sense of unease or insecurity. Altogether, about six per cent thought that the event would have a very strong lasting impact upon their lives, but less serious lasting changes in behaviour were reported by higher proportions. For example, a quarter went out less, and 20 per cent were less likely to invite people into their homes. Finally, when we used a version of the Middlesex Hospital General Health Questionnaire, the scores of victims of the above types of crime, particularly female victims, were strikingly high on average, indicating much higher probabilities of psychiatric disturbance than those found among the general population, or even among patients at doctors' surgeries.

The smaller number of interviews carried out three months or a year after the event generally supported the 'crisis theory' postulation that the majority of victims will recover fully from the 'trauma' of an offence within a few weeks or months. Nevertheless, a small proportion suffering lasting effects did not seem to be recovering at all, and were experiencing persisting fear and anxiety, even after having had some support from VSS at an early stage. This was most common among victims of violence who had been badly affected early on, and suggests that Schemes might consider routinely recontacting such people after a few months in order to offer further support if necessary.

Finally in Chapter 3, we returned to the slippery concept of victims' 'needs', which we deemed, under one possible definition, to exist when practical problems had not been solved within a reasonable period of time, or emotional effects had not been ameliorated by support from friends or relatives. It was calculated that about 20 per cent of victims of burglary and violent crime had been badly affected and lacked a sympathetic 'listening ear', and a further five per cent needed outside support in addition to help from family and friends. When 'practical needs' were added, we estimated that 30 - 40 per cent of victims of these more serious offences 'needed' VSS assistance: this accorded well with the 33 per cent of victims of such offences in the BCS who said that they would have liked a visit from a volunteer. Finally, among all personal victims of recorded notifiable offences, the need for Victims Support defined in this way might be put at 10 - 15 per cent.

In Chapter 4, we described the 'filtering processes' by which the total numbers of possible VSS 'clients' were whittled down to those actually contacted or visited. It was argued that Schemes generally paid insufficient attention to the shape of their body of referrals from the police, often being content to 'take what they were given', rather than to plan referral systems carefully in consultation with the police, informed by knowledge of local crime patterns and the true volume of offences. Indeed, other Scheme policies often tended to reflect local police views and attitudes - e.g. as regards practices in response to self-referrals.

'Automatic' referral systems were seen to be much more effective than 'selective' systems in providing regular flows of cases, and were less vulnerable to hiccups caused by changes in police personnel, personal prejudices, or declining interest. They did contain the risk of becoming too rigid, and, unless properly prepared for, a change from a selective to a blanket referral system could swamp Co-ordinators with work. Nevertheless, they are clearly superior in a well organised Scheme.

Allocation of cases within Schemes reflected different ideas about VSS aims and priorities, as well as a number of practical constraints. As letters to victims produced few replies (about 10 per cent), it was generally agreed that volunteers should be sent to visit, unannounced, those 'most likely to need support'. These, however, were identified in different ways. Co-ordinators tended to give priority to older victims (to the extent in one case of guessing ages from names) but most also had an idiosyncratic set of other criteria affecting allocation, varying from the social class of the victim to aspects of the offence. Most also agreed that the information on police crime reports was not the most suitable for VSS purposes, wanting instead to know whether the victim was, for example, handicapped, socially isolated, a single parent, or having language difficulties. This kind of information, ironically, was more often available where victims were referred 'by consent' through individual police officers, than where there was automatic referral. The ideal system, we concluded, was one with the 'best of both worlds' - i.e. automatic referral but with routine identification of priority cases by investigating officers marking crime reports accordingly.

Considerable variation was found between volunteers in attempts to contact victims, with some routinely giving up after one unsuccessful visit, and others trying numerous times and methods. Where telephoning was used, there were large differences in rates of 'conversion' into visits.

Co-ordinators often knew little about actual contacting practices or contact rates, owing to failures to return forms.

Overall, in the Schemes we studied in depth, only a third of victims referred were actually seen in person. However, the filtering processes within Schemes seemed to work to the extent that 60 per cent of our sample of referred victims, and 79 per cent of our sample of visited victims, rated themselves badly affected by the offence.

In Chapter 5, we discussed problems in the internal structure of Schemes, mainly confusions in the roles of Co-ordinator and Committee member, the excessive load that tends to fall on Co-ordinators' shoulders, loss of volunteer morale, and failures of communication between Committees, Co-ordinators and volunteer visitors. Some Schemes had partly overcome these problems through the use of job descriptions, by Co-ordinators refusing to take on certain tasks on principle, by co-opting more visitors on to the Committee, by using a smaller Executive Committee (meeting more often that the full Management Committee), and/or by getting volunteers to help Co-ordinators regularly with their routine tasks.

We discussed also common problems in the supervision of volunteers, including that of maintaining their sense of 'involvement'. These were minimised in some Schemes through (a) regular personal telephone contact between volunteer and Co-ordinator (e.g. some form of 'debriefing' after every visit), (b) visiting rotas, to reduce overuse of some and underuse of other volunteers, (c) insistence upon the prompt return of report forms, (d) regular, well-run volunteer support meetings, with strong encouragement to attend and (e) regular newsletters, social gatherings, experienced members' involvement in training, and other opportunities for all members to meet and pass on news.

In Chapter 6, we constructed a 'victim's-eye view' of VSS and asked to what extent Victims' Support could be said to 'work'. We found that the great majority of reactions to unannounced visits, after (understandable) short-lived suspicion by some burglary victims, were positive. Some 17 per cent of victims contacted by telephone had a negative reaction, but 71 per cent were pleased to receive the call. Very few reacted negatively to postal contact. However, there was some misunderstanding of the nature or purpose of VS among those who had been contacted by post or telephone.

Only about half of those visited said that they had discussed their feelings in depth, although few of those who had not, blamed the volunteer. Indeed, most were very complimentary about the manner of volunteers, 71 per cent saying that they had made it 'easy' to talk (if the victim wanted to). Furthermore over 60 per cent said that they had felt better as a result of the visit, although only 12 per cent had felt 'very much' better. We calculated that volunteers had given specific and useful practical help (as opposed to general advice) to 18 per cent of all those visited, and in a third of these cases the victim said that he or she had been saved some money. Seventy six per cent were very satisfied with the service, and only 15 per cent could think of anything else the volunteer might have done to assist them.

The 'typical' visit was short (half an hour or less), 'one-off' (although victims of violence were more likely to receive follow-up visits, mainly in connection with CICB claims) and relatively 'low-key'. Other agencies were contacted in only 23 per cent of cases (most often Social Services). And 'the gesture' was seen by most victims as the most important aspect (although nearly a quarter said that the opportunity to express their feelings had been the most important). On the other hand, in a small number of cases a great deal of intensive discussion and follow-up work had been carried out.

Finally, we described an exercise in which 26 victims who had not been visited by VSS were compared with a 'matched' group of 26 who had. Although this was only a small-scale experiment, and the results must be treated with some caution, the indications are that the visited group, although worse affected initially, had recovered better than the non-visited group by three weeks after the offence. Their attitudes were also 'softer' towards the offender and towards the idea of mediation.

In Chapter 7, we discussed the work of VSS in relation to victims of rape. It was shown that the effects of rape are generally far worse than those of any of the offences discussed previously, and we argued that VSS should put a high priority upon training volunteers to support these victims. Although Rape Crisis Centres already offer a rather different service to rape victims, we concluded that there was a place for both organisations, each of which tends to appeal more or less strongly to different types of woman.

We found that the present level of training of volunteers who wish to deal with rape victims is generally inadequate. While some Regions or other groups have set up very useful seminars or workshops, it is important to create more

223

intensive courses with a strong component of counselling skills - perhaps best organised at county (or similar) level. The rape victims we interviewed who had been supported by VSS volunteers had clearly benefited greatly, and despite high numbers of visits to each, the volunteers seemed to have avoided one of the main risks involved - that of creating dependency in the victim. However, most of these were very experienced and we argued that to send out volunteers without special training or previous counselling experience was unwise unless there was very close supervision by a properly qualified group leader. Indeed we stressed throughout the importance of supervising and supporting volunteers, however well trained. This may be best achieved, at least in Schemes which deal with relatively high numbers of rape cases, by the task being removed from the Co-ordinator dealing with the normal work of the Scheme, and passed on to another supervisor - ideally himself or herself having access to advice and support from a qualified psychiatrist or counsellor.

Other subjects discussed in Chapter 7 included the treatment of rape victims by the police, referral practices in rape cases, and the use of male volunteers to help counsel husbands or boyfriends.

Finally, attention is drawn to the Appendix, where findings on a variety of subjects are presented briefly. These include the treatment of victims by the police, victims' attitudes to mediation, and the recruitment and training of new volunteers. The section on training is the fullest, and in it we identify weaknesses in some of the courses we observed. These include failure to make the information presented relevant to the everyday reality of VSS visiting, a tendency to 'over-dramatise' the work, unbalanced courses, and failure to brief outside speakers (such as police officers) adequately about what subjects they should cover. We also draw attention to the importance of continuing training (e.g. in volunteer meetings) over the first few years of practice. Nevertheless, in general we conclude that most Schemes equipped their new volunteers adequately for the task, and that some courses were excellently planned and executed.


## Concluding remarks

We have suggested a number of ways in which VSS might be able to improve their operation or the services they provide: for example, by better awareness of local crime patterns and firmer agreements with the police about referral systems; by providing more assistance to overworked

Co-ordinators; by better organisation of volunteers' workload and more efficient supervision of their visiting; by more inter-Scheme co-operation and joint ventures; by more 'relevant' and better integrated training courses, and so on. However, until they are on a firm financial basis, with all large Schemes possessing a paid Co-ordinator, working from an office with at least part-time clerical help, and, equally important, reasonably sure that funding levels will be maintained for a period of several years, the effectiveness of most is likely, as at present, to wax and wane with the energy of dedicated individuals.

Our study, we believe, shows that there is a genuine and widespread need for VSS work and that even at its simplest level it is important to victims. Moreover, the area in which they are most needed is the most demanding in terms of skills and resources - the longer term support of victims of very serious crime. While it is possible (though not desirable) for volunteers to continue 'one-off' visiting of victims of burglary or theft within a fairly loose organisation and with minimal supervision, the support of rape victims or of the relatives of murder victims requires a more 'professional' background organisation. Although the current VSS 'model' includes the attractive idea of Schemes as agencies which 'refer on' badly affected victims to other agencies with, say, professional counselling resources, this is in many Scheme areas difficult to achieve in practice. In other words, Schemes are having faute de mieux, to develop their own resources and their own expertise in these fields, often at the same time as dealing with increasing numbers of 'ordinary' referrals. The need for regular and reliable funding, at least among large urban Schemes, is thus growing stronger and more urgent. While a fair amount of public money (in the region of £1 million in 1985) does reach Schemes indirectly, mainly through payment of Co-ordinators under the Urban Aid and MSC Schemes, this is both inadequate for their needs and unsatisfactory in terms of continuity of staff. The obvious solution seems to be direct funding of Schemes by the government. In the context of the estimated £3000 million spent annually (Home Affairs Commitee 1984/5) on agencies concerned with processing offenders - police, courts, probation and prisons - a commitment at least to provide a paid Co-ordinator for every Scheme above an agreed size would not seem extravagant and would be in accord with the widely held view that it is time to redress the balance a little in favour of the victim (see also Maguire 1986).

# Appendix: Miscellaneous findings

## 1. Mediation

Over the last few years, reparation and mediation projects have been springing up across the country, latterly with the encouragement of central government, which has financed four projects on an experimental basis (Leeds, Coventry, Cumbria, Wolverhampton - see Marshall, 1985; Marshall and Walpole 1985 ). There has also been much discussion about the possible involvement of Victims Support Schemes in these ventures. The connection has been maintained partly by enthusiasm for the idea among some probation members of Victims Support Management Committees and partly through the setting up of the Forum for Initiatives in Reparation and Mediation (FIRM), to which a number of Victims Support members belong. However, at a local level, uncertainty about the prospective role of VSS in reparation and mediation projects (some attention has centred on VS volunteers training as arbitrators) and the concern of some that mediation is not always in the interests of victims, has led most Schemes to remain cautious about the idea. Thus currently, where local reparation or mediation projects exist, Victims Support involvement is usually limited to a member sitting on the committee to keep watch on developments and to ensure that the interests of victims are kept strongly to the fore.

All BCS respondents who recalled an offence were asked whether they would have accepted the chance of meeting the offender in order 'to agree a way in which the offender could make a repayment for what he had done.' Overall, 49 per cent said that they would, the equivalent figure being 52 per cent among those who had reported the offence to the police. Within this latter group, there were only slight differences in enthusiasm for the idea, between males (55 per cent) and females (48 per cent), and almost none between those who had previously been aquainted with the person responsible and those who knew it to be a stranger.

There were, however, considerable differences according to the type of offence involved. The following table shows the proportions of victims of each BCS offence category who would have accepted the opportunity of a meeting:

## Percentage of victims willing to meet offender

| Offence type | Offence reported to police | Offence not reported to police | All (Unweighted N = 3,515) |
|---|---|---|---|
| | % | % | % |
| Theft of bicycle | 67 | 57 | 64 |
| Theft of vehicle | 59 | ** | 59 |
| Other personal theft | 67 | 53 | 58 |
| Burglary/theft dwelling | 57 | 59 | 57 |
| Vandalism | 53 | 58 | 57 |
| Theft from vehicle | 56 | 56 | 56 |
| Other household theft | 50 | 53 | 53 |
| Attempted burglary | 37 | 43 | 40 |
| Assault, wounding | 31 | 36 | 33 |
| Robbery/snatch theft | 44 | 24 | 31 |
| Threats | 29 | 27 | 28 |
| Common assault | 29 | 25 | 26 |
| All | 52 | 48 | 49 |

** Numbers too small for analysis.

Victims of violent offences were much less likely than victims of property crime to find the idea attractive. Under one third of victims of assault and robbery would have accepted a meeting. Similarly, people who had been threatened seemed to have little desire to meet the offender. At the other end of the scale, most victims of bicycle theft, car theft and other personal theft would have done so. And, encouragingly for proponents of mediation, 57 per cent of victims of burglary - one of the offences for which the process is believed to be most rewarding - would have been willing to participate.

228

The only major difference according to the sex of the victim was to be found in the case of minor vandalism reported to the police: men were three times as likely as women to answer 'yes' to a meeting. The only offences where higher proportions of women than men said they would take part were assaults and household theft - although here the differences were not enormous.

Similarly, whether or not the offender was previously known to the victim made little difference, except where assaults and threats were concerned: here, considerably smaller proportions of people who knew the offender wanted to have anything to do with mediation. Many such cases, presumably, involved neighbourhood or family disputes, in which one is faced with a complex situation requiring conflict resolution, rather than with a simple victim-offender relationship.

We included two other reparation-related questions in the BCS. The first, asked only of those who said 'no' to a meeting with the offender, was:

> 'If an out of court agreement like this could be arranged without you having to meet the offender(s), would you like this to happen or not?'

It emerged that 40 per cent of those who had reported the offence to the police (but did not wish to meet the offender) would have liked such an agreement to take place. Again, victims of property offences were considerably more likely to wish it than those of violent offences. Altogether, then, 69 per cent of all victims who reported the offence to the police would have agreed to some form of reparation (i.e. 49 per cent who wanted a meeting, plus 40 per cent of the remainder who wanted an agreement without a meeting).

Finally, to what extent did these acceptors of reparation/mediation accept it also as an alternative to prosecution, rather than simply an addition - i.e. were in favour of a form of 'diversion' from the criminal justice system? They were asked:

> 'If an agreement could be reached, would you want the offender(s) to be prosecuted and punished as well?'

The responses were as follows (offences reported to the police only):

|            |     |
|------------|-----|
| Yes        | 58% |
| No         | 30% |
| Don't know | 12% |

229

Those whose offender was definitely a stranger were rather more likely to want prosecution than were those who knew him or her, and women were marginally more likely to want prosecution than men. Finally, victims of assault, burglary, robbery and car theft were, not unnaturally, more likely to want their pound of flesh than victims of plain property offences. But overall, the message was that the concept of mediation/reparation is acceptable to quite a large proportion of victims of crime.

A little more can be added from our own interviews with victims. Our first question was slightly different, referring not to 'repayment', but to 'making personal amends', the aim being to get closer to the idea of mediation rather than simply financial restitution. Possibly for this reason, or possibly because the offences in our sample were more serious, the proportion of burglary victims among our interviewees prepared to meet the offender was somewhat lower the BCS figure. The results for violent offences, however, were almost identical:

### Percentage who would accept a meeting

|  | BCS (reported to police) | Our interviews |
|---|---|---|
|  | % | % |
| Burglary (loss) | 57 | 44 |
| Assault, wounding | 31 | 32 |

As mentioned in Chapter 6, there was some difference in willingness between those who had and had not been visited by Scheme volunteers (43 per cent and 32 per cent respectively). There were no significant differences according to the sex of the victim.

Victims were also asked to give reasons for their answers. Among those favourable to the idea, the most frequent (unprompted) responses were that they wished to 'know why he did it' or - among burglary victims - to 'see what he was like'. Those who would not have accepted a meeting were most likely to say that they were fearful of coming face to face with the offender (again), that they were 'not interested' or could 'see no point' in a meeting, or that they would be 'too angry' or 'too upset'.

We next prompted interviewees with a list of seven possible reasons for such a meeting, as shown in the following table:

Q. Can you think of any reasons why you would like to meet the offender(s)?

% answering yes

| Might you want a meeting... | Burglary | Violence |
|---|---|---|
| (a) To arrange for offender to pay money in compensation | 32 | 19 |
| (b) To arrange for offender to carry out some service (e.g. reparing damage or gardening) | 4 | 7 |
| (c) To give an apology | 7 | 9 |
| (d) To see what he was like | 32 | 16 |
| (e) To ask why he did it | 28 | 31 |
| (f) So he could see the effect the crime had on you | 30 | 23 |
| (g) To 'give him a good piece of your mind' | 38 | 13 |

The major differences between prompted and unprompted responses (apart from, as one would expect, a higher proportion giving each reason) were that a considerable number responded positively to the suggestion of compensation, although few had mentioned this unprompted as a reason for meeting; and a high proportion of burglary victims, once prompted, said that they would have liked to meet the offender to 'give him a good piece of their mind'.

231

## 2. Treatment of victims by the police

BCS respondents who had reported an offence to the police were asked:

'Overall, were you satisfied or dissatisfied with the way the police dealt with the matter?'

The answers were:

|  | % |
|---|---|
| Very satisfied | 32 |
| Fairly satisfied | 35 |
| A bit dissatisfied | 13 |
| Very dissatisfied | 14 |
| Don't know/can't say | 6 |

The answers varied somewhat by type of offence (see table below). The most satisfied customers were victims of attempted burglary, car theft and bicycle theft, of whom about 80 per cent professed themselves satisfied (and almost half the victims of car theft were 'very satisfied'). On the other hand, about a third of victims of threats, assaults and burglaries were dissatisfied overall. In the case of assault, both serious and minor, this was offset to some extent by the fact that victims tended to answer at the two extremes: thus over 40 per cent said that they were very satisfied and almost a quarter that they were very dissatisfied:

| Type of offence | Satisfied % | Dissatisfied % | (Very dissatisfied) (%) |
|---|---|---|---|
| Attempted burglary | 82 | 12 | (2) |
| Theft of vehicle | 80 | 17 | (11) |
| Theft of bicycle | 79 | 18 | (8) |
| Household theft | 74 | 21 | (8) |
| Robbery/snatch | 71 | 29 | (15) |
| Vandalism | 71 | 25 | (16) |
| Other personal theft | 67 | 23 | (9) |
| Theft from vehicle | 66 | 23 | (9) |
| Burglary/theft dwelling | 63 | 32 | (15) |
| Common assault | 57 | 35 | (26) |
| Assault, wounding | 56 | 39 | (21) |
| Threats | 56 | 41 | (25) |
| All | 67 | 27 | (14) |

(Unweighted N = 2,075)

The high satisfaction level of victims of attempted burglary may reflect the quick response of the police when told that an offender has been disturbed, as there is a good chance of an arrest. By contrast, the dissatisfaction of victims of threats and common assault is interesting, for we pointed out in Chapter 3 that these are among the types of crime which, when reported to the police, are least likely to be recorded officially as offences. It was also noted that threats in particular have a considerable emotional effect upon many victims.

We turn now briefly to our interviews with victims in VSS areas. In response to a general question on how they felt they had been treated by the police after the offence, the majority of victims we spoke to were evenly divided between those who felt that the police had simply 'done their job' and those who remembered the treatment as sympathetic, courteous or helpful. In addition, 20 per cent made negative remarks, these coming more frequently from burglary victims than from victims of violent crime (a reversal of the BCS result - perhaps because several of our interviewees who were assaulted were quite badly hurt and the police took trouble to see they received medical attention). The major complaint was that the police 'didn't seem to care' - an interesting reversal of the most frequent comment made by victims about VSS that 'it's nice to know someone cares' (Chapter 6).

When asked how they had felt as a result of the police visit, almost half reported feeling 'no different', and about a third 'very much' or 'a bit better'. Almost 20 per cent said that they had felt 'worse' afterwards, three-quarters of them attributing this to the behaviour or attitude of the police. (The remainder, particularly people who lived alone, said that they had felt worse because of suddenly being left alone.) Those who had felt better often remarked on the 'interest' taken in them and the offence by the police or that the police had acted in a reassuring manner. By contrast, the most common single reason given for having felt worse afterwards was that the police had in some way devalued the incident, the perception being that they had treated it or the victim as 'unimportant'. This was apparent particularly among victims of burglary (almost ten per cent), and probably owes a lot to police officers' overfamiliarity with this type of offence. Other reasons mentioned were that they had felt disbelieved, that the police had made unwelcome 'jokey remarks', or that victims' fears had been raised. For instance:

'He made me feel worse, but it was unintentional. He told me basement flats are worst for getting burgled

233

and being on the corner made it worse, and that the front door was inadequate. It wasn't the right time to tell me that because he knew I was on my own for the rest of the weekend and I was already really frightened.'

'He implied that I had been stupid and he didn't reassure me. I wasn't comforted at all.'

'They laughed when I asked whether the bag might be returned, which upset me.'

'I was surprised that they were so relaxed about it. They didn't pay attention and were a bit jokey. I felt fairly disappointed. I expected them to take it a bit more seriously.'

Asked whether the treatment they had received had altered their views about the police, three-quarters reported that their views remained unaltered. However, victims of violence were almost three times as likely as those of property offences to report a positive change of views (24 per cent and nine per cent respectively) and, vice-versa, three times as many property victims as victims of violence now felt less favourable towards the police (13 per cent and four per cent).

Previous studies (e.g. Maguire 1982, Shapland et. al. 1985) have shown that police failure to inform victims of the outcome of their investigations is a major reason for dissatisfaction. In our study, only a quarter had received any reports of progress (or lack of it). Altogether, 87 per cent felt that they should have been kept informed, irrespective of the outcome, and half of these had expected this information to be given - only, in most cases, to be disappointed. For example:

'I had no complaints about the police at all when they first came, but I was very annoyed I wasn't kept informed, it's not business-like. Having written three times, enclosing stamped addressed envelopes, not once did I get a written reply.'

In sum, most interviewees were broadly satisfied with the overall police treatment they had received, but a significant minority had some form of complaint, and indeed a few had acquired more negative views about the police as a result of the treatment received. The main reasons for discontent were that the police showed an uncaring attitude or devalued the incident.

## 3.    Recruitment of volunteers

As stated in Chapter 2, when asked to name the worst problems facing their Scheme, one-third of respondents to our national survey mentioned, unprompted, a shortage of volunteers. Moreover, in response to pre-coded questions, nearly 40 per cent admitted that recruitment was a 'major' or 'considerable' problem.

Victims Support has, to some extent unfairly, acquired the reputation of being a 'middle-class' organisation. This is undoubtedly true in many of the smaller Schemes, particularly in rural and small-town areas (cf. Mawby and Gill, forthcoming), but there is also an increasing number of Schemes with a predominantly young, working-class, volunteer force. In fact, as in many voluntary organisations, local branches tend to take on a distinct character of their own. The explanation for this seems to lie partly in the natural tendency for people to be attracted to groups made up of people broadly like themselves, but partly also in the methods normally used to recruit new volunteers.

As is often the case in voluntary organisations (Jackson 1985), the most successful method of recruitment of volunteers among Schemes was word-of-mouth (see Chapter 2). Individuals approached in person tended to fit in well with existing members, and were more likely than those responding to advertisements, for example, to 'stay the course' of selection and training and become volunteer visitors. However, the very success of personal contact, combined with poor results from other methods, holds certain dangers. Where friends and acquaintances of current volunteers were the major source of recruits, we sometimes found Schemes lacking in social 'mix'. One Scheme's volunteers were predominantly middle-aged or elderly, many with local church connections. Another's were almost exclusively middle-class (or above!). A less wealthy member of the latter Scheme said that she had nearly been 'put off' joining by her first impressions of the 'type of people involved'. By contrast, such problems were not found in two Schemes which had close links with their local Council for Voluntary Services Bureau, where potential volunteers from various backgrounds were headed towards Victims Support if it was thought that the work would suit them.

The tendency of some Schemes to draw members from relatively narrow social circles - in our experience, it should be stressed, without any deliberate intention - is well illustrated by failure to recruit black or Asian members. This problem is being examined by the NAVSS Ethnic

Minorities Working Party, which was set up to discuss the general role of VSS in relation to racial issues (including harrassment). In 1984, the Working Party sent a questionnaire to 140 Schemes, only 60 of which responded. Very few regarded recruitment from among the ethnic minorities as a 'problem', even where, despite a substantial black population in the area, there was a conspicuous absence of black visitors among their volunteers. What many such Schemes had failed to tackle was their basic unattractiveness to people from different backgrounds - caused partly by their image of 'middle-classness' and partly by their apparent close association and alignment with the police and police views.

Despite the lower returns of recruitment methods other than 'word-of-mouth', there is still clearly a need for VSS to use them, in order to achieve a wider social mix. In order to lose as few potentially good volunteers as possible, we would emphasise that Schemes need to have interview and training procedures well organised in advance of any recruitment drive. Pre-planning should have two aims - first, to make the Scheme as attractive as possible to potential volunteers, including those unknown to present members; second, to avoid incidents which could dissuade visitors-in-training from continuing. Some of the pitfalls to be avoided - which certainly helped to lose potential visitors in areas we visited - are delays in sending out application forms or literature about Victims Support, delays in starting training courses, and failure to explain clearly the rules for payment of expenses and other points concerning 'terms of membership'. In some areas, invitations to volunteer support meetings were successfully used to help intending volunteers decide if they would like to join the organisation. A textbook example of how not to conduct a recruitment drive was provided by one Scheme which was at the time in a somewhat disorganised state. One of the more enterprising members of the Management Committee interested a local newspaper in giving the Scheme a front-page spread, but were then upset by the sensationalist coverage, which attracted a number of clearly unsuitable applicants. Nevertheless, more than 25 genuine enquiries were received. Delays in dispatching literature and application forms reduced the number completing the formalities to nine. Training was then badly delayed and poorly structured, and eventually only four volunteers completed the course. Finally - after, as one put it, 'being messed about' and 'offered no guidance' for their first few months of visiting - all four lost interest, a confusion over claims for travel expenses being the last straw.

Two categories of visitor require separate mention. These are recent victims (usually people who have been visited or assisted by existing volunteers) and MSC-funded visitors. We estimated that people referred to Schemes as victims who had later volunteered their services as visitors made up seven per cent of all trained volunteers. Schemes differed in their policy towards the recruitment of recent victims, who have had little time to work through either their own feelings about the offence or their motives for joining VSS. While most were happy to accept them, two Schemes had decided as a matter of policy that victims should wait at least six months before training as volunteers. In view of the importance, emphasised by NAVSS, of avoiding the creation of a 'victim identity' (Reeves 1985), some waiting period seems a good idea, unless the offence in question was very minor and had little effect upon the victim.

As far as we know, the only paid visitors existing in Schemes are those supplied through the Manpower Services Commission. These people tend to be young and on the long-term unemployment register, and are usually provided with a job for a one-year period. At a time when most Schemes are on an uncertain financial footing, expansion or development aided by the MSC can be very tempting, but many within Victims Support feel that the marrying of this Government employment scheme with a voluntary organisation is inappropriate. One major concern is that in the case of paid visitors, 'helping the victim' need not be paramount. Certainly, among a small group of MSC-paid visitors with whom we discussed the question, while half did seem dedicated to helping crime victims, the others affirmed that they were not particularly interested in this type of work, and did it simply 'as a job'.

Tension between paid and unpaid visitors working alongside each other is also likely to damage cohesion and group identity. Fairly open resentment by unpaid visitors was apparent at one Scheme we visited, the feeling being that many of the incoming MSC workers would be paid for a lower standard of work than that achieved by the volunteers. Schemes' control over the employment of specific individuals is limited,[1] and they may sometimes be obliged to take people with whom they are not completely happy. Another problem with MSC-paid visitors is the high turnover of personnel, workers having to be replaced after a year. Although Management Committee members of some MSC-funded Schemes to whom we spoke said that this had not caused them any undue difficulties, it has been blamed elsewhere for serious setbacks in the administrative functioning of Schemes, in police-VSS relationships, and even for the total collapse of one Scheme.

For these reasons, the NAVSS Policy Committee has not given encouragement to Schemes to forge links with the MSC, believing that alternative sources of funding must be sought. However, it is important not to ignore an important argument in their favour. These visitors are mainly young, working-class and poor, and also include a considerable number from ethnic minority groups. They therefore belong to the groups least represented among many (though not all) Schemes. Their presence can bring new life to a Scheme, as well as improve its image with local groups not at present well-disposed towards VSS. And it should not be forgotten that large numbers of victims come from a similar social background to the MSC workers. It is not altogether surpising if paid young people from the unemployment register receive a cool reception from some middle-aged, middle-class volunteers. However, provided that they are not 'foisted' upon the existing volunteer group, but introduced after full discussion and in (at first) small numbers, and provided that they meet the same standards as everybody else, we see no reason why MSC-paid visitors should not be encouraged and welcomed. What is needed ultimately is better agreement between the MSC and Schemes as to selection procedures, leaving the latter more opportunity to employ people clearly motivated towards the work.

# 4.  Selection and assessment of visitors

We found that Schemes varied widely in the care exercised in the selection of volunteer visitors.  The problem for many Schemes was that, as one Co-ordinator commented:

> 'We're hard-pressed to get anybody, so we can't be too choosy in the initial stages.'

Some also justified their lack of care with the arguments that unsuitable volunteers would 'self-select themselves out', and that for the bulk of routine referrals, visitors of the highest calibre were not essential.

The selection of visitors usually took place in two stages - before and after training - although 'clearance' by the police was required before visiting of victims could commence.  Assessment usually proceeded by formal interviews and/or 'informal chats' (usually by the Co-ordinator), and most permutations of 'interviews' and 'chats' before and after training were found at the Schemes we visited. However, few used both initial and final formal assessment interviews.

At the Schemes which did conduct formal assessment at the end of training, selection was taken very seriously.  At one recently established Scheme, the Co-ordinator impressed on new trainees at the outset that they might not be found suitable.  Three of a training sub-committee of five members took turns to run each training course.  At the final interview, the other two sub-committee members interviewed the trainee 'blind' to form first impressions, and immediately afterwards they discussed the candidate with the three group trainers.  Any disagreement between them and the trainers would then be ironed out.

In the absence of a final panel interview, rejection of unsuitable applicants after training appeared embarrassing for Co-ordinators to handle informally on their own, and these difficult situations were dealt with in different ways.  At two Schemes studied, a straight but sensitive approach was adopted where the Co-ordinator was matter-of-fact about the volunteer's unsuitability.  At another Scheme the solution was to ask the volunteer to attend another training course before commencing visiting, but elsewhere a common approach was to avoid the issue.  One Co-ordinator commented:

> 'Some are just unable to listen, so we deal with this by not referring them any victims, although they are welcomed to the volunteer meetings. We could always use

239

them for something - minor cases perhaps,or something other than visiting, like fund-raising.'

In fact, one visitor who fell into this category was perplexed and upset when talking to the researcher about why she had not been used since completing training many months previously. Avoiding referring victims to those who are judged unsuitable does not seem the kindest way to deal with this situation. The new training manual firmly states that the selection of volunteers should become the responsibility of the Management Committee, who should set up a sub-committee for the purpose. This would remove the burden of selection from the shoulders of Co-ordinators and for many would be a welcome move.

Before any volunteer can begin visiting, clearance must be obtained from the police that the individual has no previous convictions that might affect his or her suitability as a visitor. Despite Co-ordinators invariably informing trainees that the police would need to 'clear' them, most Schemes visited had been through the experience of having at least one applicant rejected in this way. (At one Scheme, a warrant existed for the arrest of one trainee!) The police rarely informed Schemes of the precise reasons for refusing to accept volunteers, and, although understandable, this sometimes caused resentment at the loss of an apparently good volunteer as well as on the part of some rejected candidates. One solution might be that the rejected candidate, if desired, could have the right to know on what precise grounds he or she was being rejected by the police, and, subsequently, recourse to an appeal - perhaps taking the form of an open discussion between the applicant, the Chief Constable of the area, and a regional or Scheme representative.

## 5. Training of visitors

The basic training given to most volunteers has three main aims. First, Schemes aim to impart information about the philosophy and background of the Victims Support movement. Second, training attempts to equip visitors with practical information of use to victims. The third and, in many eyes, the most important aim is to sensitise intending visitors to the feelings that victims are likely to experience, and to develop their capacity for offering emotional support, in particular the skill of 'listening'.

Courses vary considerably, but a fairly typical course would consist of six weekly sessions, each dealing with one or two topics. These might include details of the local, regional and national structure of the VSS movement; the police role; the impact of different crimes on victims; the development of listening skills; advice on how to help with insurance and criminal injuries compensation claims; and information about local voluntary and statutory agencies.

Training of visitors does not stop with completion of the basic preparation course. Between the issue of the initial and updated training manuals, there has been a growing awareness of the need for futher training opportunities and support for volunteers, and the updated manual now advocates that training should comprise a three-part package of initial preparation, continuing training/support meetings and specialist preparation. The earlier edition paid scant attention to the latter components, and said of volunteer support meetings only that 'in some areas these meetings are recognised as essential'. By contrast, the updated version states that 'participation in a minimum number of support meetings should be regarded as a pre-requisite to their continued volunteering and as an essential extension of the initial training'. Thus efforts to formalise and strengthen the training programme for visitors are now seen as vital.

Although the Code of Practice for Schemes stipulates that Management Committees should ensure that adequate training is given, as yet no Scheme has been disaffiliated for not complying with the Code. Nevertheless, our national survey found that four Schemes still did not offer a basic training course. Three of these had been formed before 1980 and the other in 1983. None was apologetic, as they seemed to represent the 'old school' view that Victims Support is primarily a matter of 'neighbourliness' and requires no special skills. They commented, in turn, 'We have little formal training', 'None is offered', 'Advice is given rather than training' and 'We have no need to establish a training course'.

We asked the 40 volunteers we interviewed for their views on the programmes in which they had participated. The responses were varied: few enthused, some had been bored, but the majority thought that the training had been adequate. To the question 'how confident did you feel on your first unaccompanied visit?' two main types of response appeared. Some, including nearly all those with relevant voluntary or professional experience, said that they had had few qualms. For example, a nurse and a social worker both remarked that they had felt very confident - 'being used to that kind of situation'. By contrast, most of the others admitted that they had felt some trepidation:

'I was scared beforehand, but once the door opened I felt fine.'

'I quaked a bit at first. I felt people might think I was a nuisance but nobody ever does - that amazed me.'

'I felt very unconfident, but when I arrived I was OK.'

'I realised I had a lot to learn.'

'It was in a rough area and I felt nervous, so I was relieved when they weren't in.'

However, this natural apprehension usually gave way to the feeling that they could 'cope' with the visit on arrival at the victim's home, suggesting that, generally speaking, the preparation had been adequate.

We turn now to our own observations of the initial preparation programmes, concentrating on general course structure, the task of trainers and speakers and audience participation levels.

Most courses we attended comprised six sessions, each lasting one and a half to two and a half hours. This length of course was first recommended in the initial training manual, although the 'period of training would vary according to local needs'. Six sessions should probably remain the minimum, since we found that attempts to reduce the number of sessions were not successful. For example, one Scheme tried a 'mini-course' of four sessions to cater for a small group of intending visitors. After the final meeting most of the group lacked confidence to go out and visit and requested further meetings before commencing. In situations where only a few intending visitors are awaiting training at each Scheme, preparation courses provided on a regional basis or shared between neighbouring Schemes, might resolve this problem. In the West Midlands, for instance, one or two trainees from each of several local Schemes participated in a regional programme of five sessions; a sixth session was then held at each individual Scheme.

At the other end of the scale, one Scheme studied always insisted on eight sessions before volunteers could begin visiting, this being possible through having a large and very active training sub-committee. Feedback from the volunteers indicated that the course was not thought overly long, and indeed most had enjoyed all the meetings.

One factor which we noted had a big impact on audience participation levels was the physical surroundings in which courses were conducted. Interaction between volunteers and trainers was more animated in the informal setting of the Co-ordinator's lounge than in a large, draughty hall where formal seating divided them. Co-ordinators themselves occasionally commented that one training course was better than another precisely because of the change in type of venue, making comments like 'that one didn't seem so good because of all the empty space'. While we do not recommend infringing the privacy of the Co-ordinator's home, attention to the planned venue could nevertheless affect the attractiveness of courses to visitors-in-training.

Most Schemes typically used a combination of Scheme members and outside speakers to conduct the training programmes, but it appeared that few had the luxury of choice of trainers. Co-ordinators often led two or three sessions each - usually on the background of Victims Support, daily routine of the local Scheme and the referral system. In a few cases they were relieved of training duties, another Scheme member - perhaps a social worker or probation officer member of the Management Committee - taking overall responsibility for the programme. While most trainers other than Co-ordinators talked knowledgeably about the work of the Scheme, in some instances they appeared to hold misconceptions of the work of Victims Support in general, and seemed ill-briefed as to the contribution they were expected to make. There were also a number of basic practical issues on which trainers did not always seem to have clear ideas about the policy of the Scheme, and sometimes confused the new volunteers. Examples were the number of visits they were expected to make to individual victims, whether they or the Co-ordinator should make referrals to other agencies, and whether their general aim should be to 'normalise' or to 'improve' the victim's situation (e.g. if the 'needs' identified are not related to the offence, but are caused by running damp or rats in the kitchen, to what extent should a Scheme become involved in helping with such problems?). During several courses contradictory edicts were issued not only by different trainers but also by the same person. Certainly these are difficult points to convey clearly, especially where no rigid rules exist, and when in practice the answers often depend on the nature of the specific case. However, trainees and researchers alike were often left feeling confused and it seemed that trainers were sometimes inadequately prepared to answer what were eminently predictable questions from the recruits.

At several Schemes the aim of equipping new visitors with practical information that would be essential to them in helping victims was achieved admirably well. One trainer asked them to contribute ideas about the range of problems that might be experienced, and what the visitor or Scheme could do, and then went systematically through the type of information one would need in order to resolve different kinds of problems. The discussion was concentrated upon problems that they were likely to meet frequently in reality, such as stolen documents, repairs and insurance claims. Another Scheme advised trainees of the range of circumstances which could lead to someone obtaining state benefits or emergency grants following a crime, and provided a clear hand-out of local voluntary and statutory services to accompany the discussion.

However, elsewhere there was a fairly common tendency to overload volunteers with detailed information about matters with which they would be unlikely to deal in their first few months of visiting. For example, one Scheme spent a whole session discussing the minutiae of criminal injuries compensation claims, even though few assault victims were ever referred to the Scheme, and then these were handled by the more experienced visitors. Other Schemes, too, spent a great deal of time on details of court procedure, although hardly anybody at the Scheme had ever acompanied a victim to court. Obviously, in some Schemes it is important to impart this sort of information at an early stage, but in these cases it seemed sensible to leave details to later 'in-service' training.

The police contributions to preparation programmes also frequently exemplified the inadequate tailoring of input to visitors' immediate practical requirements. Many police officers who were invited to conduct a session were unsure of what was expected of them and how to make their talk useful to trainees. At one Scheme, a senior officer treated the audience to a long, colourful review of his police career, which although very interesting was hardly relevant to the work of the visitors. Sometimes, too, officers sounded patronising, saying things like 'We haven't got time

to go and visit victims so I'm just here to give you moral
support', or 'You're the lady with the cup of tea', which
did not impress the audience. Other talks were criticised
by trainees afterwards as simply public relations exercises
on the part of the police. What appears to be required, but
was rarely given, is chronological information on what
happens after an offence is reported, information on local
crime rates and prevalent offences and general crime
prevention advice. Morevoer, it would be helpful for the
police to equip trainees to answer questions that might be
worrying crime victims, such as 'Do burglars often come
back?', 'Are they violent?' and 'Are they likely to be
watching the house?'

We found that most trainers were successful in gearing
sessions to the abilities of new visitors-in-training, but a
few met problems. The role play session at one Scheme,
while attempting to illustrate useful and important points,
unfortunately misfired through the trainer assuming that
trainees had previously covered the practical aspects of
helping that they were now expected to role play. Because
relatively serious cases were presented which had required
much follow-up in real life, the confidence of intending
visitors was somewhat undermined by their lack of knowledge.
This underlines the importance of the co-ordination of the
training programme, and shows that tailoring role play cases
to the level of new trainees needs care.

One other problem worth mentioning arose from
misconceptions held by outside trainers about the normal
caseload of VSS. There was a tendency to overdramatise the
'normal diet' of day-to-day visiting. Trainers would often
use grievous bodily harm and rape cases as examples rather
than more 'ordinary' cases of burglary, which is the crime
that new visitors will most often encounter. One police
officer enthusiastically gave a thorough account of what
happens 'when your victim is killed in a fatal accident',
but as one visitor commented:

> 'He told us what happened when victims were dead on
> arrival at hospital, but that's a bit late for the
> volunteer. I don't see how that's training.'

One introductory session was an alarming experience for
initiates. No background information on the national or
regional perspective was offered, and the impression given
was that visitors would be working almost in isolation.
Trainees were reassured that they would be personally
insured from the moment they stepped outside their door
(creating unnecessary anxiety at this stage). Moreover,
they were told that they would be able to ring a Social

Services contact person in the middle of the night if need be, and that some visitors had 'broken their holidays' to visit victims. Thus the atypical was portrayed as typical. Volunteers were left wondering what Victims Support was all about and what dangerous tasks visitors would actually be expected to undertake.

Various techniques were used to increase audience participation levels - an important ingredient for maintaining the interest of trainees. The first session at many courses included an exercise for effecting introductions among the group. Trainees would take it in turn to find out as much about their partner as possible and then would report back to the group on what they had discovered. Sometimes this exercise was carried out in groups of three with another trainee acting as observer and commenting on the performance of the other two. This technique also served to sensitise intending visitors to the art of listening - one of the skills essential to supporters - to increase awareness of body language and to break the ice. By contrast, the trainers at another course did not even attempt to introduce participants to each other, causing one visitor to remark in the penultimate session that she still did not know anyone's name.

The 'brainstorming' technique was one successful way of encouraging the involvement of the audience and of prompting trainees to empathise with victims' feelings. They would be asked to call out the range of feelings they might experience or had experienced if a previous victim themselves, and when a list was compiled the group would discuss each one separately. Elsewhere, the impact of the offence on the victim was usually dealt with by way of a lecture, which, although interesting, did not encourage participation and may have been less successful in this context as a teaching tool.

Role play was a method used at nearly all of the programmes we attended, but while this had advantages over the use of straight talks to demonstrate certain points or skills, not all trainees were enthusiastic about taking part. Interestingly, the updated training manual, recognising occasional volunteer resistance, suggests 'practice at helping' as an alternative title. We noticed that the use of role play seemed more successful and less intimidating at Schemes where visitors got together in twos or threes than when one pair was watched and evaluated by the others. In particular, group discussion flowed more easily after role playing in pairs. During the later sessions at one Scheme studied, role play concentrated on important issues like what to do if a victim maintains that he or she is quite all right and does not need help when clearly this is not the case, and what to do if the named victim declines help but his or her partner is really the one badly affected. Role playing these situations alerted trainees more forcefully to these possibilities than just hearing about them in passing.

Another Scheme which made considerable use of the telephone as a contact method, role played introduction techniques using a real telephone. This is an idea which we feel could be taken up at all Schemes regularly using the telephone to contact victims, since people have varying ability to communicate clearly and warmly without visual contact and, as reported in Chapter 6, victims were generally less happy with a telephone call than either an unannounced visit or a letter.

While the updated training manual stresses the importance of 'ongoing training and support meetings' for visitors, only three of the eight Schemes studied offered training of this nature. Among the sessions we attended were workshops designed to improve visitors' confidence and assertiveness, including how to say 'no' to excessive demands and how to deal with manipulative victims, a meeting where local services and facilities available to ethnic minority groups were discussed, and a seminar on the special problems of personal violence victims. These topics which, through time limitations, fell outside the remit of the basic preparation were found extremely useful by pariticipants. Interestingly, at these Schemes, several experienced visitors told us that they were more likely to attend these training sessions than ordinary support meetings, since the problems of new volunteers became less stimulating on repeated hearing.

The third component of the new training package is specialist preparation. This has been discussed to some extent in Chapter 7, where we recommend that visitors who intend to support rape victims should be well equipped in counselling skills, although undoubtedly these take much more time to assimilate than the one or two sessions devoted to them in many preparation programmes. Indeed, we also feel that visitors who provide longer-term support to other victims, perhaps of personal violence, would benefit from a specialist training course with a counselling component. This seems to us a matter which deserves considerable priority as Schemes gain the confidence of the police and are referred more serious cases.

To summarise: while, generally speaking, the basic training sessions we observed seemed adequate, certain weak

247

features were quite common. Some trainers were either ill-briefed about the input they were expected to make, failed to concentrate on the essential needs of new visitors (especially with regard to practical help to be offered), and sometimes appeared to have little knowledge of the reality of the day-to-day work of Victims Support Schemes. It also seems more beneficial to place the emphasis on routine rather than exceptional work.

A final point we would make is that it seemed useful for neighbouring Schemes to pool their training resources, which removes some pressure from individual Schemes and saves new volunteers waiting for several months for sufficient recruits to be available to make it 'worthwhile' setting up a new course.

**Notes to Appendix**

1.   In some circumstances where only one worker is to join the Scheme, no choice is allowed.  However, where the recruitment of a group of workers is agreed, Schemes may have several months to take up this full quota.

# Appendix tables

**What would you say are the most difficult problems facing your Scheme at the moment?**

| | Percentage of Schemes mentioning problems* |
|---|---|
| | % |
| Financial Problems | 36 |
| Volunteer recruitment | 34 |
| Police referral problems | 22 |
| Co-ordinator problems (workload, recruitment, remuneration) | 12 |
| Volunteer morale/interest/quality | 11 |
| Lack of public awareness about the Scheme | 9 |
| Management Committee problems | 5 |
| Problems related to MSC-funded workers | 5 |
| Co-operation from statutory agencies | 3 |
| Other | 3 |

\* Column sums to more than 100%, as some Schemes mentioned more than one problem.

N = 163 Schemes and districts responding to 1984 questionnaire.

## Table B

**Difficulties in recruiting volunteers by type of area and age of Scheme**

|  |  | Percentage finding recruitment a 'major' or 'considerable' problem % | Percentage finding recruitment 'no problem at all' % |
|---|---|---|---|
| **Schemes in large cities** |  |  |  |
| Under 3 years old | (N = 26) | 50 | 19 |
| 3-4 years old | (N = 14) | 64 | 0 |
| 5+ years | (N = 19) | 68 | 16 |
| All ages | (N = 59) | 59 | 14 |
| **Schemes in medium-sized towns** |  |  |  |
| Under 3 years old | (N = 29) | 21 | 41 |
| 3-4 years old | (N = 8) | 25 | 12 |
| 5+ years old | (N = 19) | 26 | 21 |
| All ages | (N = 56) | 23 | 30 |
| **Schemes in small towns/rural** |  |  |  |
| Under 3 years old | (N = 23) | 22 | 39 |
| 3-4 years old | (N = 13) | 54 | 15 |
| 5+ years | (N = 12) | 17 | 25 |
| All ages | (N = 48) | 29 | 29 |
| **All Schemes** |  |  |  |
| Under 3 years old | (N = 78) | 31 | 39 |
| 3-4 years old | (N = 35) | 53 | 9 |
| 5+ years | (N = 50) | 40 | 20 |
| All ages | (N = 163) | 38 | 24 |

## Table C

## Schemes' experience of different methods of recruiting potential volunteers

### Outcome

| Method | very successful % | Fairly successful % | Not very successful % | Very unsuccessful % | Not tried % | (Percentage of those trying method who found it very or fairly successful) % |
|---|---|---|---|---|---|---|
| Word of mouth | 39 | 44 | 9 | 2 | 6 | (88) |
| Advertisements | 9 | 29 | 19 | 9 | 34 | (57) |
| Talks to local groups | 8 | 31 | 28 | 12 | 20 | (49) |
| Voluntary services bureaux, etc. | 14 | 24 | 22 | 20 | 19 | (47) |
| Other voluntary agencies | 3 | 17 | 20 | 11 | 49 | (40) |
| Posters | 1 | 6 | 20 | 16 | 57 | (17) |

N = 163 Schemes and districts replying to questionnaire, mid-1984

251

## Table D
**Rates of retention of volunteers over 12-month period by type of area in which Scheme is based**

| | Percentage of volunteers still active after one year | | | |
|---|---|---|---|---|
| Type of area | Under 50 per cent % | 50 - 79 per cent % | 80 per cent and over % | Total % |
| Inner city | 17 | 52 | 31 | 100 (N=29) |
| Other parts of large city | 10 | 35 | 55 | 100 (N=20) |
| Town of 50,000-250,000 pop. | 7 | 37 | 56 | 100 (N=43) |
| Small town/rural | 7.5 | 37.5 | 55 | 100 (N=40) |
| All areas | 10 | 40 | 50 | 100 (N=132) |

## Table E
**Frequency of volunteer meetings; by whether (and how) Co-ordinators were paid (urban Schemes only)**

| | Frequency of volunteer meetings | | | |
|---|---|---|---|---|
| Status of Co-ordinator | Under 4 per year % | 4 - 9 per year % | 10 or more per year % | Total % |
| Full-time paid | 3 | 26 | 71 | 100 (N=31) |
| Part-time paid | 6 | 29 | 65 | 100 (N=17) |
| Honorarium | 10 | 39 | 52 | 100 (N=31) |
| Unpaid | 11 | 36 | 53 | 100 (N=36) |
| All | 8 | 33 | 59 | 100 (N=115) |

## Table F

### Selected activities of Schemes; by status of main Co-ordinator (urban Schemes only)

| | | Status of main Co-ordinator | | |
|---|---|---|---|---|
| | | Paid (full-time or part-time) % | Unpaid or honorarium % | All % |
| Number of CICB claims helped with in past six months | Nil | 11 | 50 | 34 |
| | 1-10 | 71 | 45 | 56 |
| | 11 or more | 18 | 5 | 10 |
| | Total % | 100 (N=66) | 100 (N=45) | 100 (N=111) |
| Number of times victims accompanied to court | Many/several times | 13 | 6 | 9 |
| | Once or twice | 40 | 36 | 38 |
| | Never | 47 | 58 | 53 |
| | Total % | 100 (N=66) | 100 (N=47) | 100 (N=113) |
| Number of times support offered to relatives of murder victims | Nil | 63 | 84 | 75 |
| | Once or twice | 28 | 14 | 20 |
| | Several | 9 | 2 | 5 |
| | Total % | 100 (N=67) | 100 (N=48) | 100 (N=115) |

## Table G

**Proportions of incidents in which victim or household 'very much' affected, by type of offence and prior acquaintance (or not) with offender**

| Type of Offence | Offence known to police: % affected 'very much' | | Offence not known to police: % affected 'very much' | |
| | offender stranger % | offender known to victim* % | offender stranger % | offender known to victim* % |
|---|---|---|---|---|
| Burglary/theft dwelling | 44 | 50 | 15 | 15 |
| Wounding | 20 | 57 | 7 ) | 15 |
| Common assault | 9 | 18 | ) | 15 |
| Threats | 24 | 54 | 6 | 20 |
| Vandalism | 42 | 29 | 4 | 14 |
| Theft (personal, household,m/v) | 14 | 24 | 6 | 13 |
| All BCS offence categories | 22 | 39 | 7 | 16 |

\* Includes cases where some offenders were known, others not.

Weighted data, based on all BCS offences where victim is able to 'say anything at all about the people who did it'.

## Table H

Best estimates of numbers of A) personal crimes and B) household crimes occurring in England and Wales 1983, in which respondent or member of household was 'very much' affected over first few days; by whether or not offence known to the police and whether or not recorded

Estimated number of offences in which victim/household 'very much' affected: England and Wales 1983

| | Recorded | Reported but not recorded | Not reported |
|---|---|---|---|
| **A. Personal Offences** | | | |
| Wounding | 40,000 | 50,000 | 20,000 |
| Theft person/robbery | 25,000 | 30,000 | 30,000 |
| Other personal theft | 40,000 | 15,000 | 60,000 |
| Sexual offences | 5,000a | b | 20,000c |
| Common assault | b | 35,000 | 120,000 |
| Threats | b | 125,000 | 125,000 |
| | 110,000 | 255,000 | 375,000 |
| | | | |
| **B. Household Offences** | | | |
| Vandalism | 75,000 | 85,000 | 120,000 |
| Burglary | 160,000 | 10,000 | 15,000 |
| Theft from m/v | 50,000 | 10,000 | 20,000 |
| Theft of m/v | 60,000 | - | - |
| Other household theft | 30,000 | 10,000 | 45,000 |
| Bicycle theft | 20,000 | 5,000 | 5,000 |
| | 395,000 | 120,000 | 205,000 |
| Total (all offences) | 505,000 | 375,000 | 580,000 |

All figures rounded to nearest 5,000.

a.   Informed guess rather than estimate: BCS has insufficient data.
b.   Numbers too small for analysis.
c.   BCS data considered unreliable, due to known under-reporting of these offences.

Sources: Our interviews and <u>Criminal Statistics</u> 1983, BCS 1984, Hough and Mayhew (1985).

## Table I

**Proportions of cases in which respondent - unprompted - mentioned a specific emotional problem: by type of offence and sex of respondent (incidents known to police)**

|                               | Female % | Male % | All % |
|-------------------------------|----------|--------|-------|
| Threats                       | 76       | 47     | 64    |
| Burglary loss                 | 67       | 49     | 58    |
| Robbery/'snatch' theft        | 88       | 29     | 57    |
| Wounding                      | 77       | 49     | 55    |
| Vandalism                     | 65       | 30     | 51    |
| Burglary attempt/nil stolen   | 49       | 42     | 46    |
| Other h/hold, personal theft  | 37       | 32     | 34    |
| Theft of motor vehicle        | 34       | 21     | 27    |
| Theft person ('sneak')        | 34       | 27     | 33    |
| Bicycle theft                 | 25       | 27     | 26    |
| Common assault                | 44       | 21     | 25    |
| Theft from motor vehicle      | 23       | 26     | 25    |
| All BCS offences known to police | 49    | 33     | 41    |

Source: BCS 1984. Weighted data.

## Table J

**Types of offence (known to police) where selected kinds of emotional effect most often mentioned; by sex of respondent**

|                                                          | Male (% mentioning)         |    | Female (% mentioning)        |    |
|----------------------------------------------------------|-----------------------------|----|------------------------------|----|
| Anger                                                    | Personal theft              | 17 | Major vandalism              | 23 |
|                                                          | Theft of motor vehicle      | 12 | Personal Theft               | 16 |
| Worry, fear, loss of confidence                          | Threats                     | 37 | Wounding                     | 53 |
|                                                          | Wounding                    | 37 | Threats                      | 46 |
|                                                          | Burglary                    | 28 | Burglary                     | 37 |
| General health problems, stress depression, sleeplessness | Wounding                   | 12 | Wounding                     | 33 |
|                                                          | Burglary                    | 7  | Threats                      | 29 |

Source: BCS 1984. (Weighted data).

## Table K

### First reactions after discovering or experiencing the offence; by offence and sex of victim

|  | Burglary | | | Assault, robbery theft from person* | | |
|---|---|---|---|---|---|---|
|  | Male % | Female % | All % | Male % | Female % | All % |
| Shock, shaking, confusion, panic | 22 | 43 | 34 | 48 | 49 | 49 |
| Anger, annoyance | 45 | 23 | 33 | 39 | 18 | 31 |
| General upset, tears | 32 | 34 | 33 | 3 | 33 | 21 |
| Fear, nervousness | 6 | 36 | 22 | 13 | 27 | 21 |
| Surprise, disbelief | 26 | 10 | 17 | 19 | 27 | 23 |
| Revulsion, feeling sick | 13 | 20 | 17 | 19 | 16 | 17 |

* The majority of assaults were committed against males, while the majority of thefts from the person were committed against females.

Columns sum to more than 100% as some respondents mentioned more than one effect.

Unweighted N = 175 victims of offences of burglary, assault and theft from the person recorded by the police or referred 'automatically' to Schemes ('composite' sample, Chapter 3).

## Table L

### Worst aspect of the offence, from the victim's viewpoint

| 'Worst thing' | Burglary % | Robbery, assault % | Theft from the person % |
|---|---|---|---|
| | | Type of offence | |
| The offence itself/ discovering it | 23 | 43 | 59 |
| Continuing fear, insecurity | 11 | 12 | 11 |
| Sense of 'intrusion' | 29 | 0 | 0 |
| Pain/difficulty caused by injury | 0 | 17 | 0 |
| Effect on people close to self | 6 | 9 | 0 |
| Attitudes of authorities/ other people | 10 | 5 | 0 |
| Financial loss | 3 | 0 | 4 |
| Other practical problems/ inconvenience | 2 | 2 | 7 |
| Sentimental value of property stolen | 7 | 0 | 4 |
| Loss of trust in others | 1 | 3 | 4 |
| Blaming self | 2 | 2 | 0 |
| Other/N.A. | 6 | 7 | 11 |
| | 100 | 100 | 100 |
| (Unweighted N) | (N=90) | (N=58) | (N=27) |

Weighted data: 'composite' sample of 175 victims, weighted to approximate to a representative sample of above offences from police records.

## Table M

Proportions of victims (not visited by VSS) experiencing each of a list of prompted effects 'very much' or 'not at all', 3-6 weeks after offence

| | Burglary | | Robbery, assault, theft from person | |
|---|---|---|---|---|
| | very much % | not at all % | very much % | not at all % |
| Unable to get it out of your mind | 18 | 42 | 8 | 49 |
| Feeling afraid or nervous generally | 12 | 49 | 5 | 41 |
| Feeling unsettled or uneasy | 15 | 54 | 5 | 54 |
| Feeling angry | 18 | 45 | 10 | 54 |
| Feeling unable to trust other people | 12 | 58 | 10 | 56 |
| Being afraid to go out | 12 | 76 | 3 | 59 |
| Feeling sad about losing something important to you | 12 | 54 | 13 | 59 |
| Feeling depressed | 12 | 70 | 5 | 74 |
| Afraid to come into house/room | 3 | 67 | 0 | 82 |
| Difficulty sleeping | 3 | 76 | 3 | 79 |
| Afraid to stay in the house | 6 | 76 | 0 | 87 |
| Not wanting to be alone | 6 | 67 | 3 | 92 |
| Headaches/feeling ill | 3 | 85 | 3 | 87 |
| Feeling helpless or vulnerable | 3 | 67 | 3 | 64 |
| Feeling weak/loss of strength | 6 | 91 | 8 | 87 |
| Feeling guilty/it was your fault | 3 | 91 | 0 | 85 |
| Unable to do ordinary tasks | 3 | 88 | 8 | 92 |
| Loss of interest in work/hobbies | 3 | 88 | 5 | 90 |
| Loss of memory of what happened | 0 | 94 | 3 | 95 |
| Feeling contaminated or dirty | 3 | 94 | 0 | 97 |
| Crying/on verge of tears | 3 | 94 | 0 | 97 |
| Loss of appetite | 3 | 94 | 0 | 100 |
| | (N = 33) | | (N = 39) | |

## Table N

### Pscyhological changes resulting from offence: victims not assisted by VSS

| | Percentage answering yes | |
| | Burglary<br>% | Robbery, assault,<br>theft from person<br>% |
|---|---|---|
| Q. Do you feel generally: | | |
| Less cheerful than you did before? | 33 | 15 |
| You have less energy than you had before? | 18 | 18 |
| Less in control of your own life? | 33 | 18 |
| Less warm in your relations with others? | 27 | 15 |
| More afraid of unpleasant things happening to you? | 45<br>(N=33) | 49<br>(N=39) |

N = 72 victims of burglary, robbery, theft from the person, and assault not visited or assisted by volunteers, and interviewed 3-6 weeks after the offence.


## Table O

Q. Have you changed your previous lifestyle in any way as a result of the crime? (Victims not visited or assisted by Schemes)

| | Percentage answering yes | |
| | Burglary<br>% | Robbery, assault,<br>theft from person<br>% |
|---|---|---|
| Go out less during the day | 21 | 10 |
| Go out less at night | 24 | 38 |
| Go out less alone | 12 | 31 |
| Avoid certain places you used to go | 3 | 26 |
| Avoid answering the door/ telephone | 18 | 13 |
| Invite fewer people into your home | 21 | 5 |
| Lock up more carefully | 67 | 44 |
| Sleep in a different room/ with the light on | 15<br>(N=33) | 3<br>(N=39) |

N = 72 victims of burglary, robbery, theft from the person, and assault not visited or assisted by volunteers, and interviewed 3-6 weeks after the offence.

General Health Questionnaire scores at 3-6 weeks after the offence, among burglary and assault/robbery victims not visited by VSS

|  | Males | | Females | |
|  | Burglary | Assault/ robbery | Burglary | Assault/ robbery |
| --- | --- | --- | --- | --- |
|  | % | % | % | % |
| GHQ.60 score:[a] | | | | |
| 0 - 12 | 77 | 75 | 50 | 47 |
| 13+ | 23 | 25 | 50 | 53 |
| which translates as:[b] Probable prevalence of psychiatric disturbance among our sample | 16 | 18 | 45 | 48 |
| Compared with: Probable prevalence of psychiatric disturbance in Goldberg's random community sample[b] | 11% | | 23% | |

(N = 72 victims of burglary, robbery and assault not visited by VSS volunteers.)

a. Scores above 12 are indicative of possible psychiatric disturbance using 60-item GHQ.

b. These probable prevalence rates are based on Goldberg's (1978) calculations using a random sample of the population of Manchester. The likely prevalence of psychiatric disturbance was, for males, 70% of those scoring 13 or over on the GHQ.60, and, for females, 90% of those scoring 13 or over.

### Table Q
**Reasons why victims who would have liked to talk more to family or friends about their feelings, did not in fact do so**

|  | % |
|---|---|
| They have no time to spare/ don't want to know/ victim sees them rarely | 19 |
| Victim doesn't want to impose/ doesn't want to worry them | 36 |
| Victim finds it difficult to talk about feelings/'keep myself to myself' | 22 |
| They will blame victim/make jokes/think victim stupid | 8 |
| Other/don't know | 14 |

N = 36: all victims interviewed after 3-6 weeks, excluding rape victims, who would have/might have liked to talk more about their feelings with family or friends.

### Table R
**Proportions of unannounced visits resulting in personal contact with victim**

| Scheme | Immediately successful | Contact established later* | No contact achieved | Total |
|---|---|---|---|---|
|  | % | % | % | % |
| B | 66 | 6 | 28 | 100 (N = 120) |
| D | 60 | 5 | 24 | 100 (N = 99) |
| E | 56 | 4 | 39 | 100 (N = 99) |
| F | 70 | 11 | 20 | 100 (N = 66) |
| Total % | 63 | 6 | 31 | 100 (N = 384) |

\* Either from a further unannounced visit or following a response to a message left after first attempt.

# Bibliography

Armstrong, P. (1982) "The Myth of Meeting Needs in Adult
    Education and Community Development."    Critical Social
    Policy, vol. 2, no. 2, p.29

Atkeson, B. K., et al. (1982) "Victims of Rape: Repeated
    Assessment and Depressive Symptoms." Journal of Con-
    sulting and Clinical Psychology, vol. 50, p. 96.

Bard, M. and Sangrey, D. (1979)  The Crime Victim's Book.
    New York: Basic Books.

Blair, I. (1984)  Investigating Rape: A New Approach for
    Police.  London: Croom Helm.

Block, R. L. (1983)  "Studies of Victimisation and Fear of
    Crime."  Washington, D.C.: Department of Justice.

Blumberg, M. L. (1979)  "Injury to Victims of Personal
    Crime: Nature and Extent" in Parsonage, W. H. (ed.),
    Perspectives on Victimology.  Beverly Hills: Sage.

Bourque, B. B., Brumback, G. B., Krug, R. E. and Richardson,
    L. O. (1978)   Crisis Intervention: Investigating the
    Need for New Applications.  Washington, D.C.:   American
    Institute for Research.

Brown, S. D. and Yantzi, M. (1980)  "Needs Assessment for
    Victims and Witnesses of Crime."   Kitchener, Ontario:
    Mennonite Central Committee.

Bradshaw, J. (1972)  "The Concept of Social Need."   New
    Society, 30  March 1972.

Burgess, A. W. and Holmstrom, L. L. (1974)  "Rape Trauma Syndrome." American Journal of Psychiatry, vol. 131, pp. 981-986.

Burgess, A. W. and Holmstrom, L. L. (1976)  "Coping Behaviour of the Rape Victim." American Journal of Orthopsychiatry, vol. 133, no. 4, pp. 413-417.

Burgess, A. W. and Holmstrom, L. L. (1978)  The Victim of Rape: Institutional Reactions.  New York: Wiley.

Burgess, A. W. and Holmstrom, L. L. (1979)  "Rape: Sexual description and recovery." American Journal of Orthopsychiatry, vol. 49, no. 4, pp. 648-657.

Burns-Howell, A. J. et al. (1982)  "Policing Strategy: Organisational or Victim Needs?"  Bramshill: Police Staff  College.

Burt, M. R. (1980)  "Cultural Myths and Supports for Rape." Journal of Personality and Social Psychology, vol. 38, p. 217.

Burt, M. R. and Katz, B. L. (1985)  "Rape, Robbery and Burglary: Responses to Actual and Feared Criminal Victimisation, with Special Focus on Women and the Elderly." Victimology, vol. 10, nos. 1-4, pp. 325-358.

Butler, S. and Tuck, M. (1984)  "Report of Visit to the Council of Europe 16th Research Conference on Research into Victimisation."  26-29 November 1984.

Calhoun, K. S., Atkeson, B. M. and Reswick, P. A. (1982)  "A Longitudinal Examination of Fear Reactions in Victims of Rape."  Journal of Counselling Psychology, vol. 29, p. 655.

Campbell, J. C. (1985)  "Beating of Wives: A Cross-Cultural Perspective."  Victimology, vol. 10, nos. 1-4, pp. 174-185.

Canadian Federal-Provincial Task Force (1983)  Justice for Victims of Crime.  Ottawa: Canadian Government Publishing Centre.

Caplan, G. (1964)  Principles of Preventive Psychiatry.  New York: Basic Books.

Carlen, P. (1983)  Women's Imprisonment: A Study in Social Control.  London: Routledge and Kegan Paul.

Chambers, G. and Millar, A. (1983) Investigating Sexual Assault. Edinburgh: Scottish Office Social Research Study.

Chesney, S. and Schneider, A. L. (1981) "Crime Victim Crisis Centres: The Minnesota Experience" in Galaway, B. and Hudson, J., Perspectives on Crime Victims. St. Louis: Mosby.

Clarke, R. and Hope, T. (1984) Coping with Burglary. Boston: Kluwer-Nijhoff Publishing Company.

Clarke, R. G., Eckblom, P., Hough, M. and Mayhew, P. (1985)" Elderly Victims of Crime and Exposure to Risk." The Howard Journal, vol. 24, no. 1, February 1985.

Conklin, J. E. (1975) The Impact of Crime. New York: Macmillan.

Council of Europe (1985) Recommendation No. R (85) 11 on the position of the victim in the framework of criminal law and procedure. Strasbourg: Council of Europe.

Culyer, A. J., Lavers, R. and Williams, A. (1972) "Health Indicators" in Shonfield, A. and Shaw, S. (eds.), Social Indicators and Social Policy. London.

Cumberbatch, G. and Beardsworth, A. (1976) "Criminals, Victims and Mass Communications" in Viano, E. C. (ed), Victims and Society. Washington, D.C.: Visage Press.

Cunningham, C. (1976) "Patterns and Effect of Crime against the Elderly: the Kansas City Study" in Goldsmith, J. and Goldsmith, S. (eds.), Crime and the Elderly. Lexington, Mass.

Denton, A. R. (1979) "What They Think/What They Do: A Study of the Perceptions and Service Utilizations of Victims of Violent Crime." Ph.D. thesis, Case Western Reserve University (quoted in Villmow, op. cit.).

Doyal, L. and Gough, I (1984) "A Theory of Human Needs." Critical Social Work, summer issue.

Draper, J. (1985) "Burglary Victims and Their Reactions." Unpublished Master's thesis, University of Houston.

Duddle, M. (1985) "The Need for Sexual Assault Centres in the United Kingdom." British Medical Journal, vol. 290, 9 March 1985.

Duff, P. (1984) "The Victim Movement - An Unresolved Problem." Unpublished paper to Cambridge conference on Victims, Compensation and Criminal Justice.

Durlak, J. A. (1979) "Comparative Effectiveness of Paraprofessional and Professional Helpers." Psychological Bulletin, vol. 86, No. 1, pp. 80-92.

Elias, R. (1983) "The Politics of Evaluating Victim Programs." Paper to conference on Victims of Crime, International Society of Criminology, Vancouver, 1983.

Ellis, E. M. et al. (1980) "Sexual Dysfunctions in Victims of Rape." Women and Health, vol. 5, pp. 39-47.

Ellis, E. M. (1983) "A Review of Empirical Rape Research: Victim Reactions and Response to Treatment." Clinical Psychology Review, vol. 3, no. 4, pp. 473-490.

Fairhead, S. (1981) "Persistent Petty Offenders." Home Office Research Study No. 66. London: HMSO.

Fattah, E. A. (1979) "Some Recent Theoretical Developments in Victimology." Victimology, vol. 4, no. 2, pp. 198-213.

Fattah, E.A. (ed., 1986) From Crime Policy to Victim Policy: Reorienting the Justice System. London: Macmillan.

Fields, R. (1981) "Research on Victims: Problems and Issues", in Salasin, S. E. (ed.), Evaluating Victim Services. Beverly Hills: Sage.

Frank, E. et al. (1981) "Past Psychiatric Symptoms and the Responses to Sexual Assault." Comparative Psychiatry, vol. 22, pp. 479-487.

Friedman, K., Bischoff, H., Davis, R. and Person, A. (1982) Victims and Helpers: Reactions to Crime. New York: Victim Services Agency.

Galaway, B. (1985) "Victim Participation in the Penal-Corrective Process." Victimology, vol. 10, nos. 1-4, pp. 617-630.

Gay, M. J., Holtom, C. and Thomas, M. S. (1975) "Helping the Victims." International Journal of Offender Therapy and Comparative Criminology, vol. 19.

Genn, H. (1982) "Meeting Legal Needs." Centre for Socio-Legal Studies, University of Oxford.

Gill, M. and Mawby, R. I. (1985) "Victim Assistance through Voluntary Organisation: The Role of Volunteers in Britain." Paper presented at Fifth International Symposium on Victimology, Zagreb.

Goldberg, D., Kay, C. and Thompson, L. (1974) "Psychiatric Morbidity in General Practice and the Community." Psychol. Med., vol. 6, pp. 565-569.

Goldberg, D. (1978) Manual of the General Health Questionnaire. London: NFER Publishing Company.

Greater London Council Police Committee (1983) Racial Harrassment in London: Report of a Panel of Inquiry set up by the GLC Police Committee.

Hall, R. E. (1984) Ask Any Woman: A London Enquiry into Rape and Sexual Assault. Bristol: Falling Wall Press.

Harding, J. (1982) "Victims and Offenders: Needs and Responsibilities." NCVO Occasional Paper Two. London: Bedford Square Press.

Hassell, R. A. and Reswick, P. A. (1981) "The Impact of Stranger versus Nonstranger Rape: A Longitudinal Study." Unpublished manuscript, Medical University of South Carolina.

Haward, L. R. C. (1981) "Psychological Consequences of being the Victim of a Crime" in Lloyd-Bostock, S. (ed.), Law and Psychology. Oxford: SSRC Centre for Socio-Legal Studies.

Home Affairs Committee (1984) Report on Compensation and Support for Victims of Crime. London: HMSO.

Hough, M. (1983) "Victims of Violent Crime: Findings from the British Crime Survey." Paper presented at the 33rd International Course in Criminology, Vancouver, B.C., Canada.

Hough, M. (1985) "The Impact of Victimisation: Findings from the British Crime Survey." Victimology, vol. 10, nos. 1-4, pp. 488-497.

Hough, M. and Mayhew, P. (1985) "Taking Account of Crime: Key Findings from the 1984 British Crime Survey." Home Office Research Study No. 85. London: HMSO.

Irving, C. (1977) "The State of Victims." Prison Service Journal, vol. 28, pp. 2-4.

Jackson, H. (1985) Recruiting Volunteers. Home Office Research Study No. 31. London: HMSO.

Katz, S. and Mazur, M.A. (1979) Understanding the Rape Victim: A Synthesis of Research Findings. New York: Wiley.

Kelly, D. P. (1982) "Victims' Responses to the Criminal Justice Response." Paper presented at Annual Meeting of the Law and Society Association, Toronto, Canada.

Kilpatrick, D. G., Veronen, L. J. and .Reswick, P. A. (1979) "The Aftermath of Rape: Recent Empirical Findings." American Journal of Orthopsychiatry, vol. 49, no. 4.

Kilpatrick, D. G., Veronen, L. J. and Reswick, P. A. (1981) "Rape-induced Fear: Its Effects upon Behaviour and Life-style." Paper presented at Association for Advancement of Behaviour Therapy, 15th annual convention. Toronto, Canada.

Kilpatrick, D. G., Veronen, L. J. and Best, C. L. (1984) "Factors Predicting Psychological Distress among Victims" in Figley, C. R. (ed.), Trauma and Its Wake. New York: Brunnel/Mazel.

Kilpatrick, D. G. and Veronen, L. J. (1984) Treatment of Fear and Anxiety in Victims of Rape. Final Report. Rockville: National Institute of Mental Health.

Kilpatrick, D. G. (1985) "Research on Long-Term Effects of Criminal Victimization: Scientific, Service Delivery, and Public Policy Perspective." Paper presented at colloquium sponsored by the National Institute of Mental Health, Washington, D.C., February/March 1985.

Kilpatrick, D. G. and Amick, A. E. (1985) "Rape Trauma" in Hersen, M. and Last, C. G. (eds.), Behavior Therapy Casebook. New York: Springer.

Kilpatrick, D. G., Best, C. L., Veronen, L. J., Amick, A. E., Villeponteaux, L. A. and Ruff, G. A. (forthcoming) "Mental Health Correlates of Criminal Victimization: A Random Community Sample." Journal of Consulting and Clinical Psychology.

King, H. E. and Webb, C. (1981) "Rape Crisis Centers: Progress and Problems." Journal of Social Issues, vol. 37, no. 4, pp. 93-104.

Knudten, R.D., Meade, A.C., Knudten, M.S. and Doerner, W.G. (1977) Victims and Witnesses: Their Experience with Crime and the Criminal Justice System. Washington, D.C.: Government Printing Office.

Knudten, M. S. and Knudten, R. D. (1981) "What Happens to Crime Victims and Witnesses in the Justice System" in Galaway, B. and Hudson, J. (eds.), Perspectives on Crime Victims. St. Louis: Mosby.

Launay, G. (1985) "Bringing Victims and Offenders Together: A Comparison of Two Models." The Howard Journal, vol. 24, no. 23, August 1985

Lejeune, R. and Alex, N. (1973) "On Being Mugged: The Event and its Aftermath." Urban Life and Culture, vol. 2, pp. 259-287.

Lerner, M. J. (1980) The Belief in a Just World. New York: Plenum Press.

Lerner, M. J. and Simmons, C. H. (1968) "Observers' Reaction to the Innocent Victim: Compassion or Rejection?" Journal of Personality and Social Psychology, vol. 4, pp. 203-220.

London Rape Crisis Centre (1979) Rape Counselling and Research Project: First Annual Report, March 1977.

London Rape Crisis Centre (1982) Rape Counselling and Research Project: Third Report, October 1982.

London Rape Crisis Centre (1984) Sexual Violence: The Reality for Women. London: Women's Press, Handbook Series.

Maclean, B., Young, J. and Jones, T. (1986) The Islington Crime Report. London: Centre for Criminology and Police Studies, Middlesex Polytechnic.

Maguire, M. (1981) "Victims of Residential Burglary" in Lloyd-Bostock, S. (ed.), Law and Psychology. Oxford: SSRC Centre for Socio-Legal Studies.

Maguire, M. (1982) Burglary in a Dwelling: The Offence, the Offender and the Victim. London: Heinemann.

Maguire, M. (1984) "Meeting the Needs of Burglary Victims: Questions for the Police and Criminal Justice System" in Clarke, R. V. G. and Hope, T. (eds.), Coping with Burglary. Boston: Kluwer-Nijhoff.

Maguire, M. (1985) "Victims' Needs and Victim Services: Indications from Research." Victimology, vol. 10, nos. 1-4, pp. 539-559.

Maguire, M. (1986) "Victims' Rights: Slowly Redressing the Balance", in Crime UK 1986. Newbury: Policy Journals.

Marshall, T. F. (1984) "Services for Victims of Crime: Research Plans." Home Office, London.

Marshall, T. F. (1985) Alternatives to Criminal Courts. Aldershot: Gower.

Marshall, T. F. (1984) "Reparation, Conciliation and Mediation." Home Office Research and Planning Unit Paper No. 27. London: HMSO.

Marshall, T. F. and Walpole, M. (1985) Bringing People Together: Mediation and Reparation Projects in Great Britain. Home Office Research and Planning Unit Paper no. 33. London: Home Office.

Mawby, R. I. (1982) "Crime and the Elderly: A Review of British and American Research." Current Psychological Review, vol 2, pp. 301-310

Mawby, R. I. (1983) "The Victim in a Mixed Economy of Welfare." Paper presented to International Congress on Criminology, Vienna.

Mawby, R. I. (1984) "Victims' Needs, Entitlement and Merit: Towards a Justice Model." Paper to International Workshop on Victim Rights, Dubrovnik, 1984.

Mawby, R. I. and Gill, M. L. (1986) "Volunteers in Victim Services: a British Survey." Paper to World Congress of Victimology. Orlando, July 1986.

Mawby, R. I. and Gill, M. L. (forthcoming) Crime Victims: Needs, Services and the Voluntary Sector. London: Tavistock.

Maxfield, M.G. (1984) Fear of Crime in England and Wales. London: HMSO.

May, T. P. (1986) Neglected Territory: Victims of Car Theft. Dissertation for the Degree of MSC in Social Research Methods, Department of Sociology, University of Surrey.

Mayhew, P. (1984) "The Effects of Crime: Victims, the Public and Fear." Council of Europe, Sixteenth Criminological Research Conference: Research on Victims, Strasbourg, November 1984.

McCahill, T. W. et al. (1979) The Aftermath of Rape. Lexington, Mass.: Heath Lexington Books.

McIntyre, J., Myint, T. and Curtis, L. A. (1979) Victim Response to Sexual Assault: Alternative Outcomes. Washington, D.C.: Bureau of Social Science Research.

Metropolitan Police (1985) Extract from Police Orders published on 26 February 1985: 16: Victims' Support Schemes - Enhancement of Categories to be referred.

Miers, D. R. (1980) "Victim Compensation as a Labelling Process." Victimology, vol. 5, no. 1, pp. 3-16.

Miers, D. R. (1984) "The Criminal Injuries Compensation Board." Paper presented at conference on Victims, Restitution and Compensation in the Criminal Justice System.

Miller, W. R. and Williams, A. M. (1984) "Marital and Sexual Dysfunction Following Rape: Identification and Treatment" in Stuart, I. R. and Greer, J. G. (eds.), Victims of Sexual Aggression: Treatment of Children, Women and Men. New York: Van Nostrand Reinhold Company.

Ministry of the Solicitor-General (1984) Awareness and Use of Crime Compensation Programs. User Report No. 2 on the Canadian Victimization Survey. Ottawa: Research and Statistics Group.

Nass, D. R. (1977) The Rape Victim. Iowa: Kendall/Hunt Publishing Company.

NAVSS (1983) "Job Description for Co-ordinators." London: National Association of Victims Support Schemes.

NAVSS (1985) Fifth Annual Report 1984/85. London: National Association of Victims Support Schemes.

NAVSS (1986) Sixth Annual Report 1985/86. London: National Association of Victims Support Schemes.

Norquay, G. and Weiler, R. (1981). Services to Victims and Witnesses of Crime in Canada. Ottawa: Ministry of the Solicitor-General.

271

Notman, M. and Nadelson, C. (1984) "The Rape Victim: Psychodynamic Considerations." American Journal of Psychiatry, vol. 133, pp. 408-413.

Pahl, J. (1979) "Refuges for Battered Women: Social Provision or Social Movement?" Journal of Voluntary Action Research, no. 8, pp. 25-35.

Parliamentary All-Party Affairs Group (1984) A New Deal for Victims. London: HMSO.

Peters, J. K. (1975) "Social Psychiatric Study of Victims Reporting Rape." Paper to American Psychiatric Association, 128th annual meeting, California.

Reeves, H. (1985) "Victims Support Schemes: The United Kingdom Model." Victimology, vol. 10, nos. 1-4, pp. 679-686.

Reeves, H. (1984) "Victims Support Schemes." Paper to Howard League Conference, Oxford, August.

Resick, P. A. et al. (1981) "Social Adjustment in Victims of Rape." Journal of Consulting and Clinical Psychology, vol. 49, pp. 705-712.

Resick, P. A. (1984) "The Trauma of Rape and the Criminal Justice System." The Justice SystemJournal, vol 9 no. 1

Rich, R. F. (1981). "Evaluating Mental Health Services for Victims: Perspectives on Policies and Services in the United States" in Salasin, S. E. (ed.), Evaluating Victim Services. Beverly Hills: Sage.

Rock, P. (1986). " A View from the Shadows." Oxford University Press.

Rock, P. (forthcoming) "Mediation, Reparation and Victims Support Schemes."

Russell, D. E. and Miller, D. L. (1979) "The Prevalence of Rape and Sexual Assault." Final Report. National Institute of Mental Health, RO1-MH-28960.

Salasin, S. E. (ed.) (1981) Evaluating Victim Services. Beverly Hills: Sage.

Sales, E. et al. (1984) "Victim Readjustment Following Assault." Journal of Social Issues, vol. 40, no. 1, pp. 117-136.

Scherer, J. (1985) "Themes in Social Vulnerability: Research Avenues in Victimology." Victimology, vol. 10, nos. 1-4, pp. 26-33.

Sebba, L. (1982) "The Victim's role in the penal process: a theoretical orientation." American Journal of Comparative Law, vol. 30, pp. 217-240.

Shapland, J. M. (1984) "The Victim, the Criminal Justice System and Compensation." British Journal of Criminology, vol. 24, pp. 131-149

Shapland, J. M., Willmore, J. and Duff, P. (1985) Victims in the Criminal Justice System. Farnborough: Gower.

Shapland, J. M. (1985) "The Criminal Justice System and the Victim." Victimology, vol. 10, nos. 1-4, pp. 585-599.

Shapland, J. M. (1986) "Victims and Justice: Needs, Rights and Services." Paper for conference '100 Jaar Wetboek Van Strafrecht' Amsterdam, September 1986.

Shapland, J. M. and Cohen, D. (1986) "Facilities for Victims: the Role of the Police and Courts". Criminal Law Review (in press).

Skogan, W. S. (1985) "The Impact of Victimization on Fear." Paper presented at International Symposium on Victimology, Zagreb.

Skogan, W. S. et al. (1985) "Detecting Adverse Program Effects in a Police Service for Victims." Unpublished paper.

Skogan, W. S. and Maxfield, M. G. (1981) Coping with Crime. Beverly Hills: Sage.

Skogan, W. S. and Wycoff, M. (forthcoming) "The Victim Re-Contact Experiment in Houston." Washington, D.C.: Police Foundation.

Silver, R. L. and Wortman, C. B. (1980) "Coping with Undesirable Life Events", in Garber, J. and Seligman, M.E.P. (eds.), Human Helplessness. New York: Academic Press.

Smith, B. L. (1985) "Trends in the Victims' Rights Movement and Implications for Future Research." Victimology, An International Journal. vol. 10, nos. 1-4, pp. 34-43.

Smith, C. B. (1985) "Response to Victims: Are the Institutional Mandates of Police and Medicine Sufficient?" Victimology, vol 10, nos. 1-4, pp. 560-573.

Smith, D., Blagg, H. and Derricourt, N. (1985) South Yorkshire Probation Service: Victim-Offender Mediation Project Report to Chief Officers Group.

Smith, G. (1980) Social Need: Policy, Practice and Research. London.

Sonnichsen, P. (1984) "An Overview of the Victims Initiative in Canada." Paper presented to conference at Sidney Sussex College, Cambridge, August, 1984.

Sparks, R. (1982) Research on Victims of Crime: Accomplishments, Issues and New Directions. Rockville, Maryland: National Institute of Mental Health.

Sparks, R., Genn, H. G. and Dodd, D. J. (1977) Surveying Victims. London: Wiley and Sons Ltd.

Stanko, E. A. (1985) Intimate Intrusions. London: Routledge and Kegan Paul.

Stein, J. H. (1981) "Victim Crisis Intervention: An Evaluation Proposal" in Salasin, S. (ed.), Evaluating Victim Services. Beverly Hills: Sage.

Stuebing, W. K. (1984) Victims and Witnesses: Experience, Needs and Community/Criminal Justice Responses. Working Paper No. 9. Ottawa: Department of Justice.

Sutherland, S. and Scherl, D. J. (1970) "Patterns of Response among Victims of Rape." American Journal of Orthopsychiatry, vol. 40, pp. 503-511.

Symonds, M. (1982) "Victim Responses to Terror: Understanding and Treatment" in Ochberg, F. and Soskis,D. (eds.), Victims of Terrorism. Boulder: Westview.

Taylor, M. B. (1979) "Caring Society: A study of the inception and growth of the Victims Support Schemes in England and Wales, with some observations on the police role in their operation and administration." Unpublished paper. Bramshill: Police Staff College Library.

Toner, B. (1977) The Facts of Rape. London: Arrow Books.

Townsend, P. (1972) "The Needs of the Elderly and the Planning of Hospitals" in Canvin, R. and Pearson, N. (eds.), Needs of the Elderly for Health and Welfare Services. Exeter.

United Nations (1985) Declaration of Basic Principles of Justice. (A) Relating to Victims of Crime and (B) Relating to Victims of Abuse of Power.

Van Dijk, J. J. M. and Steinmetz, C. H. D. (1983) "Victimisation Surveys: Beyond Measuring the Volume of Crime." Victimology, vol. 8, nos. 1-2, pp. 291-309.

Van Dijk, J. J. M. (1983) "Victimology in Theory and Practice." Justitiele Verkenningen, no. 6, pp. 5-35.

Van Dijk, J. J. M. (1984) "Compensation by State or Offender? The Victim's Perspective.' Unpublished paper.

Van Dijk, J. J. M. (1985) "Regaining a Sense of Community and Order." General Report of the 16th Criminological Research Conference of the European Committee on Crime Problems, The Hague, February 1985.

Vennard, J. (1976) "Justice and Recompense to Victims of Crime." New Society, 19 February 1976, pp. 378-380.

Veronen, L. G., Kilpatrick, D. G. and Reswick, P. A. (1979) "Treating Fear and Anxiety in Rape Victims" in Parsonage, W. H. (ed.), Perspectives on Victimology. Beverly Hills: Sage.

Veronen, L. G. and Kilpatrick, D. G. (1983) "Rape: A Precursor of Change" in Callman, E. and McCluskey, K. (eds.), Life Span Development Psychology: Nonnormative Life Events. New York: Academic Press.

Viano, E. (1978) Victim/Witness Services: A Review of the Model. Washington, D.C.: Department of Justice.

Villmow, B. (1984) "Criminal and Social Policy with regard to Victims." Council of Europe, Sixteenth Criminological Research Conferences: Research on Victims, Strasbourg, November 1984.

Volunteer Centre (1976) "The Bristol Victims' Support Scheme." Berkhamstead: The Volunteer Centre.

Walklate, S. (1985) "The South Liverpool Victims Support Scheme: A Consumer Evaluation." Unpublished report of the Crime, Justice and Welfare Unit, Liverpool Polytechnic.

Waller, I. and Okihiro, N. (1978) Burglary: The Victim and the Public. Toronto: University of Toronto Press.

Waller, I. (1979) "Victimisation Studies as Guides to Action: Some Cautions and Suggestions." Paper presented at Third International Symposium on Victimology, Munster, Germany.

Waller, I. (1982) "Crime Victims: Needs, Services and Reforms. Orphans of Social Policy." Paper at 4th International Symposium on Victimology, Tokyo.

Waller, I. (1984) "Assistance to Victims of Burglary" in Clarke, R. and Hope, T. (eds.), Coping with Burglary. Boston: Kluwer-Nijhoff Publishing Company.

Walmsley, R. (1986) Personal Violence. Home Office Research Study No. 89. London: HMSO.

Weisaeth, L. (1985) "Psychiatric Studies in Victimology in Norway: Main Findings and Recent Developments." Victimology, vol. 10, nos. 1-4, pp. 478-487.

Williams, K. (1983) Community Resources for Victims of Crime. Home Office Research and Planning Unit Paper 14. London: Home Office.

Wright, M. (1982) Making Good: Prisons, Punishment and Beyond. London: Burnett Books/Hutchinson.

Wright, M. (1985) "The Impact of Victim/Offender Mediation on the Victim." Victimology, vol. 10, nos. 1-4, pp. 631-645.